BlackOut
Understanding The End Of The Age

By: Darren T. Carter

Foundation Publications
www.FoundaitonPub.org

BlackOut
Understanding The End Of The Age

ISBN: 979-8-218-51382-5

Published 2024 by Foundation Publications
www.foundationpub.org

All scriptures are quoted from the
English Standard Version unless otherwise noted.

CONTENTS

INTRODUCTION

The American church has been facing what could be described as an identity crisis, shaped by the influential forces of culture and political identification. Today, the church in America stands at a pivotal moment, encountering significant confusion. Its deep entanglement with both sides of the nation's culture and political identity has contributed to its current struggle over its true identity.

In this book, I aim to demonstrate that the key to our spiritual survival lies in placing the cross at the center of our faith. During times of upheaval, it's easy to become lost, confused, or misled. That's why I believe we must return to the basic foundations of our faith, where clarity and stability can be found. The cure to the identity crisis is to find our identity solely in the cross of Christ.

The Rise of the Kingdom Now Movement

It was the summer of 1989 that I was introduced to a system that has now become popular and trendy in parts of the church. I was introduced to Randy Shankle, one of the first ministers that I was aware of at the time calling himself an apostle.

Randy Shankle became a popular speaker on the Trinity Broadcasting Network during the late 1980's and was one of the leaders of what had emerged in Charismatic circles which came to be known as the 'Kingdom Now Movement'. The 'Kingdom Now Movement' was a mixture of Christian Reconstructionism with Charismatic Theology, and it spawned some extreme ideas. It's what I consider incorrect views of the role of the church in the world along with the role of the gifts of apostles and prophets. I spent 2 years at Randy's discipleship school in East Texas. It was a mixture of Mars Hill masculinity and IHOP Kansas City spirituality.

The school was designed around what Randy called a heavenly vision. In the auditorium where we had school daily there were six large paintings. 3 on one wall and 3 on the opposite wall. The paintings were revelations that Randy was given through dreams, angelic visitations and out of body experiences. Randy and the staff he had trained used the Bible, but it was a twisted Charismatic version of Dominion Theology based on Randy's spiritual experiences. It became a spiritually abusive church system. I witnessed a lot of damage to people's lives because of false prophecy, false teaching and abusive authoritarian control.

I watched a lot of people walk away from Christ and completely give up on church because of the spiritual abuse. Randy's sin wasn't sexual, but it was the sin of pride and arrogance. Spiritual authoritarianism can be just as damaging as sexual abuse, and it took me years to detoxify from the false ideas of spiritual covering that places too much of a reliance on man. It was a man centered gospel and was focused on having the correct church structure. Sure, Jesus was talked about, but it was Jesus, and the Bible filtered through Randy's revelations.

The Dangers of False Spirituality and Manipulative Hierarchical Systems

I've witnessed the devastation that can happen to people's faith when it is placed upon false systems and a false spirituality based on accountability to hierarchical systems. It becomes even more dangerous when authority is claimed through spiritual experiences. It then becomes a spirituality that is used as a weapon to manipulate, control and dominate people's lives. It has the appearance of truth, but it's a shadowy spirituality manifested through power hungry people to take advantage spiritually, financially and sexually.

I tell this story because I've witnessed firsthand the power of deception and how people can twist the Bible for power and control. I know that I am not alone in these experiences and what happened to me on a small scale 35 years ago has played out over and over to where there are literally millions of believers laying wounded across this nation. It's a sad tale of what happens when we become focused around personalities and spiritual movements instead of the person of Christ.

What I am encouraging you to do is follow the teachings of Jesus. He told us that we should judge a tree by its fruit. I hope to equip you through this book to be able to test and examine spiritual experiences. I hope to provide you with a framework to help you investigate teachings. Paul summed it up when he told the Thessalonians too, "test all things; hold fast what is good" (I Thess. 5:21). It is our duty to evaluate the causes, teachings and spiritual activity we encounter. Our spiritual health depends on discernment, a solid understanding of the Bible and critical thinking skills.

The goal I have in writing this book is to help you identify false, abusive and extreme ideas no matter where you find them. I hope to equip you to live in the foundational truth of sound doctrine established by Christ and the apostolic fathers. If you listened to the radio in the early 1990's then you probably heard of Hank Hangergraff aka 'The Bible Answer Man'. He was one of the first ministries on a national scale to focus on heresy in the church.

The Internet: A Double-Edged Sword for Spreading the Gospel and Spreading Heresy

The internet brings accessibility to a variety of spiritual views, and it creates what I consider a double edge sword of the good along with the bad. Is it confusing? Yes, it can be, but the opportunity to spread the gospel has never been so great. At the same time, I do see a bit of an accountability factor with the internet because fact checking can happen quick and we've seen corruption exposed today at lightning speed.

I've always been a seeker, but I'm also one who always questions. I encourage you to do the same. We need to pray for wisdom along with the discernment of the Holy Spirit. However, having critical thinking skills is also a key to keeping free from deception and staying away from spiritually abusive groups. If a spiritual leader has a problem with you asking questions, then red flags of caution should be raised. Humility and transparency are some of the main signs of healthy leadership because true servants have nothing to hide.

We tend to put labels on people and group them together because it helps us define things. I am a Continuist which means I believe in the continuation of all the gifts in Ephesians chapter 4:11, Romans chapter 12 and I Corinthians chapter 12. I have a master's degree in theology from a Pentecostal school, but I am not a classic Pentecostal. I am a Covenant Theologian, but I am not Reformed. I am an oxymoron on so many levels and live between the tension of varying ideas. It would be hard to box me into a group because I am the sum-total of a lifetime of learning, and I've never been a good groupie.

In this book I don't want to label people and box them into certain groups that they may not be completely a part of because as I said guilt by association is wrong. What I am going to be doing is confronting what I consider to be wrong and dangerous ideas that can produce spiritual abuse along with apostasy. I'm writing about my journey of faith over the last 35 years and hopefully I can help you avoid the ditches of extremism that I found myself stuck in and climbing out of over the years.

The Impact of Deconstructionism on Biblical Interpretation and Progressive Christianity

I've spent many years deconstructing my experiences. Now let me explain what I mean by deconstruction, so we are on the same page. Deconstruction has become a buzzword in recent years. [1]The foundational idea of deconstructionism as proposed by the French philosopher Jacques Derrida is built on the idea that everything is subjective to one's personal experience and therefore truth is subjective.

Deconstructionism rejects objective truth and does not present a way to reconstruct a text. It's completely different from contextualization which is understanding an author's audience, language and cultural setting. You must employ contextualization to understand the author's original intent on by examining the author's audience, language and cultural setting which is one of the main keys to interpreting the Bible.

Deconstructionism rejects objective truth and does not present a way to reconstruct a text so when applying this to Biblical interpretation it leaves you with nothing. The ideas work well with Gnosticism as I will explain in this book. Gnostic ideas lean towards inward and private revelation over sound doctrine. You see this especially in spiritual movements that emphasize special inside knowledge. [2]Whenever Christians claim new secret revelation beyond Scripture or twist Scripture to their preferred meaning the church moves toward ancient heresies. New Testament scholar Ben Witherington III is quoted as

---

[1] Kenneth Taylor, Derrida and Deconstruction, p. 1.
[2] Michael Horton, Christless Christianity, p. 47.

saying: "A text without a context is just a pretext for whatever you want it to mean."

[3]The Gnostic impulse is alive wherever salvation is sought through secret knowledge or elite spiritual experience and spiritual enlightenment. If you detach a text from its context and strip it from the redemptive story found in Christ it leaves room for subjective spirituality to make the Bible, say just about anything you want it to say. It is how you wind up with Progressive Christianity and the over spiritualized Mystic Christianity both being a departure from the faith. It's what we are witnessing on a large scale in America today.

I believe that the fundamentals of our faith are non-negotiable and reconstructing our faith plays a vital role in spiritual restoration to those who have veered off the foundation. It is one of the reasons I am writing this book because I am concerned about the level of apostasy that I am witnessing among large portions of the church which is a departure from foundational truth.

In this book I am going to make a clear and concise defense of the gospel as presented by Jesus along with his apostles. The book I am writing is a companion book to my other books and 'Foundation Publications School of Discipleship' which I will be directing you to quite often for additional learning.

I've witnessed over the years many people turn away from the faith because of abusive spiritual leaders and their own personal dysfunction. The experience I had at the age of 19 changed my heart so powerfully I never questioned my salvation or that Jesus the resurrected Christ was real. Turning back to the world was not an option for me because for me it meant death. I had seen the abyss, and I had seen Christ, so I had nowhere to go, but forward following Christ. I'm not saying I never struggled with the flesh because I did, but I never questioned my salvation.

Protestant Reformation and Priesthood of the Believer

One of the ideas that was recaptured during the Protestant Reformation was the priesthood of all believers. The idea was clearly presented by Jesus and the apostles. Unlike under the Old Covenant the New Covenant was founded on the body and blood of Christ being

---

[3] Douglas Groothuis, Confronting the New Age, p. 134.

established on a foundation of loving God with all our hearts and serving others. [4]All believers constitute God's priestly people and there is no hint of a distinct priestly class. It's not excluding spiritual leadership (I Timothy 3; I Peter 5:1-4), but it's emphasizing every member being a useful part of the body of Christ. The New Covenant is not to be built upon a clergy class set above the people, but a kingdom of priest with every member using the gifts that God had freely given them. The idea of the priesthood of all believers was recaptured during the Protestant Reformation, but it has rarely been implemented.

The predominant model that has prevailed in the modern American church has been the CEO model. The rise of the Charismatic leader has built a version of Christianity that draws great crowds but produces a very shallow form of faith. I don't think it's necessary for me to point out the obvious, which is that model has some major flaws. The main flaw is the over dependence on one individual and the idolatry that it promotes. [5]There is no clerical caste in the New Testament, and [6]the New Testament knows nothing of a sharp clergy-laity distinction.

The Bible simply does not tell us specifics on how to perform services, when to meet, where to meet or the types of structures we are to follow. Yes, there are some basic guidelines for spiritual leadership and worship, but very minimal so that leaves me to conclude we have been given freedom to contextualize. It's the idea of flexibility depending on the culture and particulars of any group you are trying to reach. It's having a missionary mindset.

The priesthood of the believer is embedded in the New Testament. It's the clear teaching of the New Testament that we have one Mediator, one High Priest and one King. Jesus is our one foundation because he is our all in all and we are all equally established on him. Jesus did not say a lot about building the church, but he clearly said that it was to be established on humility and serving. The kingdom of God is to be antithetical to the kingdom of this world who thrives on systems power, submission and control.

One of the things I deconstructed during my journey is looking at why we do ministry and what motivates us? I can't tell you how important 'the why' and 'the what' is to our spiritual health. The

---

[4] Thomas Schreiner, 1, 2 Peter and Jude (NAC), p. 110.

[5] John Stott, The Living Church, p. 36.

[6] Howard Snyder, The Problem of Wineskins, p. 117.

priesthood of the believer is that we are one body yet diversely gifted. Every member of the body needs to identify, develop and put into practical use the gifts that God has given them. However, in doing that we need to always ask ourselves why are we doing what we are doing and what is motivating us?

Yes, I believe in spiritual leadership because to accomplish tasks leadership is needed. Leadership is primarily about service and sacrifice. To be a leader in the first century church did not mean notoriety and power, but sacrifice, service and it could cost you your life. Paul said it was a noble thing to want to lead and Jesus told us to count the cost. Leadership is about setting an example for others to follow and Paul in I Timothy 3:1-7 lays out clear qualifications

If I was giving advice to a young man or woman who feels like they are called to spiritual leadership within the church the first thing I would tell them to do is to find a way to make an income. Find a way to make an income that is not solely centered around others giving to you.

I am not against full time salaried positions for ministry and giving is to be part of our New Testament sacrifices. We are all part of a new priestly order built around the body and blood of Christ. We are to give our lives and resources for the furtherance of the gospel. Paul said in I Timothy 5:17 that spiritual leaders who rule well should be "considered worthy of double honor, especially those who labor in preaching and teaching." Galatians 6:6 says: "Let the one who is taught the word share all good things with the one who teaches."

Paul lived off the financial support of those he ministered to at times, but he did not see himself as a privileged class set above the people. He accepted and encouraged giving, but he also worked with his hands, making his own way when necessary. It's not either or and it could be both, but regardless leaders are examples that others can relate to. The New Testament rejects the idea of a two-tiered system dividing the body into a priestly clergy class and the laity who are subservient to them.

We don't have a Levitical Priesthood in the New Testament, and the scriptures are absent of this clergy class distinction. One thing we've done is make being paid a salary for ministry as some sort of holy grail that separates you into some higher form of believer. We've made working a job seem like it is non-spiritual while full time paid staff are the real spiritual clergy. Paul demonstrated a life of hard work and service. He set an example for those he taught to follow. Paul demonstrated that he was not some kind of a hierarchical leader or hireling, but a co-laborer with those whom he led.

The bedrock of the church is built on fellowship. If there is a pattern for us to follow, then it is the cross and the cross is about fellowship which is teamwork. Paul spoke of the church as a flexible body where every part was needed. Paul was building the church not his ministry and he built a team that could outlive him. You can't help but see teamwork as the normative way regarding the organizational framework that Jesus and the apostolic fathers built.

We need money to operate and for the Missional church to move forward it's going to have to be built wisely. Building wisely will mean figuring out how to best utilize the resources that we need to get the job done. One thing I learned in business is that we need to utilize all our resources and be flexible. To survive and thrive in the coming days we must be nimble, changing very quickly. In addition, it's going to be those who utilize all its members and prepare them for service.

I am writing this book as a Continuist. I spent a lot of years deconstructing and in so doing I have concluded that to truly implement the priesthood of the believer you can't do it without the gifts of Ephesians chapter 4:11, Romans chapter 12 or I Corinthians chapter 12. One of the main questions for Continuist is what to do with the hot topic of apostles and prophets? It's the third rail and when you start talking about the topic then you are automatically pushed into certain ideological boxes. To get more details on this subject I recommend reading my book: Empowered – Discover You Gifts, Develop Your Gifts and Do Your Part.

Embracing A Continuist Position

To me it's a wrong perspective and a false argument to reject portions of the Bible due to extremes. Paul corrected the Corinthians for their extreme positions, but never said certain ministries and spiritual gifts would pass away. I can show you a lot of extreme ideas among many different groups. One thing you do not find a shortage of today and that is extreme positions. I am simply going to stick with 'Sola Scripture' which was the heart cry of the Reformation.

I am writing this book as a teacher, but it also has some prophetic tones and insights to it. The primary gifting that I operate in is that of a teacher, but I also have a prophetic gifting. The gift of the prophet as spoken of in Ephesians 4:11 is not an Old Testament prophet, but just one of the five gifts Paul says Christ gave to individuals when he ascended to help equip his body to fulfill the Great Commission. The Ephesians 4:11 gifts of apostle, prophet, evangelist, pastor and teacher are not a hierarchical structure of authority nor are they offices.

The APEST gifts are an individual expression of Christ given to members of his body to help the body function properly (To get more details on this subject I recommend reading my book: Empowered – Discover You Gifts, Develop Your Gifts and Do Your Part). Every member of the body of Christ has been given spiritual gifts. Each member of Christ body should identify, understand, develop and put into practical use their gifts because gifts help explain how we function. As a part of the New Testament priesthood each member is to be an offering laying their lives down at the altar of the cross, but we must also be faithful to use the gifts that we are freely given by the grace of God.

Ultimately, we are all going to be held accountable to Christ. We will be judged for our faithful surrender to his gifts in our lives and his rule over our lives. Your life is your message. Our life's circumstances and culture in which we live is part of what makes us who we are. None of us live in a vacuum of time. In this book I am going to be sharing with you how I have learned to navigate some complex topics in times that are moving towards increasing confusion and instability.

Being born in 1969 gives me a unique perspective of modern America because it was a pivotal year that planted the seeds to a cultural divide that has come to full maturity within our populace, our politics and the church. I lived through what is going to be looked back at as the height of the American Empire. I spent years as a missionary outside of America, but America is my home and the place I will rest should the Lord tarry. America has been the greatest missionary sending force in history taking the gospel to the nations of the earth. Yes, it's been a mixed bag, but nonetheless multitudes responded to the call.

America is at a great turning point in its history and the church must respond to the times in which we live. The Chinese word for crisis is the same word as opportunity. In the days ahead I believe if the church turns back to embracing the cross and focuses on the original mission of the gospel that the harvest is plentiful. We need a missionary movement in America with the same dynamic of sacrifice, service, commitment and sending force that Americans of former generations gave their lives to in going to the nations.

The Transition from the Mega to a People's Movement

What is happening in the American Church is the transition from the Mega church centered around celebrity to the Missional church centered around a people's movement. It's happening very quickly and its why foundations are so important. Crisis is about returning to basics. The church has one simple mission, and the author left us telling us to stay focused on that one mission. It's why I am writing this book because it's what has kept me on track during my journey.

I've been stuck in some extreme ditches, and it was only by turning back to the centrality of the cross that I found my way back to soundness of truth. I hope that through my journey I can help others find their way back to the solid ground of a Christ centered message focused on the cross and being established on sound doctrine.

In my years of deconstruction, I realized we have complicated the gospel and as a result have impeded the intent of Jesus' message. I'm not saying I have all the answers because I don't, but I am saying we don't have to have all the answers. It's okay to not know everything because that's what the walk of faith is all about.

One of the key takeaways I learned training people over the years is that simplicity is one of the main keys to learning retention. I am not writing this book for academics, but for fishermen, the tax collector, the farmer and those who have not been educated in Theological Seminaries. I'm writing to the nurse, customer service rep, factory worker, the mother, schoolteacher, construction worker and truck driver who simply wants to be an ambassador of the risen king.

The priesthood of the believer is about every member of the body identifying, developing and putting into practical use their gifts for the furtherance of the gospel. An apostolic movement is where every member is an active part in getting the job done. Jesus did not commission a clergy class, but he commissioned his body. I hope this book is an encouragement for you to join me in staying focused around our common mission of Christ the Alpha and Omega.

Chapter 1

UNDERSTANDING OUR TIMES

"Look carefully then how you walk, not as unwise but as wise, making
the best use of the time, because the days are evil."

~ Ephesians 5:15-16 ~

I started my journey of faith in the late 1980's and spiritual
warfare along with a real focus on the end times was all the rage. The
Soviet Union had collapsed, revival was sweeping the globe, and Jesus
was going to rapture his church at any moment, thrusting the world into
'the great tribulation'. At the same time the modern American church
was hit with some of its greatest scandals to date with Jim and Tammy
Baker along with the Jimmy Swaggart fiascos. The scandals were both
very public and ugly. What I was witnessing in live time was apostasy
and revival happening simultaneously. In the last 35 years so much has
changed in the world and the church, yet so much has remained the
same.

What I am hoping to do as you read is cause you to examine
your walk with God. I am not using this book to point the finger at
others, but I am hoping to have a conversation about what our faith looks
like in a world that is rapidly changing. We are living in times when
rapid changes are taking place. Think about what happened to the
children of Israel living in Egypt who had become slaves in that land for
400 years. In the fullness of times God raised up the prophet Moses as
his representative to bring them out of slavery back to the land promised
to Abraham.

The Passover sacrifice was the final moment when they were
separated from the hold of the Pharaoh's power. However, it was the Red
Sea that was the final separation from his ability to control their lives.
The true challenge started in the wilderness, as they found themselves
battling their own inner conflicts.

The Importance of Finding Stability and Guidance in Life's Challenges

Life is about struggle, hardship, and a series of choices. During momentous change, we need to have our footing. We need something on which to securely plant our feet or we are going to fall. During great darkness, we need something to guide our path, or we are going to get lost. Paul in I Corinthians chapter 10 uses Israel's struggles through the wilderness as an example of indiscretions and our susceptibility to the same ones. He said: "Now these things happened to them as an example, but they were written down for our instruction, on whom the end of the ages has come. Therefore, let anyone who thinks that he stands take heed lest he fall."

Paul wasn't telling us to point fingers and say, "man how could they have acted this way". He says that we need to take notes so that we can learn from others' mistakes. Don't assume that you're immune—it could happen to anyone. If you remain unaffected, stay vigilant and humble so that you don't stumble as well. In this book what I want to do is what Paul was doing in I Corinthians chapter 10. Like Paul I am asking us all to take heed, lest we too fall.

I'm not just talking about living in duplicitous sinful disobedience but living in the shadows of deceptive lies. I've witnessed a lot of good people get caught up in what I call the fantasy land of faith and become part of the lunatic fringe. Did everyone in the crowd that shouted to crucify Christ really understand what was happening or were they just caught up in the chaos of the moment? I think many had succumbed to Groupthink just like the crowds in the days of Hitler's Third Reich. How about America's bloodiest war? The Civil War where both sides were certain that God was on their side.

None of us are above tripping in this present darkness and succumbing to deception. In fact, we are all going to struggle, trip, lose our way and sometimes fall If you have fallen, I want to encourage you to get up. If you have tripped or you are struggling to find your way because you're walking a dark path, I hope to shine some light on your path. If you are discouraged because you feel like others, you looked up to have let you down then I have some words of hope and exhortation for you.

The journey of faith is a journey and one thing I've learned along this journey is that every situation we face in life there is a lesson to be learned. The pathway of following Christ is not for the faint of heart and it's through the struggles, the trials, suffering and difficulties that we learn to truly trust in his ability. It's called the walk of faith and good fight for a reason.

The Crucial Decision Facing the Church in America

The church in America is at a major crossroads and we are all going to have to decide if we are going to continue in the faith. John chapter 6 opens with Jesus performing the miracle of feeding the 5,000 with 5 loaves of bread and 2 fish. The next day people were following him around for what he could give them. It's the sad state of the church in America. Far too many people follow him for what they can get, thinking that godliness is a means of gain. Sadly, it's what many have been taught and their faith will be greatly tested when the American gospel is shown to simply be a mirage amid a wilderness.

In John chapter 6 Jesus compared himself to the manna that the children of Israel partook of walking through the wilderness. Jesus then told them that following him is not about what you can get, but it's about laying down your lives and sacrifice. He started talking about his flesh being the true food and his blood being the true drink. In verse 63 he says, "It is the Spirit who gives life; the flesh is no help at all. The words that I have spoken to you are spirit and life". Verse 62 says, "After this many of his disciples turned back and no longer walked with him".

Jesus began to explain the heart of the gospel to them. Yes, you get delivered from the enemy. Yes, you are given the power of the Spirit. Yes, God is going to provide for you, but you must lay down your life in covenant. It's life for life. It's when the gospel started challenging their self-indulgent carnality is when it got real.

The gospel means Christ died for you, but it's also that you die. It's what Jesus told Nicodemus that you must be born from above. Just like natural childbirth, being born from above is the pathway of blood and sacrifice. I, like you, have grown up in an American society of privilege, safety and security where we've not really known what it means to pay a price to identify with Christ.

Jesus then turned to the 12 disciples and said, "Do you want to go away as well?" I love Peter's answer because I understand it so very well. Verse 68 and 69 it says: "Simon Peter answered him, "Lord, to whom shall we go? You have the words of eternal life, and we have believed, and have come to know, that you are the Holy One of God." I don't know about you, but I've stood at that place many times. I've wanted to turn around because it was hard, it was lonely, sin looked so attractive, the church was a mess, and I wasn't sure about the way forward. It was at those times when I reflected on the power of the cross delivering me from the powers of darkness and realizing this present evil age is not my home.

I know what living in darkness is like and I don't ever want to go back there. I've tasted the power of the age to come. I know the gentle Spirit of heaven. I know the fire of God that shines in darkness. If your heart has been captivated by the Living God then your answer will be like Peter's, "Lord, I have nowhere else to go".

Once you've truly tasted the flesh of Christ and drank in that living blood nothing else will satisfy. Like Paul we must be dead men walking and crucified with Christ. If we want to walk in the light and have glory upon our lives, we must embrace the cruciform way of life. We have to grasp the understanding that the only way we can live in this present darkness is by allowing Christ to live his life in us.

The crossroads the church is facing is the choice between living our lives or being willing to lay them down. It's always been the choice of those who would follow the God of Abraham, but as we approach the end of the age there will be no middle ground.

Embracing the Humility of the Cross

The American McGospel has produced and promoted celebrity, prosperity and fame. It's had its day, but it's been found lacking the humility of the cross. The New Covenant is about a kingdom of priests that will truly reflect the glory of the coming king. It's a message founded in the humility, transparency and sacrifice of the cross. Remember, the first sin was pride, and the root of deception is pride. It's putting self-first. Pride blinds you and darkens your understanding.

It's what compels me to write this book because this book is about deception. Deception has become so widespread that it affects all of us today. In a world of confusion, distortion of facts, extremism and outright falsehood the church is supposed to be a place of sound truth. Paul in I Timothy 3:15 called the church "a pillar and foundation of the truth". In our modern architecture we don't see many buildings that Paul was more than likely reflecting upon as he wrote this letter to Timothy.

Paul had left Timothy in Ephesus to establish the body of believers in that city. The imagery of these terms for the church would not have been lost on the Ephesians. In their city was the impressive temple of the goddess Artemis called by the Greeks and later called Diana by the Romans. The temple was one of the seven wonders of the ancient world, located in the city of Ephesus which is modern day Turkey.

William Barclay gives the following description of it: "One of its features was its pillars. It contained one hundred and twenty-seven pillars, every one of them the gift of a king. All were made of marble, and some were studded with jewels and overlaid with gold. Each pillar acted as a tribute to the king who donated it. The honorary significance of the pillars, however, was secondary to their function of holding up the immense structure of the roof." The pillars were securely placed upon the foundation and they both supported the immense structure.

The Church: Beyond Confusion and Misconceptions

The Greek word for church is *ekklēsia* literally means 'called out ones'. The double-k in the word gives it a two-fold meaning, which is called out of the world and called unto God. The church then, is a group of people who have been called out of spiritual darkness through the gospel of the kingdom and brought into fellowship with the King of the kingdom. The church is a group of people who have come under the present reign of Christ's rule through spiritual rebirth.

The *ekklēsia* was first developed as a ruling assembly of citizens in the Grecian democracy to govern its city-states. The Greek and Roman versions of the *ekklēsia* appeared in different forms and sizes, the assemblies were not a one size fits all.

The ruling assembly of citizens could be as small as two or three gathered anywhere in the world. It only took 2 or 3 citizens for the *ekklēsia* to be considered a local expression of Rome. Even though geography separated the *ekklēsia* from the capital of the empire and the emperor, their coming together as fellow citizens automatically brought the power and presence of the Roman ruling authority into their midst. This was indeed the Roman *ekklēsia* in a microcosm.

In like manner, the *ekklēsia* is made up of followers of Christ who have received the life of the kingdom. It is those who are dedicated to the task of using the keys of the kingdom under the authority of Christ to unlock those who are bound by Satan.

Jesus said in Matthew chapter 16 that the *ekklēsia* or his church is established upon those who truly have a personal encounter with the living Christ and are changed from the inside out. Ecclesiology, which is what we believe about Christ' body and how it functions, is important. The reason is because Paul said the body of Christ is the pillar and foundation of the truth.

If you want to further understand my views, then you can go check out the following lessons in the Foundation Publications School of Discipleship. Lessons Part I and Part II of Section III: Kingdom Ministry Through The Church. Lessons 41 and 42 Part I and Part II on Spiritual Warfare. Lesson 45: The Body of Christ and Lessons 47 and 48 Part I and Part II on Order In The Church. In those lessons I thoroughly discuss Biblical Ecclesiology, which is the study of Christ and his body.

I'm simple in my views because Jesus has made this simple enough for anyone who is willing to be an active member in forming his church. We have been given great flexibility when it comes to structure, how, where and what type of meetings we are to have as his body.

Jesus did not give us a blueprint on organizational structure nor did the apostles and there is more than one way to get from point A to point B. However, Jesus and the apostles gave us some very clear blueprints regarding the truth along with the foundations of our faith. The body of Christ is an extension of the resurrected Christ in this earth. Paul said it's to be a pillar and foundation for truth.

Challenging the Concept of Truth in Today's World

We live in days when they tell us that white is black and black is white. The very core of truth is being challenged from all sides. The question that the Roman ruler Pilate asked Jesus the night before he was crucified is a question still being asked. Pilate asked Jesus, "What is truth?" If I was to do a man on the street interview and walk up to people asking them this question. "What is truth?" The answers I would get would be as varied as the person to whom I am asking the question. In today's world truth like beauty is in the eye of the beholder.

In our postmodern world truth is relative. Everyone has their own truth made in their own image so what is true to one person could be false to another person. There are no absolutes in todays' postmodern culture where relativism is the norm. Remember Satan was able to convince Eve, through his subtle and cunning speech that what was forbidden by God, would be good for her. It's the postmodern lie of relativism which says truth is whatever you make it.

Satan was the first post-modernist who destroyed truth through relativism where there are no absolutes, but just the mushy grayness of man being his own god. The father of lie's initial sin was pride and thinking that he could be like God. As a result of his pride, he became a deceiver, liar and twister of truth. The main weapons of the enemy are enticing philosophies with a scriptural foundation that have been taken out of context. Every serious Bible student knows that context means everything since you can make the Bible say just about anything you want it to say if you take it out of context.

The Guiding Light of God's Word in the Darkness

Have you ever gotten out of bed in the middle of the night to go to the bathroom in a pitch-black room? To be able to successfully walk through great darkness and not stumble, fall or get lost we need light. Psalms 119:105 says, "Your word is a lamp to my feet and a light to my path." Psalms 119:130 says, "the unfolding of your words gives light; it imparts understanding to the simple." We can trust the proven, tried and tested word of God to give us direction in great darkness.

Paul told Timothy in his second letter to him that: "all Scripture is breathed out by God and profitable for teaching, for reproof, for correction, and for training in righteousness." I like to look at it this way. Jesus is the foundation. It's not the Bible. I love the word of God, but the Bible does not save us. We are saved by encountering the living resurrected Christ who is our Great High Priest.

I love the way Eugene Peterson in the Message Paraphrased Translation interprets the text in Matthew chapter 16:15 - 18. Jesus had just come to them in the villages of Caesarea Philippi, he asked his disciples, "What are people saying about who the Son of Man is?" They replied, "Some think he is John the Baptizer, some say Elijah, some Jeremiah or one of the other prophets." He pressed them, "And how about you? Who do you say I am?" Simon Peter said, "You're the Christ, the Messiah, the Son of the living God." Jesus came back, "God bless you, Simon, son of Jonah! You didn't get that answer out of books or from teachers. My Father in heaven, God himself, let you in on this secret of who I really am. And now I'm going to tell you who you are, really are. You are Peter, a rock. This is the rock on which I will put together my church, a church so expansive with energy that not even the gates of hell will be able to keep it out."

You know everyone had their own version of who Christ was, but there is only one version that is true. Truth is a person, and we are in a relationship with a person not a book. The scriptures are able to make you wise for salvation through faith in Christ Jesus (II Timothy 3:15). [7]Scripture is the ultimate standard of truth and the final court of appeal, but the scriptures are not an end to themselves. Identifying with his broken body and poured out blood; being consecrated through the waters of baptism and being filled with the same Spirit that raised Christ from the dead makes us a member of his body here in the earth and eternally.

The word of God is the pillar of truth that holds the body of Christ together. [8]Truth is not created by the church; it is upheld by the church. I'm a sticker for sound doctrine and its why I put together a free online school of discipleship. Sound doctrine produces sound living and is like railroad tracks. It provides structure, stability, and protects us from being deceived. Gordon D. Fee says, "[9]Right belief and right behavior are inseparable." The living Christ who is the Spirit also illuminates, teaches and leads us, but never contradictory to the foundation. [10]The Spirit who inspired the Word will not lead the believer contrary to the Word.

The prophet Zechariah in 3:9 talks of a "stone with seven eyes." [11]The seven eyes symbolize the fullness of divine knowledge and the Spirit's omniscience. You can't separate the foundation of the word from the foundation of the Spirit and if you do then you are much more likely to trip, fall and be lost in the darkness. [12]Word and Spirit belong together; to separate them is either rationalism or enthusiasm. The Spirit is the glove that fits around the hand. The hand is the word that gives structure, and you can't separate one from the other.

---

[7] John Frame, The Doctrine of the Word of God, p. 9.
[8] D.A. Carson, The Gagging of God, p. 50.
[9] Gordon D. Fee, 1 and 2 Timothy, Titus (NIBC), p. 185.
[10] Gordon, D. Fee, Gospel and Spirit, p. 90.
[11] Iain Duguid, Haggai, Zecharaiah, Malachi. (NIVAC), p. 129.
[12] Michael Horton, The Chrisitan Faith, p. 558.

Understanding the End of the Age

Regarding the book of Revelation, I do consider myself somewhat of a panologist. A panologist means we'll see how it all pans out. I kind of straddle different opinions and views on the subject. I've found even the greatest of theologians don't have a complete understanding of an extraordinarily complex and fluid subject which is the summing up of all things in both heaven and earth.

In looking at the 'last days' or 'end of this age' let's get a framework for understanding. Paul in one of the scriptures we looked at earlier in I Corinthians chapter 10 saw himself as a man on whom the end of the ages has come. Peter puts himself in the last times. As he opens his first epistle in chapter 1 verse 20 speaking of the redemptive work of Christ, he says that Jesus, "was foreknown before the foundation of the world, but was made manifest in the last times for the sake of you.". He also sees the opening of the outpouring of the Spirit on the day of Pentecost bringing to birth the church as the beginning of the last days. Acts 2:17 Peter quotes the prophet Joel saying, "in the last days it shall be, God declares, that I will pour out my Spirit on all flesh".

The author of Hebrews opens his epistle saying something very similar. Hebrews 1:1 - 2 say, "Long ago, at many times and in many ways, God spoke to our fathers by the prophets, but in these last days he has spoken to us by his Son, whom he appointed the heir of all things, through whom also he created the world." A few other scriptures referring to the last days are II Timothy 3:1-9, II Peter 3:1-9, James 5:1-6. The apostolic writers saw themselves in the last times, at the end of the ages and last days. To them it wasn't something future, but a present reality and that was 2,000 years ago.

Truth is important because it grounds us, tethers us, shines light on our pathway and keeps us from being overtaken by darkness. The flood of information today is astonishing, especially if you grew up like I did before the internet. Today the internet is just a fact of daily life and it's causing our world to change rapidly. Just like the invention of the printing press in 1436 by Johannes Gutenberg the German goldsmith transformed the world as we know it. Today we are going through a massive transformation.

A Massive Transition Every 500 Years

One author has noted that every 500 years God has a rummage sale. We are 500 years past the Protestant Reformation, and we are in the middle of a great rummage sale going on right now in the world and in the church. It's causing an upheaval which will bring drastic change as to how we practice our faith.

Think about life before the printing press and then after the printing press. Two different worlds. Think about the life in most European nations when they were ruled by kings. Then think about those nations after the Enlightenment discourse which brought about republics and democracies. Two different worlds. Think about the time when the monolithic Catholic Church controlled and ruled nations. Then life after the Protestant Reformation which produced the priesthood of all believers. Two different worlds. Think about life before the internet and life today. Two different worlds.

If we didn't have the printing press, I'm not sure we would have had a Renaissance, Protestant Reformation or the Enlightenment period. Historians conclude that the printing press had a profound impact on this period of human history. It accelerated the spread of ideas. It increased knowledge, increased literacy rates, standardized language and spelling. It had a significant impact on the arts, being a key factor in the intellectual and cultural growth of the period.

The printing press became the single most important factor in the success of the Protestant Reformation by providing widespread access to new teachings. The Bible itself was once controlled in the hands of a few, but the printing press brought truth to the masses, light shone, breaking the power of the 'Dark Ages' and the rest is history.

The technological advances from that time to present are breathtaking if you look at it in the context of human history. It was estimated that literacy rates during the period of the early church was around 10%. It was estimated throughout the Roman empire the literacy rate was around 15%. In just looking at the West literacy rates up until the time of the printing press at best were 20%. The nobility, priests and monks were the only one's literate while the rest were left in the dark. Scientific, artistic, medical, architectural and historical knowledge greatly diminished during this period. Knowledge and modes of travel hadn't changed much in the first 1500 years of the church.

In just the last 500 years things have changed in ways like no other time in human history. It's not even comparable. It was by the 1700's during the First Industrial Revolution that we went from hand production methods to machines, and it was the rise of the mechanized factory system. We went from wind powered ships to steam powered ships, from horse and buggy to locomotives so travel was increased. The first electric telegraph was invented in 1840.

The Second Industrial Revolution brought a period of rapid advancement. The period was also known as the Technological Revolution. It was a period of rapid scientific discovery, standardization, mass production and industrialization from the late 19th century into the early 20th century which ended at the beginning of WWI.

Information Age: Advancement at a Breathtaking Pace

Since 1947 we are living through what's come to be known as the Information Age, Digital Revolution or some call it the Third Industrial Revolution. As far as the increase of knowledge, communication and travel the last 70 years have exceeded the advancement in all previous times back to the beginning of recorded human history.

The modes of travel and increase in knowledge remained relatively static for all recorded human history until after the Protestant Reformation. Since the 1800's the graph I'm about to show you goes up with no end in sight. Anyone who is living today feels just along for the ride. We are all just holding on as the world moves at a pace never seen in human history.

Buckminster Fuller spoke of the "Knowledge Doubling Curve" in 1982: He suggested that in 1900, human knowledge doubled approximately every 100 years. At the end of WWII in 1945, the rate had come down to every 25 years and by 1982, every 13 months. Ray Kurzweil has suggested that with the arrival of the Internet knowledge is now doubling every 12 hours - think about that! The graph produced by author Max Roser gives you a picture of accelerated change. If you look at this graph it's breathtaking. A picture is worth a thousand words.

The Third Industrial Revolution has been a great leap forward in the way that we communicate with each other, and it has resulted in computers along the internet which has become a part of the way that we daily live. The advanced ability to communicate cannot be overestimated.

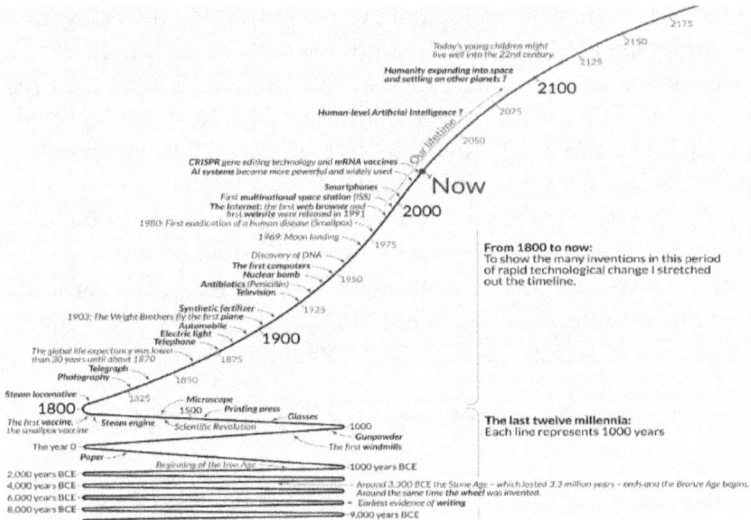

2175
2150
Today's young children might
live well into the 22nd century.
2125
Humanity expanding into space
and settling on other planets ?
2100
Human-level Artificial Intelligence ?
2075
Our lifetime
2050
CRISPR gene editing technology and mRNA vaccines
AI systems become more powerful and widely used
Smartphones
Now
First multinational space station (ISS)
The Internet: the first web browser and
first website were released in 1991
2000
1980: First eradication of a human disease (Smallpox)
1969: Moon landing
1975
Discovery of DNA
The first computers
Nuclear bomb
Antibiotics (Penicillin)
1950
Television
Synthetic fertilizer
1925
1903: The Wright Brothers fly the first plane
Automobile
Electric light
Telephone
1900
The global life expectancy was lower
than 30 years until about 1870
Telegraph
Photography
1875
Steam locomotive
Microscope
1800
1825
1500
Printing press
The first vaccine,
the smallpox vaccine
Steam engine
Scientific Revolution
Glasses
The year 0
1000
Paper
Gunpowder
The first windmills
Beginning of the Iron Age
1000 years BCE
2,000 years BCE
4,000 years BCE
6,000 years BCE
8,000 years BCE
9,000 years BCE

Around 3,300 BCE the Stone Age - which lasted 3.3 million years - ends and the Bronze Age begins.
Around the same time the wheel was invented.
Earliest evidence of writing

From 1800 to now:
To show the many inventions in this period
of rapid technological change I stretched
out the timeline.

The last twelve millennia:
Each line represents 1000 years

In the year 2024 as I am writing this, we are walking through the door of the Fourth Industrial Revolution with Artificial Intelligence taking on a greater role. It's truly hard to grasp the momentous transformation the entire world is going through. We are moving through rapid change at a pace that makes your head spin just trying to keep up. It's why the church must be established on the foundation of our ancient faith that is constant and unchanging.

We are quickly moving into a world where it will be extremely difficult to know fact from fiction. In looking at the words of Isaiah the great darkness seems to be worldwide, so it's not isolated to Israel. It is a darkness that is going to be felt on a global scale, and we seem to be living in those days when it has the potential to come to pass. In studying the Bible and history I've tried to imagine myself living in those times.

Living Through Historic Moments

People living through history many times don't realize exactly what they are living through. When history is being made and I'm talking about dramatic world changing events it's very confusing. The old saying hindsight is 20/20 applies which means in the fog of war it's not clear to understand exactly what's happening since many times it's only after the fact that you see clearly. I believe we are walking through such a time in world history.

The book of Revelation was written by John the apostle with whom Jesus had a special relationship out of all the rest. In his gospel we see a very intimate portrayal and clear description of the God who created all things wrapped in human flesh. The Deity of Christ and Humanity of Christ is clearly articulated through the writings of John. It's also through John's gospel that we get some of the clearest understanding of God the Holy Spirit. John makes following the risen Christ a very intimate reality. He truly shows us that our journey of faith is about a living relationship with a living personal God.

John's gospel compares us to branches dependent on the Vine for its source of life (John 15:1-17). He compares Christ to manna and tells us that we are dependent on partaking daily of the bread of life just like the Israelites were sustained by manna in the wilderness. He tells us if we want eternal life then we must eat Christ flesh and drink his blood which is a total identification with him. It's a merging of our lives with His life and living the cruciform way of life (John 6;31-58).

John says that by coming to Christ and humbly submitting to him then we can have rivers of living water flowing through our hearts (John 7:37-39). He says that we are sheep dependent on following our Shepherd who will care for us, protect us and lead us (John 10:1-18). John showed us that Jesus is The Way, The Life and The Truth which was a reference to the still standing Temple (John 14:6). John's gospel clearly showed us that Jesus' body is the new temple (John 2:19-21), that he was the final sinless Passover sacrifice to cleanse not just the nation of Israel, but the sins of the world (John 1:29). It's only in John's gospel 8:12 that Jesus is recorded as saying: "I am the light of the world. Whoever follows me will not walk in darkness, but will have the light of life." In this same chapter verses 31 and 32 he says: "If you abide in my word, you are truly my disciples and you will know the truth and the truth will set you free."

The Risen Christ: The Central Focus of Revelation

The central focus of the book of Revelation is not a secret letter to conceal, but to unveil the risen Christ. The central theme, consistent with all of John's writings, is that the culmination of all events is fundamentally centered on the Lamb, who was sacrificed prior to the foundation of the world. [13]The Revelation stands as a canonical capstone, intentionally summarizing and re-presenting the entire Biblical story in apocalyptic form rather than introducing new doctrines.

It's not intended to be a literal chronological account of future history but a symbolic portrayal of the conflict between God and the forces of evil. [14]John does not provide a timetable of the end but a theological interpretation of the redemptive story from the perspective of the end summing it all up in Christ. It's a clear focus on the supremacy of the risen Christ as the victorious Lion from the tribe of Judah who is going to return as the king of Kings to judge the nations. In the midst of his judgment of justice there is going to be redemption, restoration and the brightness of His glory.

John opens the book with this his intent: The revelation of Jesus Christ. In this book I am not doing a deep dive into the book of Revelation. What I am doing is something I've practiced over the years. It's my attempt to help us understand the times in which we live and to use the Bible as our guide for faith in daily living. As we look at the Bible as our guide and lens by which we view the world, we must understand this one truth: The Bible does not tell us everything about world history nor does it tell us everything about how to live life. The Bible is history, but it's telling us the story of God's redemptive history in time. It's God's love story to humanity showing us His redemptive hand through the Hebrew people, his chosen vehicle to redeem a fallen humanity bringing us back to Himself.

John is the author that coined the term antichrist which when looking at the book of Revelation it will be a question that many will want to understand. John spoke of the 'antichrist' as both a present and future reality. In I John 2:18 - 19 he says: "Children, it is the last hour and as you have heard that antichrist is coming, so now many antichrists have come. Therefore, we know that it is the last hour. They went out from us, but they were not of us; for if they had been of us, they would have continued with us. But they went out, that it might become plain that they all are not of us". John's readers had already heard that antichrist is coming so it was not a topic that they were ignorant about. However, it is the only reference to the 'last hour' in the Bible.

[13] G.K. Beale, The Book of Revelation, NIGTC, p. 40, 48
[14] Richard Bauckman, The Theology of the Book of Revelation, p. 8

To many scholars John's usage of the term 'last hour' is in reference to the prophecy of Daniel from which John draws strongly from in the book of Revelation. John draws inspiration from Daniel and Ezekiel who were contemporaries writing their prophecies as captives in Babylon.

Daniel 12:1-4 says: "there shall be a time of trouble, such as never has been since there was a nation till that time. But at 'that time' your people shall be delivered, everyone whose name shall be found written in the book. And many of those who sleep in the dust of the earth shall awake, some to everlasting life, and some to shame and everlasting contempt. And those who are wise shall shine like the brightness of the sky above; and those who turn many to righteousness, like the stars forever and ever. But you, Daniel, shut up the words and seal the book, until the time of the end. Many shall run to and fro, and knowledge shall increase."

Insightful Commentary on the Text of Daniel

I want to comment on a few things in this text before I move on.

1. Daniel sees a time of trouble coming upon the earth that has never been seen.
2. It's going to be a time when the children of Israel will be delivered.
3. He speaks of the resurrection from the dead and judgment.
4. He speaks of great glory upon his people.
5. It says we are not going to truly understand these words until this period.
6. He concludes with a rise in knowledge and travel.

What I am hoping to do through this book is to help give you a framework for understanding our times in light of the word of God. It's a view that has helped me navigate throughout the years keeping me centered, grounded and established in Christ.

I'm not doing a comprehensive study on the book of Revelation. However, I do think having a framework for understanding the last days and the book of Revelation is important in keeping us out of the ditches of extremism. We live in an age of cultural, political, economic and theological extremes. I understand the book of Revelation and message of the end of the age is a complex and confusing topic or there would not be so many differing opinions.

What I hope to do is give you a clear focus on how to walk in these times and grow closer to God. I'm hoping that as you read this book you will be illuminated so that you can shine in the midst of a dark and confused world.

Chapter 2

THE THRESHING FLOOR

"His winnowing fork is in his hand, and he will clear his threshing floor and gather his wheat into the barn, but the chaff he will burn with unquenchable fire."

~ Matthew 3:12 ~

We live in an age of cultural, political, economic, and theological extremes. If you are like me then you are often confused due to the excessive amounts of information flowing towards you daily. It's what I call information overload. It's like a power circuit that can't manage the electricity flowing through it, so it shuts down before it creates a fire. Instead of creating a fire it creates a blackout.

The Multifaceted Nature of Prophecy

What I am doing in this book is attempting to make the complex subject of prophecy as simple as I can. One Jewish method of interpretation concerning prophecy is called Midrash: To the ancient Jewish mind, prophecy was a pattern which keeps repeating, a prophecy having multiple fulfillments with each fulfillment, each cycle, teaching something about the ultimate fulfillment. [15]Midrash is not primarily historical commentary but interpretive expansion that makes the ancient text speak to the present.

It's the concept that history repeats itself. If you have ever sliced an onion, then you'll see there are layers. Prophecy is like that in how God fulfills them. [16]Israel's story was understood as a recurring drama awaiting its final decisive act. This layered structure—sometimes described as multiple horizons—reveals prophecy as organic and progressive rather than flatly linear. Each historical fulfillment functions as a partial realization that both teaches and anticipates the ultimate

---

[15] Daniel Boyarin, Intertextuality and the Reading of Midrash, p. 12.
[16] N.T. Wright, Jesus and the Victory of God, p. 139.

fulfillment in the eschatological purposes of God. [17]The fulfillment is not a simple one-to-one prediction but a recapitulation of Israel's history in Jesus. Midrash assumes that Scripture is a living text whose words continue to speak to new situations since [18]Biblical writers often see earlier events as patterns that are escalated and intensified in later redemptive history.

One of the main things that blinded many of the Pharisees was pride. The Pharisees searched the scriptures for their coming Messiah but couldn't see the very essence of truth; God manifested in human flesh. Jesus taught, performed miracles and demonstrated the love of the Father right in front of them for three and a half years, but many missed their day of visitation. He did not fit in the boxes of their preconceived ideas. It's because they thought they had it all figured out.

I've seen that when you think you have it all figured out, God peels back a layer of the onion. It's why you are going to hear me talk about humility of heart throughout this book because humility is a key to living in the truth and walking in the light. Truth is not always having everything figured out. Truth is learning to abide in Christ, the one who knows the end from the beginning.

One of the layers of the 'fullness of times' is that God stepped into history at the right time. It was by the predetermined plan and purpose of the heavenly counsel that Christ was to step into time as the God-Man and he did it during the rule of the Roman Empire. The Roman Empire at the time was connected by what has come to be known as the Roman Roads. The light of the gospel spread like a wildfire throughout the known world as the disciples obeyed the command of the risen Christ to take his message to the ends of the earth. It was the unseen hand of God bringing to pass his predetermined plan to deliver, redeem and restore his creation.

God had promised that a Redeemer would come, who would reunite Mankind with Him by His sacrificial death. The Old Covenant, written over a 1,000-year period, contains 332 distinct predictions of the promised Redeemer. In his life, death, burial, resurrection and ascension Jesus the Christ, the son of the Living God has fulfilled 300 of those prophecies. The rest of those prophecies will be fulfilled when he returns to this earth as the ruling king of Kings.

---

[17] D.A. Carson, Matthew (EBC), p. 91.
[18] G.K. Beale, A New Testament Biblical Theology, p. 17.

Methods of Interpreting the Book of Revelation

As you look at how to interpret the book of Revelation there are two main contradictory views which are the Preterist and Dispensational methods. In theological circles you have two main ways to interpret the Bible from Genesis to Revelation which are Covenant Theology and Dispensational Theology. As I said in chapter one when I got delivered from addiction at the age of 19 and I was immediately thrust into this debate concerning the last days. I started my journey of faith 35 years ago in the late 1980's and spiritual warfare along with a real focus on the end times was all the rage.

I was hungry to know the truth, so I found what was considered the best books at the time on these subjects. We are talking about pre-internet days, so I had to go to a bookstore. So I ordered Clarence Larkin's book 'Dispensational Truth' written in 1918 and consumed it in a matter of days front to back. It really was very well written, documented and convincing. Clarence liked to write with pictures and illustrate the truth he was trying to convey. I liked the pictures and graphs because it did help you understand, although I don't agree with all his timelines and charts. The book was very informative and helped me grow in my understanding of Biblical history and how the unseen Hand of God has moved through time, through differing nations along with the different ages.

I then ordered David Chilton's book written in 1987 called 'The Days of Vengeance: An Exposition of the Book of Revelation'. It was a very thick book, so it took me several weeks to read. At that time David Chilton was the premier scholar writing from the preterist view and he used a lot of big words which made it a long hard read. He thoroughly documented his views with tons of source material, and it was a very compelling viewpoint. In the end I was left with whiplash.

The two books could not have been more contradictory in their interpretation of the book of Revelation and the way to interpret scripture. I was 20 years old at the time and was trying to understand how you could come up with two completely different views of the same book? I found both books to be helpful in growing in my faith and both gave me understanding that I did not have before I read them.

It's been 35 years since I read those two books and so much has changed yet so much has also remained the same. I don't consider either of these authors who are now deceased to have been heretics, which is the label that is thrown around so quickly just because you disagree with someone's viewpoints. I think they were both sincere in their beliefs and both presented a clear portrayal of faith in the risen Christ.

The dilemma that faced me was how to view the book of Revelation. I was convinced that understanding this subject was important, so I had to figure out how to find my way forward in understanding Biblical Prophecy. What I discovered was what Paul taught us in the love chapter of the Bible. In I Corinthians 13:9 he says, "we know in part". Prophecy is many times an enigma and it's meant to be. It is mysterious, puzzling and often difficult to understand so you must walk by faith. You must walk in the light that you have because you simply are not going to have everything figured out.

The Importance of Humility in Understanding Prophecy

Humility of heart is a must, so you must be careful with prophecy because it's in God's hand and he brings it to pass. The dogmatic prideful attitude thinking you have it all figured out and you have all the answers is what blinds you. His ways are not our ways therefore humility of heart is a necessity to truly understand.

Extremism develops when we try to carry to logical conclusions that which God has only revealed in part. I could see valid positions to both views, and I could see flaws in both views. However, it's been my desire and search for the truth which has helped to mold my current views. I'm going to end this series by covering five differing views used to interpret the book of Revelation because I think it's important for us to be informed and to have a basic framework for interpreting scripture.

As I was doing my bachelor's and master's degree in theology, I had to figure out the language they were using. If you are studying, for example to be a medical doctor, there is a certain vocabulary that the medical community speaks and writes in. Its medical terminology used to describe anatomical structures, procedures, conditions, processes and treatments in the medical field. It's the same way with Theologians, who have developed their own theological terminology.

Like the Pharisees and even medical doctors today, Theologians tend to argue among themselves. Books and papers are written trying to prove who has the correct interpretation of scripture. A Theological language develops because they are writing among themselves. I've come to realize most people don't understand the big Theological words used by Theologians. One of my goals is to produce material that is simple, attainable and applicable. I want to help you understand so that what you are learning affects your day-to-day life. Knowledge is good, but applied knowledge is even better because it's the wisdom to live life.

Over the years I've developed some fixed positions concerning the end of the age along with the book of Revelation which I will share with you in this book. I have some flexible positions waiting for a clearer picture to develop regarding the fulfillment of Biblical prophecy. In saying that I don't have it all figured out. If you are expecting me to provide every solution, you may find yourself disappointed. I am on a journey of faith with an open humble heart to learn as I walk and I'm inviting you to walk with me. I hope that I am simply giving you some light so that you can finish your race and not find yourself in the ditch. We live in days when there are a lot of obstacles and confusion on the road to sound Biblical truth.

John opened the book of Revelation saying, "Blessed is the one who reads aloud the words of this prophecy, and blessed are those who hear, and who keep what is written in it, for the time is near". It is clear from scripture that the apostolic writers viewed themselves in the last days. It is one of the main arguments that the Preterists emphasize to validate how they interpret the book of Revelation. It is one of the main reasons I had a hard time disagreeing with their viewpoint. You have different degrees of Preterism, but the basic belief is that much of the book of Revelation has already happened and the prophecy Jesus gave in Matthew 24 has been fulfilled.

I agreed with the Preterist position for many years and would still be one had it not been for a few texts that I just could not cut out of the Bible. The texts that refused to fit in their puzzle of interpretation were:

- Jesus' prophecy in Matthew chapter 24 concerning Israel.
- Jesus' last words to the apostles in Acts 1 concerning Israel
- Paul's discussion to the Romans in chapters 9 thru 11 concerning Israel.

Theological Views on the Second Coming and Resurrection of the Righteous

I do consider myself a Covenant Theologian and I tend to combine Amillenial views with Historic Premillinial views, not taking an overly literal view of the text in Revelation 20:4. I have a post-tribulation view of the second coming of Christ and the catching away of the living saints at that time. I see the rapture and resurrection of the dead righteous believers as simultaneous events. Yes, that's a mouthful if you are not used to any of those terms and by the end I will teach you some Theological terminology. You will find I am not dogmatic on such complex issues and will give you other views so you can decide for yourself.

What you will find out about me is I don't have a Theological camp I am trying to defend. I'm simply trying to understand to the degree that I can understand so that I can live my life to the fullest. I simply want to fulfill the will of God for my life and share it with others. The bottom line is that we will all stand before Christ one day and give an account. I simply want to be a faithful steward over all that I have been given and that's what motivates me. Hopefully, I set an example that motivates you to do the same. If you have not been through the Foundation Publications School of Discipleship Lesson 33: Stewardship I fully cover this subject.

Let's take a quick look at the words of Christ on the temple Mount as he prophesied in Matthew chapter 24 concerning the end of the age. In Matthew 24 while Jesus was on the Mt. of Olives, he made a series of predictions concerning the 'end of the age'. Jesus spoke of things that were about to happen and things that were far off in the future. Earlier I said, prophecy is like an onion, that you peel off in layers. [19]Walter Kaiser states that, "prophecy may contain a near and far fulfillment blended together in the prophet's vision."

Just prior to Jesus' crucifixion it is recorded in John's gospel that he cleansed the Jewish temple due to the leadership corrupting Israel's worship for power and profit. The Jewish leaders, being upset about this act of exposing their fraud said to him, "What sign do you show us for doing these things? Jesus answered them, destroy this temple, and in

---

[19] Walter C. Kaiser, Toward an Old Testament Theology, p. 106.

three days I will raise it up. The Jews then said, it has taken forty-six years to build this temple, and will you raise it up in three days?" But he was speaking about the temple of his body."

Now in Matthew's gospel chapter 24:1-2 it records a conversation between Jesus and his disciples. "Jesus left the temple and was going away, when his disciples came to point out to him the buildings of the temple. But he answered them, You see all these, do you not? Truly, I say to you, there will not be left here one stone upon another that will not be thrown down".

[20]The discourse begins with a clear reference to the destruction of the temple, which occurred in AD 70 some 40 years later. The city of Jerusalem was overthrown, and the temple was completely destroyed by the Roman armies. The Jews were scattered, and the nation of Israel ceased to exist. Jesus's prediction was fulfilled, and it was a 'day of judgment' upon the nation of Israel.

The Preterist interpretation of these events saw this as a fulfillment of the 'day the Lord'. The Latin word for Preterist means past and it's a view that sees the book of Revelation as having already been fulfilled except for the Second Coming of Christ, Final Judgment, Resurrection of the dead along with the New Heavens and New Earth. I do not agree with their view, but I do see the events of AD 70 as a peeling back of the layer of the onion when it comes to prophetic events.

At Christ' second coming he will return to the Mt. of Olives in Jerusalem which can be found in Zechariah 14:4. In Matthew chapter 24 we are seeing Jesus as the Prophet. Jesus' prophecy was speaking about **both present and future** events blending them together. The judgment upon Israel in 70 AD and the end of the age when God comes to judge the nations have quite a lot in common. [21]The coming of the Son of Man in Matthew 24:30 cannot be exhausted by AD 70.

The Jewish Concept of the 'Day of the Lord'

The Old Testament prophets used a common phrase the 'day of the Lord'. The 'day of the Lord' which the prophets spoke of was to be a time when the full restoration of Israel, the earth, the heavens and the resurrection of the dead would occur under a Messianic figure. It was

---

[20] R.T. France, The Gospel of Matthew, (NICNT), p. 893.
[21] D.A. Carson, Matthew, p. 501.

also to be a time when the nations of the earth would be judged, and justice would reign under a messianic king like David. This was the dream the Zealots had of Jewish nationalism. The Jewish concept of the kingdom of God explains why the Jews tried to make Jesus king by force during the early part of his ministry because they wanted him to lead them out from Roman oppression and establish a political kingdom greater than David's.

The Bible is the story of redemptive history in time through the Hebrew people, remedying Adam and Eve's decision to disobey, resulting in the corruption of all creation. It is the story of how God is going to vindicate his own righteousness and judge the sins of humanity. He will fix what we have broken, and he will correct what we have corrupted. The deep longing for creation to be made right is the driving force behind the scriptures. The Bible is essentially prophetic in nature "declaring the end from the beginning "as it says in Isaiah 46:10. The prophets looked forward to the full restoration between God and man along with a renewal of creation itself.

[22]The term 'day of the Lord' becomes the focal point of prophet's with similar terms like 'that day,' 'the day of,' and 'the day when,' appearing nearly 200 times in the writings of the Hebrew Prophets. In the prophetic writings there is an expectation that God will reveal himself and set right that which humanity has made wrong through Adam's sin. It's what lies at the heart of the 'day of the Lord' concept developed in prophetic literature.

We see this in Isaiah 2:12 when he declares, "For the LORD of hosts has a day against all that is proud and lofty, against all that is lifted up—and it shall be brought low. . . The haughtiness of man shall be humbled, and the lofty pride of men shall be brought low, and the LORD alone will be exalted 'in that day'." It will be a humbling of humanity's sin and pride is spoken of in the context of God's coming judgment. It will be a judgment upon Israel, the nations and will affect even creation itself. It will be a redemptive judgment setting them free from the powers of darkness that have held them captive.

It was very similar terminology used by John the Baptist preparing the way for Jesus. John said to the crowds: "You brood of

---

[22] John P. Harrigan, The Gospel of Christ Crucified: A Theology of Suffering Before Glory, p. 45.

vipers! Who warned you to flee from the wrath to come? Bear fruits in keeping with repentance. And do not begin to say to yourselves, 'We have Abraham as our father.' For I tell you, God is able from these stones to raise up children for Abraham. Even now the axe is laid to the root of the trees. Every tree therefore that does not bear good fruit is cut down and thrown into the fire."

Christ stepped into time as God (Luke 1:26-38) and when He did it opened the door of the 'day of the Lord'. His arrival was declared by the heavens (Matthew 2:1-12), and the prophetic scriptures were fulfilled one after another. His death, burial, and resurrection gave him the keys of the kingdom to unlock the door. At his death the heavens made a declaration as the sun did not shine for 3 hours, and an earthquake took place with creation itself groaning (Luke 23:44).

Over 300 prophecies in the Hebrew Bible concerning his coming were fulfilled. The Hebrew prophets had been vindicated and shown to be servants of the living God. Jesus' ascension to the right hand of the Father and outpouring of the Spirit was the opening act of the 'day of the Lord'. Peter, in preaching the first sermon of the Messianic age, speaks of the 'day of the Lord'. He explains that the promised outpouring of the Holy Spirit was a result of Jesus being seated on the throne of God and an extension of his rule connecting heaven to earth (Acts 2:14-40).

The prophets saw the 'day of the Lord' as a future event. The apostles taught that 'the day' had already started, because of the Messiah suffering and entering into glory, ascending to the right hand of the Father. I Peter 1:10-12 says, "concerning this salvation, the prophets who prophesied about the grace that was to be yours, searched and inquired carefully, inquiring what person or time the Spirit of Christ in them was indicating the **sufferings of Christ** and the **subsequent glories**" (Emphasis mine). [23]The prophets saw future events as a series of mountain peaks...without always distinguishing the valleys between them.

Viewing history through a redemptive lens, the day of the Lord offers what could be called "double vision." The prophets glimpsed important milestones but didn't comprehend the time gap between these events—a gap Paul described as 'the mystery.' Biblical prophecy is fulfilled in phases, and we now live in an era where the ages overlap. Although the Messianic age foretold by the prophets has begun, it exists

---

[23] Anthony Hoekema, The Bible and the Future, p. 155.

only in its initial form; its complete fulfillment will arrive when the king of glory returns. History is steadily moving toward that climactic event. Both Jewish prophets and apostles spoke about inheriting the kingdom of God, restoring Israel, the resurrection of the dead, judgment of nations, God's glory filling the earth, and the ultimate renewal of heaven and earth.

Jesus is seated in the heavens with all power and authority both in this age along with the age to come. The Messianic age has dawned as the prophetic writings declared, but not in its fullness. The apostles describe this age where God has stepped into our time as simply a taste of the 'age to come'—its fullness awaits the culmination of the ages, at the return of Christ. Christ opened the door for the 'day of the Lord' and is ruling from heaven now over his body in the earth, the church. It's a rule over the hearts of those from all nations who will submit to his rule.

The 'Now and Not Yet' Fulfillment of Biblical Prophecy

Preterism fails to recognize this 'now and not yet' fulfillment of Biblical prophecy, but it is prevalent throughout the prophetic scriptures. The fulfillment of prophecy comes 'in stages' like the analogy of the onion I used. Today we are living in an overlap of the ages. What the prophets prophesied concerning the Messianic age has arrived, but only in its inaugurated form—its fullness awaits the consummation when the king of glory returns. History is moving towards this climatic event.

The Temple curtain of the Old Covenant was ripped from top to bottom signifying the end of the Mosaic age of law. The Torah law was simply a tutor to lead us to the Messiah who has opened the door and invites us to partake of the age to come. The final curtain dropping event of this age will be the fullness of the 'day of the Lord' when Christ returns in judgment, taking us into the age to come. The birth pangs of the new age will be complete when he sets his feet upon the Mt. of Olives to begin his rule upon this earth.

Paul told us in Ephesians 1:10 that in the 'fullness of time all things in heaven and things on earth' would be united and restored in Christ. It's what Peter referred to as the 'restoration of all the things' about which God spoke by the mouth of his holy prophets long ago.

The restoration started through the outpouring of the Holy Spirit on the day of Pentecost when the body of Christ was brought to birth. In Ephesians 1:20-23 it says that when Christ rose from the dead and ascended into the heavenlies then he was seated at the right hand of the Father. He is "far above all rule and authority and power and dominion, and above every name that is named, not only in this age but also in the one to come. And he put all things under his feet and gave him as head over all things to the church, which is his body, the fullness of him who fills all in all."

Paul, who wrote two thirds of the New Testament epistles, seemed to have an idea about this valley when he spoke about 'the mystery' in the book of Ephesians. However, he along with Jude, James and John all lived with an expectation of Christ's imminent return. Paul reveals to us that Christ's rule is first about an inward transformation and restoration in the hearts of all who call upon the name of Jesus. Paul referred to this time as 'the mystery'.

G.H. Lang in his book 'The Parabolic Teaching of Scriptures' says that: "Neither John nor Christ said that the kingdom 'is at hand', in the sense that the kingdom of glory or physical rule of Christ upon this earth could be ushered in at once." He referred to this as 'the mystery'. Paul told us in Ephesians 1:10 that in the 'fullness of time all things in heaven and things on earth' would be united and restored in Christ. It's what Peter referred to as the 'restoration of all the things' about which God spoke by the mouth of his holy prophets long ago (Acts 3:21).

G.H. Lang shows us that the Greek perfect tense cannot be translated by the English present tense. He shows us that when John and Christ said that 'the kingdom has drawn near,' it was in the sense that a king is the essence and embodiment of his kingdom. So, when the king visits a region then the kingdom and the authority the king represents is present in the person of the king. This, then, was the inclusive theme of John and Christ. [24]All their teaching was concerned with this kingdom of God and heaven, which is the case with their pictures and parables. Only there were two aspects and periods of this kingdom, as foretold by the prophets and was the necessity of the case: an inward and an outward kingdom.

The inward kingdom was spiritual in the hearts of men. The outward kingdom would deal in human affairs, and the latter must wait for the former. Let me repeat the last two sentences because they are very important to remember. There were two aspects and periods of this

---

[24] G.H. Lang, The Parabolic Teaching of Scriptures, p. 28-29.

kingdom, as foretold by the prophets and was the necessity of the case: an **inward** and an **outward** kingdom. An inward kingdom in the hearts of men. Then an outward kingdom which will affect human affairs, when Christ judges and rules over the nations. Getting this concept correct is of utmost importance in understanding what the New Testament teaches.

The 'Day of the Lord': The Culmination of Redemptive History

Now the defining event of redemptive history is what the prophets called the 'day of the Lord'. It's the icing on the cake of all the prophets foretold. It's the Jewish view of redemptive history with the arrival of the Messiah inaugurating the 'day of the Lord', splitting time between this age and the age to come. It's the primary message that ties together the Old Testament prophets and the New Testament apostles. It's the cohesive message of God's redemptive history spoken through the Hebrew prophets and understood through the apostles.

The Jewish prophet's and Jewish apostles both taught inheriting the kingdom of God, the restoration of Israel, a resurrection of the dead, a judgment of the nations and the glory of God filling the earth, along with a final restoration of the heavens and the earth.

The prophets saw the 'day of the Lord' as a future event. The apostles taught that 'the day' had already started, because of the Messiah suffering and entering into glory, ascending to the right hand of the Father. Peter started his first epistle saying, "concerning this salvation, the prophets who prophesied about the grace that was to be yours, searched and inquired carefully, inquiring what person or time the Spirit of Christ in them was indicating the **sufferings of Christ** and the **subsequent glories**" (Emphasis mine).

As you are looking through the view of redemptive history, 'the day of the Lord, gives you what I call double vision. What I mean is that the prophets saw the high points but did not understand the valley and space of time between these two events. It's what Paul called 'the mystery'. Peter in his second epistle 3:8 - 9 says "do not overlook this one fact, beloved, that with the Lord one day is as a thousand years, and a thousand years as one day. The Lord is not slow to fulfill his promise as some count slowness, but is patient toward you, not wishing that any should perish, but that all should reach repentance, but the 'day of the Lord' will come." He seemed to have a glimpse into this valley between

Christ first and second coming, but he still expected Christ to return in his lifetime.

Paul, who wrote two thirds of the New Testament epistles, seemed to have an idea about this valley when he spoke about 'the mystery' in the book of Ephesians. However, he along with Jude, James and John all lived with an expectation of Christ's imminent return.

We like to think of the apostles as demi-gods, but they were simply men just like us. I can't believe that any of them could have imagined that I'm sitting here in 2024 writing on an electronic book in real time. I'm then going to take the message that I wrote and record it. I'll then push a little button and transmit this message to the world instantly. I like to look at it this way because it helps me understand. The apostolic writers walked through the front door of the 'day of the Lord', last days and end of the ages. The times that we live in are closer to the back door; getting ready to step into the age to come at Christ second coming.

Jesus began his rule on this earth on the day of Pentecost. However, it's only a rule over those whose hearts submit to the king of glory. It's an inward rule over the hearts of those from all nations who receive his message of redemption, justification, propitiation, reconciliation and restoration. He has begun the restoration of all things through his body, but it's only a taste of what's going to happen upon his return to this earth. [25]The 'Day' has already dawned through the resurrection of Christ and the outpouring of the Spirit which is the beginning of the new creation with the Spirit being given as the downpayment of the final redemption at the return of Christ on that glorious 'Day'.

The prophets saw the first and second coming of the Messiah as one event. On one Mountain, you have the first coming of Christ as the suffering servant and on the other Mountain, you have the second coming of Christ as the ruling King. It's why the Pharisees had such a hard time reconciling these two aspects of the Messiah in one man.

It was the apostles, who accurately interpreted what the prophets had declared, concerning the 'day of the Lord'. The one thing that the teachers of Israel failed to understand was that the Messiah first had to suffer as the 'Lamb of God' before He could deliver them from their enemies as the ruling king. The period of overlap between an already

---

[25] G.K. Beale, A New Testament Biblical Theology, p. 132.

'day of the Lord' and a future 'day of the Lord' is what Paul called 'the mystery' that was hidden.

In Christ's first coming, the 'day of the Lord' has intruded in this present age and the grace of God has appeared, bringing salvation for all people, initiating the new creation within the heart of man. Nevertheless, we are still waiting for our blessed hope, the appearance of the glory of our great God and Savior Jesus Christ, when our bodies will become like His resurrection body, he raises the dead, he completely subdues his enemies and restores the kingdom to Israel. The culmination of the 'day of the Lord' is going to be about the cleansing fire of God's judgment transforming creation itself. The next great event on the calendar of redemptive history is the second coming of Christ which is going to wrap up this present age.

Empowering Words of Jesus for Discipleship

Let me share two more scriptures that have helped me to form my ideas. After Jesus' resurrection he utters some of his final words in Matthew 28:18 - 20. Jesus said to them, "All authority in heaven and on earth has been given to me. Go therefore and make disciples of all nations, baptizing them in the name of the Father and of the Son and of the Holy Spirit, teaching them to observe all that I have commanded you. And behold, I am with you always, to the end of the age."

The Great Commission should be our primary focus until he returns. However, Jesus' last conversation with his disciples on the Mt. of Olives is the icing on the cake validating the nation of Israel's place in the events wrapping up this current age.

Right before Jesus ascended to the Father the disciples asked him a question regarding Israel. Acts 1:6 - 7 says when they had come together, they asked him, "Lord, will you at this time restore the kingdom to Israel?" He said to them, "It is not for you to know times or seasons that the Father has fixed by his own authority."

Jesus didn't say. Hey guys you have it all wrong. I'm done with Israel; the church is Israel's replacement. Instead, he said it is not for you to know the times and seasons the Father has fixed. He said let the Father take care of Israel. You need to focus on the mission I've given you.

Jesus then once again defines our mission as his body. He says, "you will receive power when the Holy Spirit has come upon you, and you will be my witnesses in Jerusalem and in all Judea and Samaria, and to the end of the earth. And when he had said these things, as they were looking on, he was lifted up, and a cloud took him out of their sight. And while they were gazing into heaven as he went, behold, two men stood by them in white robes, and said, "Men of Galilee, why do you stand looking into heaven? This Jesus, who was taken up from you into heaven, will come in the same way as you saw him go into heaven."

Two things I want to emphasize about this portion of text:

- **Number one** is that our main focus should be a complete focus on the Great Commission of making disciples.
- **Number two** is that Jesus is going to restore the kingdom to Israel when he returns to this earth and he is going to return to this earth in the same location that he left. It is also the same location that he gave his final prophecy in Matthew chapter 24 concerning the end of the age which is the Mt. of Olives.

Fulfillment of Prophecy: Jesus' Arrival in the Fullness of Times

Jesus stepped into time at the right time in human history during the reign of the Roman Empire. It is one of the meanings behind Paul's usage of the term fullness of times. The prophetic conditions had come to full maturity for the Messiah to step into time and fulfill that which was spoken by the Hebrew prophets.

I find it extremely interesting that at the end of WWII the nations of the earth were realigned in dramatic fashion with the rise of the American Empire. Two things happened simultaneously. 1947 is marked as the opening of the Third Industrial Revolution, the Information Age and 1948 was the restoration of the Jewish state that had not existed for almost 2,000 years. I don't think those two events are coincidences and I do think those two events have created a context for the text of Matthew chapter 24 to be fulfilled in a whole new layer of understanding; concerning the prophecy that Jesus gave regarding the end of this present age.

Let me go off on a little side note as I start concluding this chapter. As an American and one who served as a missionary from my mid 20's to my late 30's. I want to give my perspective. As Americans we tend to think the world revolves around America. I understand it because we live in a vacuum of world history to where in our lifetimes, we have only known a world that has gravitated around American world power. Any honest observer can see that our power has been a double-edged sword. Just as Rome we have yielded that power for good and evil.

As American Christians we tend to think we are at the center of all that God is doing on the earth. Now I do think that America has had a unique place in being a vehicle to shape world events concerning the end of the age. Just as God used Rome and the Roman Roads during the infancy of the church. In like manner, the American world order which increased the free flow of travel and technology has played a part in facilitating the free flow of the Christian missionary movement in the 20th century.

The church in America has played an important role since the 1900's in taking the gospel to the ends of the earth. Sure, it's been a mixed bag, but overall, the church in America has had a positive impact in spreading the gospel worldwide. Especially after WWII with our abundant resources, free flow of thought, free flow of travel and a home base being a government that protected freedom of religion along with a population that was supportive financially.

A lot has changed since WWII in America. It's my perspective that the day of America being a mission base to reach the rest of the world is concluding. I could go through a list of reasons why I feel the way I do, but quite simply one of the main reasons is technology. The "Roman roads" of today are the Internet, the smartphone and the technological advancements to be able to communicate instantly all over the world. The vast majority of the world doesn't want, nor do they need American missionaries. It's my opinion that it's America who needs a missionary movement.

What is America's place at the end of the age? It's a good question because America is not in the Bible and not in the book of Revelation. I spent time during the mid-1990's working with a church planting team in New York City starting a church in Queen's, NY. During this period, I would go once a week to Yonkers, NY teaching at a Christian Rehabilitation Center. On Friday night's I would go to Times Square Church to help them do outreach to the New York homeless.

The famous Pentecostal preacher David Wilkerson founded the

Times Square Church in 1987 which is in the Theatre District of
Manhattan. He was also the founder of Teen Challenge which has
become a nationwide Christian rehabilitation program. I'm mentioning
this because David had a very American perspective of the book of
Revelation. He identified America and particularly New York City as
being the 'mystery Babylon' spoken of in the book of Revelation
chapters 17 and 18.

I don't agree with his interpretation, but he was a prophetic voice
to the American Church. Like Luther and many of the Protestant
Reformers who believed the Catholic Church was the 'mystery Babylon',
I think they were both correct for their times. However, I think they
were both wrong when it comes to the ultimate fulfillment and
interpretation of the 'mystery Babylon' spoken of in chapter 17 and 18 of
Revelation. Martin Luther was addressing the corruption of his time in
both the church and world. David Wilkerson was addressing the
corruption of the American church and particularly the prosperity gospel
with its excessive extravagance along with the corruption of an American
society that had made money and pleasure its god.

Jesus' Parable of the Wheat and Tares

I want to end this chapter discussing Jesus' parable about the
wheat and tares. In Matthew 13:39 Jesus is explaining his parable about
the wheat and tares to his disciples saying: "the harvest is the end of the
age." In Israel after they harvested their crops, at the end of the growing
season they took the wheat to a threshing floor. The threshing floor is
where the wheat and tares were separated. I find this a very interesting
study and there is so much to be said about this subject.

Do you know where the Temple foundations were laid? The
Temple built by Solomon, the second temple destroyed in AD 70 and
now where Islam's Dome of the Rock sits were all built in the same
location. In the last chapter of II Samuel the prophet Gad came to king
David and said: "Go up and build an altar to the Lord on the threshing
floor." David obeyed and bought the threshing floor. He then built an
altar to the Lord there and presented sacrificial offerings. Do you know
this is the same place that Abraham had offered Isaac some 700 years
earlier? It's also the same place that Jesus prophesied which is recorded
in Matthew chapter 24 some 950 years after David.

The threshing floor theme is woven throughout the Bible and

something Jesus' disciples would have understood because it was a part of Israel's culture at the time. The difference between wheat and tares in their infancy is indistinguishable. It's not until the wheat begins to produce fruit that it begins to bend over while the tares remain standing straight and tall which distinguishes the wheat from tares. You couldn't go through the field and pick out the tares or you would destroy the wheat too, you had to wait till harvest. At harvest you cut the field and brought it to the threshing floor.

The Symbolism of Threshing Floors

[26]Threshing floors were located on elevated ground where breezes could assist in separated chaff from the grain. [27]You would put your harvest on the threshing floor and either an ox would trample the stalks or workers would beat them with sticks. As the wind blew it would separate the wheat from the tares.

In our modern outlook of history, we fail to see the two-sided coin of salvation and judgment. [28]The threshing imagery conveys both separation and destruction. The cross is our foundation, yet it is a place of salvation: restoration, reconciliation, mercy, while at the same time a place of judgment: separation, sifting, holiness produced by the consuming fire of the Spirit. The book of Revelation is an unfolding of God's judgments in history meant to turn humanity back to Christ.

The Hebrew word *mishpāṭ,* which is translated into the English word judgment, can be defined as a *sifting out.* Judgment is not only a final, curtain-dropping event but also a lengthy process with God as an active investigator testing people's hearts, giving the wicked a chance to repent. Peter tells us that it is not God's heart that any would perish, but he desires all to come to the full understanding of the truth (II Peter 3:9).

Worship on the threshing floor is the great equalizer. It is a place of total surrender where the arrogant soul is humbled and the downtrodden is lifted up. Hannah, the mother of Samuel, who was a great transitional figure in the Old Testament preparing the way for the king-priest ministry of David, had a similar word as Mary the mother of Jesus. Mary celebrated *mishpāṭ* as an upside-down reversal of the current

---

[26] Victor Matthews, Manners and Customs in the Bible, p. 103.

[27] Roland de Vaux, Ancient Israel: Its Life and Institutions, p. 32.

[28] R.T. France, The Gospel of Matthew (NICNT), p. 111.

state of affairs. 'He has brought down rulers from their thrones but has lifted up the humble' (Luke 1:52)." The great equalizer is the cross. [29]The cross is simultaneously the moment of salvation and the moment of judgment.

The threshing floor is a place of crushing and separation where all things are laid open and naked before the Lord of the harvest. The threshing floor was also symbolic of the relationship between the bride and the bridegroom. It is not insignificant that Ruth came to Boaz at the 'threshing floor' (Ruth 3:6-14). Boaz represents Christ (our kinsman-redeemer) and Ruth, the bride of Christ. At the center of the threshing floor, one finds two large flat stones, one resting on the top of the other. They were fitted and joined together. The top stone was known as the female and the bottom stone the male, the grinding of grain was a depiction of the act of marriage (Job 31:10).

The foundations of the Temple were built upon a place of separation and refinement. John the Baptist's, in Matthew chapter 3, clearly defined Christ's mission saying, "He will baptize you with the Holy Spirit and fire. His winnowing fork is in his hand, and he will clear his threshing floor and gather his wheat into the barn, but the chaff he will burn with unquenchable fire." It was this picture that Jesus gave explaining that the end of the age is going to be a harvest of both wickedness and righteousness. He showed us that if we want to be sons of the light then we must bow in humility with a single focus of devotion to the risen Christ.

As I studied the preterist and dispensationalist views I was left with two choices:

- **Number one** as Preterists I had to view the church as taking over and transforming the world's systems emphasizing a theology of dominion.
- **Number two** as a dispensationalist I had to view the church as a small remnant barely holding on to the faith where most will completely fall away from the faith.

Yes, I'm painting in broad brush strokes, but that pretty much sums up the two contradictory viewpoints. I do think there is a third way to look at things. If the end of the age is about harvest, then couldn't we

---

[29] D.A. Carson, The Gospel According to John, p. 442.

have both an apostasy with many falling away from the faith and revival with multitudes coming to Christ at the same time?

Personally, I think that's the picture of the end of the age. It will be the ultimate valley of decision with the divide between light and darkness clearly evident. The winds of God will be blowing forcefully upon the threshing floor separating the wheat from the chaff. [30]The judgments of Revelation are not arbitrary acts of wrath, but responses intended to expose evil and call for repentance.

The threshing floor is about worship, and the end of the age is going to be about who you are going to worship? The book of Revelation is a worship book clearly laying out a decision between worshiping the Lamb slain before the foundation of the world or worshiping the beast. The purpose of the judgments is redemptive – to bring people to repentance. [31]God's *mishpāṭ* is the active intervention of God to put things right because [32]Yahweh's judgment is discriminating, not destructive for its own sake. [33]The Lord's coming for *mishpāṭ* refines rather than annihilates his covenant people.

Israel had three feasts: Passover, Pentecost and Tabernacles. Jesus is our Passover Lamb. Pentecost brought to birth the church with the outpouring of the Spirit. It was also called the feast of the 'first fruits'. The feast of Tabernacles was the harvest feast at the end of the growing season. Dispensationalist will put the fulfillment of the feast of Tabernacles as being strictly in the millennial reign of Christ upon the earth after Christ returns but let me pose a question.

If the Feast of Passover was fulfilled in this age and the Feast of Pentecost which birthed the church was fulfilled in this age. Then surely the Feast of Tabernacles will be fulfilled in this age? Surely it will be fulfilled prior to Christ's second coming. I take the position that it will be, and we are going to see God's wind blowing, shaking, crushing and sifting the nations. It's going to be a great harvest consummating, wrapping up this age and inaugurating king Jesus' reign upon this earth. The backdoor of the 'day of the Lord' is going to open and Christ is going to step back into time as the ruling king and an all-consuming fire

---

[30] Richard Bauckham, The Theology of Book of Revelation, p. 38.

[31] Christopher J.H. Wright, Old Testament Ethic for the People of God, p. 255.

[32] John Goldingay, Isaiah 1-39, (ICC), p. 157.

[33] Andrew Hill, Malachi, (AB), p. 259.

judging the nations with justice. [34]The judgments in Revelation express God's just response to evil and his faithfulness to vindicate his people.

One analogy that Jesus used in the prophecy he gave in Matthew chapter 24 was comparing the events that would take place prior to his coming as to a 'woman in labor'. Vs. 4-8 Jesus answered a question about his return and the end of the age. He said, "See that no one leads you astray. For many will come in my name, saying, 'I am the Christ,' and they will lead many astray. And you will hear of wars and rumors of wars. See that you are not alarmed, for this must take place, but the end is not yet. For nation will rise against nation, and kingdom against kingdom, and there will be famines and earthquakes in various places. All these are but, the beginning of birth pangs."

Jesus instructed us to make sure "that no one leads you astray" (Matt. 24:4) opening his 'last days' prophetic view not with war or signs but emphasizing deception. Paul is using very similar language to Christ drawing on his prophecy in I Thessalonians 5:1-9. [35]Paul assumes his readers already know the 'day of the Lord' tradition. Vs. 2 he says, "the day of the Lord will come like a thief in the night" then vs. 3 talks about "peace and safety" then uses the metaphor of a pregnant woman and labor pains. [29]The language echoes Jesus' parables of sudden judgment and false assurance not to mention his prophetic proclamations in Matthew 24:8 concerning birth pangs of increasing conflict, famines, natural disasters, deception and lawlessness in relation to the end of the age. Lying spirits create fanatical attitudes towards the 'day of the Lord.'

Lessons from the Birth Pains to Stay Focused

The end of the age is compared to the birth pangs of a new age and just like natural birth, it's going to be bloody and painful. Just like a woman in labor we will continue to see these events grow closer together in frequency. The main thing women are taught to do through the process of pain during the birthing process is to stay focused. It's of utmost importance that we don't focus on the waves, turmoil and confusion as these events happen more frequently, but focus on the mission. It's the opposite of sound doctrine which produces stability of mind, but Paul

---

[34] G.K. Beale, Revelation (NIGTC), p. 60.
[35] Gordon D. Fee, God's Empowering Presence, p. 744, 746.

called it 'shaken in mind'.

As we grow closer to the end of the age, winds of confusion will be blowing strongly. That's why Jesus warned us to not let anyone lead us astray because there will be many deceptive messages, calamities and distractions. It's an alarmist attitude that causes you to make irrational decisions; replacing faithful waiting and wise action, exactly what Jesus warned against (Matt. 24:23). He was warning them that deception is a reality and that people will use distorted realities to control. Language that is used to make you feel like you are in a spiritually elite movement of super saints should be a loud warning sign. Deception is a powerful force when groups of people begin to believe the same lie.

Just as the church was birthed through a great outpouring of the wind of the Spirit in Jerusalem opening the day of Christ reign from heaven through the church. In like manner, the church age will be consummated with the winds of the Spirit sweeping the entire globe bringing in the harvest of the end of the age consummating 'the day of the Lord'. Christ the foundation will clearly be revealed. It will be the unveiling of the risen Christ and the unveiling of the Antichrist. The inhabitants of the earth will have to choose between light and darkness. It will be a choice between the truth that is found only in Christ or the deceptive lives of man living independent of God following the Antichrist.

The end of the age is about a return to foundations. If the body of Christ is to fulfill its intended purpose, then it must return to a single focus on being devoted to Christ and worshiping him with our whole lives. The wheat will those who bow in humility to the king and the glory of the coming king will rest upon them. To those who refuse to bow, but want to live their own lives, darkness and the coming judgment will be their portion.

CHAPTER 3

A LAMP SHINING IN A DARK PLACE

"We have the prophetic word more fully confirmed, to which you will do
well to pay attention as to a lamp shining in a dark place, until the
day dawns and the morning star rises in your hearts."

~ II Peter 1:19 ~

Peter in his second epistle 1:17-21 says: "the voice was borne to
him by the Majestic Glory, 'This is my beloved Son, with whom I am
well pleased,' we ourselves heard this very voice borne from heaven, for
we were with him on the holy mountain. And we have the prophetic
word more fully confirmed, to which you will do well to pay attention as
to a lamp shining in a dark place, until the day dawns and the morning
star rises in your hearts, knowing this first of all, that no prophecy of
Scripture comes from someone's own interpretation. For no prophecy
was ever produced by the will of man, but men spoke from God as they
were carried along by the Holy Spirit."

The episode that Peter was referring to is recorded in all three of
the Synoptic gospels. Peter, James and John were with Jesus when he
was "transfigured before them and his clothes became radiant, intensely
white, as no one on earth could bleach them. And there appeared to them
Elijah with Moses and they were talking with Jesus. And a cloud
overshadowed them and a voice came out of the cloud, "This is my
beloved Son; listen to him." And suddenly, looking around, they no
longer saw anyone with them but Jesus only." I am not going to get into
speculation on all that took place in this powerful experience.

If you look at the context of chapters 1 and 2 of Peter's epistle,
he clarifies what he wants us to understand. He starts out talking about
the new birth of the Spirit and how that changes us from the inside out.
II Peter 1:4 says we have been made: "partakers of the divine nature,
having escaped from the corruption that is in the world because of sinful
desire."

Peter then clearly lays out the character traits that are produced
through this living relationship with a living Christ in verses 5 thru 12.
In verse 16 of this chapter, he says: "we did not follow cleverly devised

myths when we made known to you the power and coming of our Lord Jesus Christ, but we were eyewitnesses of his majesty." Peter had experienced the power of the age to come, and his faith was based on more than a fairy tale, but it was based upon the God who created all things.

The Divine Encounters on Mt. Sinai

It was Moses' visitation upon Mt. Sinai where he received the Torah (Mosaic law), and it was the entire foundation of Israel's worship of Jehovah as he met face to face with the 'Great I Am'. Like Moses, Elijah was one of the central figures of the Hebrew prophets. Just after his show down with the false prophets of Baal turning the nation back to covenant faithfulness, he has a visitation of God on Mt. Sinai also called Mt. Horeb. It's the same place where Moses experienced the burning bush and was commissioned by the God of Abraham, Isaac and Jacob.

The two main figures that the nation of Israel looked to as men who had a direct encounter with God were here with Jesus. It says a cloud overshadowed them and a voice came out of the cloud, "This is my beloved Son; listen to him." And suddenly, looking around, they no longer saw anyone with them but Jesus only."

The Law and the Prophets found their fulfillment in the Messiah. Jesus is the 'Great I Am' in person. He is God manifested in human flesh and he alone is a lamp shining in a dark place lighting our pathway. Paul says it this way in 2 Corinthians 4:6: "For God, who said, 'Let light shine out of darkness,' has shone in our hearts to give the light of the knowledge of the glory of God in the face of Jesus Christ."

I've pondered on this text and reflected on previous moves of the glory of God visiting America. America has a history of revival that has greatly affected us as a nation. The First Great Awakening in the New England colonies was led by Jonathan Edwards prior to the Revolutionary War who preached that famous sermon 'Sinners In The Hands Of An Angry God.'.

America then experienced the Second Great Awakening starting around 1795 up to around 1835. One of the greatest church planting movements started out of this visitation of the Spirit through the Wesley brothers. The Wesley brothers were simply responding to the Great Commission empowered by the Holy Spirit and making disciples. What eventually developed was the Methodist Denomination.

I'm reminded of Peter's initial response to his experience in the glory of God. Peter's initial response to the glory of God was to build a monument to Elijah, Moses and Jesus, until he heard the voice of God. I scratch my head when I look at the current state of the Methodist Church and wonder how they went from the glory of God to just an empty shell of an institution that embraces destructive heresies and something other than the foundation of Christ. I wish it was just the United Methodist, but I could write a whole book on the American church's departure from the faith. In America we have built monuments, we have beautiful buildings, and we have great wealth, but where has the glory of God gone?

In verse 13 of this chapter Peter was aware that he was about to die so he was making every effort to ensure that the glory would continue after he was gone. He wanted them to stay singly focused on Christ and he knew the church wasn't built around any one man, but on the foundation of the one who rose from the dead and entered the glory of God. Peter begins chapter 2 urging them, as Paul did in I Corinthians 10, to remain faithful and avoid the enemy's deception. He knew that false prophets and false teachers would bring in "destructive heresies, even denying the Master who bought them, bringing upon themselves swift destruction. And many will follow their sensuality and because of them the way of truth will be blasphemed. And in their greed, they will exploit you with false words" (II Peter 2:2-3).

Peter was trying to show us where our complete focus needs to be. The risen Christ can never become secondary. It's when Jesus is no longer the central focus of our lives that we lose our way. If we want to see the glory of God, then we must once again singly focus on the risen Christ. So many have lost their way because they are looking for some new thing. The latest revelation, the next great technique for church growth, the shiniest new word and the prophecy that is going to show them the way. What we need is a return to the simplicity of Christ.

The Established Foundation Of Christ

We have a sure foundation. It's Christ as he is revealed in the prophetic words of the prophets and confirmed by the apostolic writers. We don't need a new revelation or some special insight that no one has ever heard of before, but we need the Holy Spirit to open the eyes of our hearts to what's been from the beginning; the Lamb who was slain before the foundation of the world. He is the Alpha and the Omega. The one who knows the end from the beginning. It's only the resurrected Christ who overcame death and Hades that can lead us through the deception of the end of the age. He is the one who stands in the midst of the lampstands lighting our pathway in this present darkness.

The author of Hebrews starts his epistle saying: "Long ago, at many times and in many ways, God spoke to our fathers by the prophets, but in these last days he has spoken to us by his Son." He is the Word made flesh and the one who is shining with the brightness of the glory of God. In the midst of the darkness of this age we must keep our eyes fixed on Christ allowing 'the knowledge of His truth' to permeate our hearts.

I hear people talk about the Leviathan spirit, the Jezebel spirit and whatever other spiritual principality that they have uncovered. I hear them talking about angels who have given them special insight and interpretation. It's this special revelation which God has revealed to them that is going to set you free. People are chasing after the latest spiritual key and the unveiling of some mysterious code to enlighten them. As we talk about darkness and deception let's start where the rubber meets the road which is self-deception. Self-deception is our primary problem. I've had to take many hard looks in the mirror. I encourage you to go look in the mirror of the word of God and you will see that the problem is you, it's not some principality.

Embracing the Light and Fire of the Risen Christ

Let's look at I John chapter 1:5 - 8 which says: "God is light, and in him is no darkness at all. If we say we have fellowship with him while we walk in darkness, we lie and do not practice the truth. But if we walk in the light, as he is in the light, we have fellowship with one another, and the blood of Jesus his Son cleanses us from all sin. If we say we have no sin, we deceive ourselves, and the truth is not in us." It's one of those scriptures that should make us all squirm.

John doesn't leave room for the gray mushy ground of the postmodern lie of relativism. He cuts down the tree of the knowledge of good and evil taking us straight to the tree of the cross. Repentance means to turn, and we must turn back to the solid ground of Christ the only place to be truly free.

Self-deception is one of the greatest battles we will face

regarding the truth. It's easy to live in the shadows of our heart compartmentalizing our lives. It's easy to look at other people's sins while dismissing our own. If the *ekklēsia* is to be a pillar and support of the truth, then each of us as members of his body needs our lives to be supported by the truth.

The church is not an institution. It's not a building that can be burned or torn down. It's not joining some club or organization that can be dissolved. It's a living temple made up of individual members who have become partakers of his divine nature through new birth. John in this scripture clearly shows that each member of his body has a responsibility to live in the transparency of the light of the truth found in Christ. If we don't pursue the truth as a living reality in our hearts, then we begin to deceive ourselves by living in the shadows of duplicity.

James 1:22 - 24 tells us to: "be doers of the word, and not hearers only, deceiving yourselves. For if anyone is a hearer of the word and not a doer, he is like a man who looks intently at his natural face in a mirror. For he looks at himself and goes away and at once forgets what he was like." [36]James warns that hearing without doing involves a subtle self-deception, a false conclusion that hearing is sufficient. Paul also talked about self-deception. In I Corinthians chapter 3 where he was talking about the very foundation of truth in the church he says, "Let no one deceive himself. If anyone among you thinks that he is wise in this age, let him become a fool so that he may become wise." Paul was identifying self-deception as the root issue.

In chapter 1 of this book, I posed the question that Pilate asked Jesus the night before he was crucified; "What is truth?" In an age of confusion where truth is being made in the image of the imaginations of man's heart, the foundation of truth is extremely important. We must have a foundation of truth established in our lives or we are going to be swept away with the hurricane force winds of deception that will be sweeping the globe as the end of the age approaches. As we approach the end of the age foundations are going to be exposed like never before and we must make sure our feet are securely placed in Him.

The author of Hebrews ends chapter 12 saying: "See that you do not refuse him who is speaking. For if they did not escape when they refused him who warned them on earth." He was speaking of when God spoke directly to Moses on Mt. Sinai giving him the Torah (Mosaic law).

---

[36] Douglas J. Moo, The Letter of James, (PNTC), p. 95

"Much less will we escape if we reject him who warns from heaven. At that time his voice shook the earth, but now he has promised, "Yet once more I will shake not only the earth, but also the heavens." This phrase, "Yet once more," indicates the removal of things that are shaken—that is, things that have been made—in order that the things that cannot be shaken may remain. Therefore, let us be grateful for receiving a kingdom that cannot be shaken and thus let us offer to God acceptable worship, with reverence and awe, for our God is a consuming fire.""

The Bride's Preparation: Embracing a Life of Worship

The end of the age is about preparing the bride to meet the bridegroom. It's about a life completely dedicated to worship. [37]The marriage imagery of Revelation 19:7 portrays the consummation of God's covenant relationship with his people. The foundations of our hearts are revealed in the consuming fire of God's glory where we are found in Him: The Lamb slain before the foundations of the world. [38]True worship is fundamentally a response to the self-disclosure of God.

Truth is not found in a book, but it's found in a person. Please hear me out before you call me a heretic. [39]The Word made flesh does not nullify the written word; the two belong together. Yes, the Hebrew prophets declared the coming Messiah and these prophecies of scripture were written down so that we may understand. It's what we call the Old Testament portion of the Bible: The Law, Psalms and the Prophets.

The apostolic writers did not come up with something new but simply revealed and explained those previous prophetic words concerning the Messiah. [40]The early Chrisitan proclamation did not invent a new story but reread Israel's Scriptures in light of Christ. [41]The apostles believed they were announcing the climax of Israel's ancient hope. Our faith has an ancient foundation, but as Isaiah 28:15 says we have many times, "made lies our refuge, and in falsehood we have taken shelter." The birth pangs of the end of the age are designed to bring us back to a clear focus on the simplicity of the cross and the foundation of

---

[37] G.K. Beale, The Book of Revelation (NIGTC), p. 940.

[38] D.A. Carson, The Gospel According to John, (PNTC), p. 225.

[39] Kevin Vanhoozer, The Drama of Doctrine, p. 98.

[40] Richard Hays, Echoes of Scripture in the Gospels, p. 5.

[41] N.T. Wright, Paul and the Faithfulness of God, p. 804.

Christ alone; challenging the deceptive refuge of lies that have tried to cover the foundation. The first three chapters of the book of Revelation show Jesus' confronting deception in his church where the lies of corruption had begun to distort the truth affecting their faith.

John's Gospel: Christ Alone is Enough

To me the opening of John's gospel are some of the most powerful words in scripture summing up the truth. "In the beginning was the Word, and the Word was with God, and the Word was God. He was in the beginning with God. All things were made through him, and without him was not anything made that was made. In him was life, and the life was the light of men. The light shines in the darkness, and the darkness has not overcome it." I could stop right here because Christ alone is enough.

We are not in a relationship with a book. [42]The Bible is not an end in itself; it is the divinely authorized means by which we encounter the triune God. We are in a relationship with the living Christ. However, "the sacred writings are able to make you wise for salvation through faith in Christ Jesus" (II Tim. 3:15). [43]The Scriptures lead one to salvation because they bear witness to Christ.

Jesus rebuked the Pharisees telling them that: "You search the Scriptures because you think that in them you have eternal life and it is they that bear witness about me, yet you refuse to come to me that you may have life" (John 5:39). [44]The tragedy is not that they studied Scripture, but that they failed to see that Scriptures' function is to direct them to Jesus. The Scriptures have no independent saving value apart from the One to whom they point.

Sound doctrine gives us structure, stability and keeps us safe. [45]Sound doctrine safeguards to church against error and shapes godly living. Doctrinal stability protects believers from deception and instability. [46]Illumination is not new revelation but the Spirit opening our eyes to understand what has been revealed. It is the living Christ

[42] Kevin Vanhoozer, The Drama of Doctrine, p. 126.
[43] George Knight, The Letters to Timothy and Titus, p. 581.
[44] D.A. Carson, The Gospel According to John, (PNTC), p. 263-264.
[45] Andreas Köstenberger, A Theology of John's Gospel and Letters, p. 421.
[46] Sinclair Ferguson, The Holy Spirit, (IVP), p. 101.

who is the Spirit that illuminates, teaches and leads us into all truth.

[47]The Spirit does not introduce independent revelation but unfolds the significance of Christ's person and work. The Spirit's illumination is never contradictory to the foundation but helps to expose those who would deceptively twist the scriptures. As we contemplate truth in an ever-changing world, I want you to reflect upon our ancient faith. Our faith is based upon the sure foundation of the Ancient of Days.

On the Mt. of Transfiguration Jesus was transfigured before them and his clothes became radiant, intensely white, as no one on earth could bleach them. The glory of God was revealed, and it was clear that Jesus is the 'Great I Am'. He created the world. He is the radiance of the glory of God and the exact imprint of his nature, and he upholds the universe by the word of his power. In all the confusion, instability and darkness of the end of the age those who are established on the true foundation of Christ will shine as lights tethered to his unchanging glory.

The Contrasting Morning Stars

Did you know that Jesus and Satan are both referred to as the Morning Star in scripture, but the contrast between them could not be more profound. Two stars, one still shining, one fallen: Satan was referred to as a star (Isaish 14:12), but his light has been extinguished because of his pride. He was cast down into darkness according to Isaiah 14:13-15 speaking of the serpent figure in Genesis 3 when Adam sinned and the serpent rebelled in arrogance being cast down to Sheol and expelled to the depths of darkness.

[48]According to an ancient Jewish midrash (Bereshit Rabbah 20:5), the nāḥāš (serpent) in Genesis was not a lowly creature slithering in the dirt—it was a radiant, upright, possibly winged being. Some rabbis describe it as an angelic entity or a celestial creature capable of speech and glory, who was only later cursed to eat the dust of the ground.

The serpent was a twister of truth, and his tactic was to cause Eve to doubt God's word by implying that God was selfishly withholding divine secrets from her. By casting doubt and offering an illicit path to

---

[47] D.A. Carson, The Gospel According to John, (PNTC), p. 540.

[48] Dr. Eitan Bar, Hebrew Word Study: Serpent or Shining One (Nahash).

knowledge, the serpent's action mirrors the fundamental premise of divination: seeking hidden information through supernatural means that are not sanctioned by God. In ancient Hebrew, the verb form of *nāḥāš* (serpent) means "to practice divination or fortune-telling," linking the serpent with magical and prophetic practices.

Paul mentions that "the serpent deceived Eve through his cunning" (II Corinthians 11:3), and adds in the same chapter, *"Satan himself masquerades as an **angel of light**"* (II Corinthians 11:14) Satan rebelled against God and when he did, he was placed under eternal judgment in what the Bible calls pits or bonds of darkness (2 Peter 2:4). This darkness does not simply mean lightless, or areas void of light.

The eternal darkness to which scripture refers is essentially a moral darkness, but its cause is not simply the absence of light, it's the absence of God: who is light. Paul the apostle spoke of this in II Corinthians 4:3 - 4 when saying "if our gospel is veiled, it is veiled to those who are perishing. In their case the god of this world has blinded the minds of the unbelievers." It's Satan's desire to blind the minds of humanity so that they will worship him, whether knowingly or through ignorance.

Satan is called the god of this present age, and he takes advantage of man's innate need to worship. Satan always makes himself and sin look attractive. He comes as an angel of light to lead us into his dungeon of moral darkness. Satan's main weapon has always been deception. Satan was able to convince Eve through his subtle and cunning speech that what was forbidden by God would be good for her.

It's the postmodern lie of relativism which says truth is whatever you make it. Satan was the first post-modernist who destroyed morality through relativism where there are no absolutes, but just the mushy grayness of man being his own god. Satan was the first one to be self-deceived, but if we follow in the pathway of putting self-first then we choose to walk in darkness and begin to deceive ourselves.

As we await Christ's return, it sometimes seems as though Satan has won, and darkness has prevailed. Just as the cross seemed to be a bloody end it was Christ's death on that tree that sealed Satan's final fate. He has been defeated, but he still wields his main weapon of deception with effectiveness against the body of Christ. He is the twister of truth, the master of delusion and counterfeit. Sailors used to use the "morning star," which is the planet Venus, to know when dawn would come. It shines brightly just before dawn and is a sign or marker that a new day is coming.

The English Theologian Thomas Fuller once said, "It is darkest before the dawn." It's not any darker, but it feels darker because of the anticipation of a new day. Do you remember as a kid going on a long trip and always asking your parents, are we there yet? Are we there yet every fifteen minutes? The end of the age is going to feel like 'time compression' and the long great night at the same time.

As I speak of 'time compression' I'm not saying time changes. Time doesn't change, but our perception of time changes. [49]Modernity is characterized by social acceleration where the pace of life increases dramatically. In recent years, the pace of life has undeniably accelerated due to advancements in technology, increased connectivity and information overload. In our digital age, we are bombarded with constant stimuli, notifications and distractions, which may contribute to the feeling that time is slipping away.

Our frenetic modern life can make it difficult to savor and fully engage with each passing moment. It's this constant activity that gives the impression that time is being compressed. What is different for us as believers is that we know we have a destination. [50]The birth-pain metaphor emphasizes both certainty and escalation. We are anticipating a new day. As Titus 2:13 says we are: "waiting for our blessed hope, the appearing of the glory of our great God and Savior Jesus Christ."

Jesus compared the end of the age prior to his return as birth pangs. Just like a woman in labor, events grow closer together in frequency compressing time. However, as the hour approaches for the consummation of the 'day of the Lord' it will seem like time slows for the believer. [51]The tension between delay and expectation shapes Chrisitan experience of time. I've been told those moments right before the birth and the final push when the baby is being born seems like a lifetime. It's the last stage of giving birth and the most intense. The main thing women are taught to do through the process of pain during the birthing process is to stay focused.

[49] Hartmut Rosa, Social Acceleration, p. 7.
[50] Gene L. Green, The Letters to the Thessalonians, p. 223.
[51] Richard Bauckham, Jude, 2 Peter (WBC), p. 312.

Staying Focused on Christ's Mission

The end of the age is going to give us plenty of reasons to be distracted. It's of utmost importance that we don't focus on the difficulties, turmoil, false messages and confusion as these events happen more frequently but focus on finishing the mission Christ has given his church. Its why Peter told us to "pay attention as to a lamp shining in a dark place, until the day dawns and the morning star rises in your hearts."

Paul said it this way in Romans 8:18 - 23: "I consider that the sufferings of this present time are not worth comparing with the glory that is to be revealed to us. For the creation waits with eager longing for the revealing of the sons of God. For the creation was subjected to futility, not willingly, but because of him who subjected it, in hope that the creation itself will be set free from its bondage to corruption and obtain the freedom of the glory of the children of God. For we know that the whole creation has been groaning together in the pains of childbirth until now. And not only the creation, but we ourselves, who have the first fruits of the Spirit, groan inwardly as we wait eagerly for adoption as sons, the redemption of our bodies."

Christ will return as the victorious king to this earth. Justice will reign and peace will rule. The light of the glory of God will shine the brightest upon his church in the darkest of nights. The contrast will be visible and undeniable. The humble wheat will bow in dependence upon Christ being clearly distinguished from the arrogant and self-sufficient tares. The end of the age is going to expose foundations. The consuming fire of God is going to expose imposters, duplicity and the shadows of deception.

The fire of God will mercifully burn away the refuge of lies and the birth pangs of the end of the age are designed to show man that he is merely flesh. 1 Peter 1:23 - 25 says: "you have been born again, not of perishable seed, but of imperishable, through the living and abiding word of God: 'All flesh is like grass and all its glory like the flower of grass. The grass withers, and the flower falls, but the word of the Lord remains forever.' And this word is the good news that was preached to you."

Embracing the Truths of Our Faith

The mystery of the gospel is foolishness to the natural man. It's a rock of offense to those who walk in darkness as they stumble and fall over the very foundation that could be their security. Just walk with me for a moment as I contemplate the truth of the message concerning the foundations of our faith. Let's face it, we believe in some amazing realities.

No, we don't believe in space aliens that are going to come to save or destroy us. No, we don't believe man evolved from apes or that a man can be changed into a woman. We don't believe that Mother Earth is mad at us for abusing her so therefore we are seeing extreme weather and earthquakes. We don't believe angels have come to teach us some new revelation. We don't believe in fairy tales, myths and wild speculation. We don't believe in empty visions of puffed-up imaginations.

- We believe in the prophetic scriptures and the sure word of prophecy concerning the eternal Son of God.
- We believe that the God who created all things by the power of his Word took upon himself human flesh. He didn't appear as some alien or some phantom ghost. The Holy Spirit overshadowed and impregnated a young teenage virgin in the back hills of Galilee, the northern part of Israel. He was God manifested in human flesh born into the very world that he created. He was born to parents who traced their lineage back to King David, to Abraham and to Adam the first man.
- We believe the birth of Christ was declared by the heavens and the stars aligned declaring his entrance into our time and space.
- We believe that God promised, at the gates of Eden, that he would send a Seed of the Woman who would crush the Serpent's head and God had inscribed upon the patterns of the stars a message. The Magi from the east read this message and came to witness the event giving gifts to the one who was born king of the Jews. It was these costly gifts of gold, frankincense and myrrh that took care of the family as they fled to Egypt from the tyrant king Herod.
- We believe the unseen hand of God moved the chess pieces around fulfilling prophecy, after prophecy on a well-played out game. At

the age of 30 Jesus was baptized in water, filled with the Holy Spirit and power. He then for 3 and a half years demonstrated by signs, wonders and miracles that he was the Messiah. He was the one sent to deliver mankind promised by the prophets of an ancient faith dating back to the beginning of man.

As Jesus approached Jerusalem for the last time to fulfill the purpose for which he came into the world, the scriptures say he was met with shouts of Hosanna to the king as he humbly rode on a donkey. He cleansed the temple in Jerusalem, the city of the king and prophesied its soon destruction, declaring that his body would be the new temple. It was all part of his prophetic message on the Mt. of Olives recorded in Matthew chapter 24.

The Hebrew prophets' words declared over thousands of years were fulfilled as the Messiah was finally offered up. He was the Lamb slain before the foundations of the world, who stepped into time, offered up for the sins of the world, on the day of that final Passover. He was crucified on a tree and on the hill of the skull Golgotha outside of the city of Jerusalem. Creation itself declared his death just as it had announced his birth. The sun did not shine for 3 hours, the earth shook, and the temple veil was torn from top to bottom at his death. The master chess player had made his final move and the serpent of old had been checkmated. The cross wasn't a sidetrack but was the central purpose for which God stepped into time.

The Mystery of the Cross

The message of the cross is the mystery that was hidden. To us who believe it seems obvious, but that's because the eyes of our hearts have been opened to see the 'knowledge of the truth'. Paul is the one who unveils 'the mystery' to us. Paul's life exemplified the work of the cross and his example has taught us so much about the cruciform life of faith. In 1 Corinthians chapter 2 verse 7 thru 8 Paul said: "we impart a secret and hidden wisdom of God, which God decreed before the ages for our glory. None of the rulers of this age understood this, for if they had, they would not have crucified the Lord of glory."

Certainly, the prophecies about Jesus in the Old Testament were abundant. However, no one before Jesus, believed that the Messiah was going to come to die before he came to rule the earth. Biblical scholars say there are no Jewish commentators who believed that Isaiah 53 referred to the death of the Messiah. It was the hidden chess move that even Satan could not see.

We know Satan knows scripture because he quoted it during his interactions with Jesus when he tempted him in the wilderness. He along with the rulers of Israel were aware of these prophecies but having 'eyes they could not see and having ears they could not hear'. It was their pride that caused them to walk in darkness and stumble over the truth that was staring them in the face.

Have you ever gotten so drunk that you had a blackout where the lights in your understanding went out and you don't remember anything? The prophet Isaiah in chapter 28 says that pride resulted in the drunkenness of Ephraim. Matthew Henry comments on this text saying, "Pride was a sin that generally prevailed among them." In verse 15 of this chapter, it says that the leaders of Israel had made lies their refuge and in falsehood they had taken shelter. Did you hear that because it sounds so much like the world and even so many in the church who have made lies their refuge and in falsehood have taken shelter.

I'm not sure deceivers really know they are deceivers because they believe their own lies. They are drunk on their pride and power. It's like a drunk who is experiencing a blackout and is simply on autopilot. The leaders of Israel were drunk on their own pride and power. Like Satan they forget that they simply reflected the light of the Creator, but their pride deceived them.

It was pride that caused them to be more interested in retaining their position, power and pleasure instead of humbly turning back to God in repentance. Pride blinds you and darkens your understanding. It's what caused Satan along with the rulers of Israel to be blinded to the power that would be unleashed through the humble, crushed and crucified Lamb of God. I Peter 2:6-8 quotes from Isaiah chapter 28 when he says: "for it stands in Scripture: 'Behold, I am laying in Zion a stone, a cornerstone chosen and precious, and whoever believes in him will not be put to shame.' So the honor is for you who believe, but for those who do not believe, 'The stone that the builders rejected has become the cornerstone,' and 'A stone of stumbling, and a rock of offense'."

CHAPTER 4

THE SCARLET THREAD OF THE CROSS

"We preach Christ crucified, a stumbling block to Jews
and folly to Gentiles."

~ I Corinthains 1:23 ~

The central theme from the book of Genesis to Revelation is the cross and it's the focus of the redemptive story. What Paul called 'the mystery' and 'the word of the cross', is 'the faith' that Jude talked about because it's the gospel unveiling Christ redemptive work. It's this message that developed in the early church before you had a Bible, and it is the message that Jude was defending in Jude 1:4. Paul lays the foundation of the church on the bedrock of the revelation of the cross. The pillar of truth and foundation that the church is built upon is what Paul calls 'the word of the cross' (I Cor. 3:11).

Jesus came into this earth wrapped in swaddling cloth in a manger with shepherds looking on (Luke 2:8-12). He was born in the humblest of accommodations with the humblest of professions witnessing his birth. God stepped into time showing us the way of humility and he ended his journey showing us the way of humility in his surrender to the power of the cross (Luke 23:46). The cross on the hill outside of Jerusalem called Golgotha is the place where Jesus shed his blood and died for our sins, but what is implied in Paul's statement 'the word of the cross'? The 'word of the cross' is a much broader statement than just that Christ died for our sins. The 'word of the cross' is the foundation. It's the very cornerstone of 'the faith' and the central message of the apostles.

The word of the cross is Christ birth, life, death, burial, descent into Hades and resurrection from the grave breaking the power of death. It is Christ's ascension to the right hand of the Father and the subsequent outpouring of his Spirit on the day of Pentecost. It is going to bring the final union between God and man being consummated at his second coming to this earth as the ruling king of Kings. It's the message of the gospel and wrapped in that message is the power and wisdom of God (I Corinthains 1:18 – 25).

The event of the cross is understood as the supreme demonstration of the Father's love and mercy demonstrated in the Son's obedience to lay down his life. It is the embodiment of God's dealings with humanity in this age. Thus, John describes, "God's love was revealed among us in this way: God sent his one and only Son into the world so that we might live through him" (1 John 4:9, CSB). [52]The cross is the ultimate means by which God expresses his love and mercy to humanity. Since the cross typifies the acts of God in this age, we might describe this age as "cruciform," meaning "shaped like a cross."

The cross substantially represents how God relates to humanity, dealings with humanity in this The children of Israel were told to eat the whole lamb during the Passover meal. It was so that the lamb who was slain for them and the blood that covered their sin could deliver them from the death angel. It was their partaking that set them free from Pharaoh's power and actually became a part of them.

In like manner we are told to eat the flesh and drink the blood of the New Covenant. It's a partnership and participation with the Lamb of God. It's upon the revelation of that foundation that the gates of hell cannot prevail against his church. The pillar and foundation of truth that the church is established on is the 'word of the cross'. The advancing church is one who has embraced the message of him who has the keys of death and Hades. Yes, it's foolishness to the earthly minded man. It's a stone of stumbling and rock of offense.

Jesus and his apostles didn't preach a message about changing the old man, but they preached the cross. The means of salvation is sacrificial, and it's always been that way because our ancient faith originated out of the soil of sacrifice. No, we can't work our way to God, but he does call us to be completely identified with him in a covenant relationship. Jesus said except a seed goes into the ground and dies it abides alone. The message of the gospel which Jesus and his apostles taught was that the pathway to life can only be entered through the doorway of sacrificial death.

Deceptive Pride Leads to Living in the Flesh

The original man and woman were deceived, and they sinned.

---

[52] John P. Harrington, The Gospel of Christ Crucified, p. 75.

Instead of being open and transparent they immediately tried to cover their sin and then hid from God. [53]The immediate consequences of disobedience are shame and estrangement...the sewing of fig leaves is an attempt at self-remedy. Pride is the root cause of all sin. C.S. Lewis called it 'the great sin'. Self-deception happens when we partake of sin and then we begin to deceive ourselves. [54]The deception lies in blaming external forces rather than recognizing one's own desires. Sin takes us on a journey away from the cruciform life of walking with God and into darkness which Paul called "living in the flesh". Paul said that sin slays us (Rom. 7:11), it corrupts us (Gal. 6:8), it darkens us (Eph. 4:18), and it deceives us (Heb. 3:13).

To effectively deal with the flesh and sin we have to identify it's source because we are in a spiritual battle. We have three main enemies regarding spiritual warfare and the struggles we face walking out our journey of faith in this body. Satan (I Peter 5:8), the world (I John 2:15-16) and the flesh (Galatians 5:17). Satan and the world can be termed enemies from without, who come against us through the avenue of persecution, deception, temptation and all types of assaults. It's what most people focus upon regarding spiritual warfare. It's always the devil who made us do it.

Too many in the church focus on some principality that they have uncovered deceiving the church like the Jezebel spirit or the Leviathan spirit. The Bible doesn't mention either of those spirits or the multitude of other spirits the spiritual warfare gurus have discovered. Yes, there are evil spirits. Yes, we have been given authority in Christ to bring deliverance to those who have been taken captive, but the Bible does not teach many of the popular spiritual warfare techniques. Taking verses out of the Bible and making a spiritual warfare doctrine out of it doesn't make it true. Remember Satan quoted scripture, but it was always used out of context. We can't cherry pick from the Bible and make them fit our ideas.

The Bible is meant to be taken in context as Peter said, "no prophecy of Scripture comes from someone's own interpretation." We can't cherry pick the Bible trying to come up with some new fancy mystery no one has seen before so we can wow our audience. It sells and makes money in today's spiritual marketplace, but taking the word of

---

[53] Gordon Wenham, Genesis 1-15, p. 225.
[54] Douglas J. Moo, The Letter of James, p. 74.

God out of context leads down roads of darkness, error and deception. Our commission is simply prayer and proclamation of the word of the cross in the power of the Holy Spirt.

The Main Enemy in Spiritual Warfare: The Flesh

Paul showed us that the main problem is not Satan or the world, but the flesh and it's where the rubber meets the road. The flesh could be termed the enemy within and if we allow it to dominate our lives it causes spiritual decay. It brings death, deterioration and like an animal rotting on the side of the road it can make our lives stink (Gal. 6:8).

Paul in Romans 8:5 says "those who live according to the flesh set their minds on the things of the flesh." Vs 6 says, "the mind on the flesh is death." Vs 7 says, "for the mind that is set on the flesh is hostile to God." Vs 8 says, "those who are in the flesh cannot please God." The cruciform way of life is the only pathway of dealing with the flesh, but we must first get an understanding of what is the flesh from a Biblical perspective.

As we look at the Bible, we will soon discover that many times in scripture the word flesh is not necessarily referring to our physical body. You must look at the context in which the word is being used to determine if it is referring merely to our human body as in II Corinthians 7:1, outward ordinances of the Mosaic Law as in Galatians chapter 3:3 or man living independent of the redeeming work of Christ as in Romans 8:8. The Gnostics were a heretical group that fully emerged in 200 AD, which taught a false concept concerning the makeup of man and the material world.

Full fledge Gnostic views did not emerge until the Second century, but you had proto-Gnostics emerge from within Judaism as a result of the Second Temple time period. Paul specifically addresses this head on in the book of Colossians. John in his gospel and epistle confronted something similar. They are both addressing a very similar spirituality, but it results in an opposite set of ethics: one resulting in lawlessness and the other resulting in aesthetic legalism. It is a fork in the same road that comes out of Second Temple Judaism especially seen in the Qumran communities administered by the Essene's.

It was a spirituality that had many variations, but it basically taught that anything that was material or of this physical world was evil, yet everything of the spirit was good, therefore Jesus could not have come in a human body. Its why John said in I John 4:2 "that by this you know the Spirit of God, every spirit that confesses that Jesus Christ has come in the flesh is from God."

The practical result of this false spirituality in the early church and today is that people teach that your physical body is evil. The result leads you to either give in to the unrestrained cravings of our unredeemed bodies since we are powerless to overcome which is what you see in Jude and II Peter or live as an ascetic monk brutalizing the body and bringing it into subjection through self-effort since to enjoy the material world is evil which is what you see the book of Colossians.

I want us to take a holistic approach which recognizes that although this age has been corrupted by sin and is under satanic control, we are not to live lives detached from creation. Jesus came to redeem not just mankind, but eventually even the created order itself according to Romans 8:19-21. We are to live in this world, which means we can enjoy ourselves without being subject to its idolizing pleasures, adulterating power and corruptive practices.

Living a Holy Life in a Corrupt World: Following the Example of Jesus

Jesus himself as God in human flesh gave us an example to follow. Spirituality is not detaching ourselves from life's experiences or withdrawing from our communities. [55]Paul's theology taken from Christ's example is fundamentally participatory and cruciform: believers are conformed to the self-giving pattern of Christ. We don't have to be spiritual isolationists like Monks or the Amish who withdraw into their own communities having no contact with the corrupt outside world. [56]Our mission requires remaining in the world while not belonging to its rebellion.

We are to affirm creation by finding a sense of holiness in the here and now without having divisions between the sacred and secular in our lives. I want you to think of Daniel who lived a holy life in the midst of Babylon. [57]Daniel models how to maintain distinctiveness without

---

[55] Michael Gormon, Cruciformity, p. 4.
[56] D.A. Carson, The Gospel According to John, p. 566.
[57] John Goldingay, Daniel (WBC), p. 37.

abandoning public responsibility. We can live lives dedicated to God in an evil age, shining as lights in a dark world, but as I will show you we can't do it through our own ability.

The makeup of man is debated in modern Psychology, but it really is an ancient debate. In Hebraic thought, the soul refers to the whole person or individual as a living being. I Thessalonians 5:23 teaches that man is a triune being made up of spirit-soul-body. Paul emphasizes total consecration; whether he intends a strict tripartite anthropology is debated. Looking at the tri-unity of man helps us to understand that we are a spiritual being that lives in a physical body. Paul called our body a temple or a clay jar that houses our true self made in the image of God.

The whole purpose of the coming of Christ was to bring redemption to man and creation, which have both been marred by sin. What I want to address now is how sin or the flesh affects our walk and fellowship with God. We need to fully understand this area so that we can learn how to cooperate with the Spirit's work, restoring us through the work of the cross and living lives free from self-deception.

William Barclay, who is a recognized Greek scholar, wrote a book called 'Flesh and Spirit'. In a section called 'The Enemy In The Soul', he examines the way Paul uses the Greek word *sarx* which is translated flesh. Paul views the *sarx* as the enemy in the battle for the soul. Barclay gives several uses of the Greek word *sarx*. The flesh is the great enemy of the life of the Spirit.

Paul defined this battle in Galatians 5:17 saying: "the desires of the flesh are against the Spirit and the desires of the Spirit are against the flesh, for these are opposed to each other, to keep you from doing the things you want to do." He then goes on to describe the works of the flesh as a result of living lives independent of Christ.

If we take this as a general statement, then it is exactly here that we see the difference between body and flesh. The body can become the instrument of the service and glory of God — the flesh cannot. The body can be purified and even glorified, the flesh must be eliminated and eradicated. It is with the flesh that a man serves the law of sin described in Romans 7:25.

One of the most debated portions of the book of Romans is chapter 7, especially the last part of the chapter (vs. 13 - 25). Just before this portion in vs. 7-8 Paul shows us that the problem is not the Mosaic law, but sin. In vs. 12 he clearly states that "The law is holy, and the commandment is holy and righteous and good", but "sin," produced "death in me through what is good, in order that sin might be shown to be sin" (vs. 13). [58]Romans 7:7-13 is a sustained argument that the law is not the problem; sin is the problem. [59]Paul's purpose is to clear the law of any suspicion and to expose sin in its true character.

Paul then says, "the law is spiritual (vs. 14), but I am of the flesh, sold under sin." [60]Paul's problem is not Torah (Mosaic law) but the fleshly condition of humanity. The rest of the chapter is where the debate is found. I conclude that the rest of the chapter is Paul as a believer born of the Spirit expressing his struggle with the flesh or you might call it the sinful nature (14-24). This passage depicts the conflict of the believer, not the bondage of the unbeliever.

[61]The language of struggle presupposes life in the Spirit. Romans 7 anticipates Romans 8 by describing life in the overlap of the ages. It is similar to the language that Paul uses in Romans 8:5-7 then Galatians 5:17. [62]Romans 7 and Galatians 5 describe the same conflict using different rhetorical strategies. Herein lies the problem and how people take certain statements Paul makes and twist them to fit their particular views in dealing with the flesh.

The flesh cannot please God as said in Romans 8:8. Worse than that, the flesh Paul says in verse 7 is essentially hostile to God. The flesh is simply man living independent of God. It is the pride of man deceiving himself into thinking that he is his own god and doing whatever is right in his own eyes. The Phillips Translation calls the flesh the unspiritual nature. The Weust translation calls the flesh the sinful nature. I like the way the Weymouth translation explains the word flesh. He refers to the flesh as the 'lower nature' when referring to living independent of Christ.

Romans 6:12 talks about sin reining in our body. Our bodies are unredeemed, subject to corruption and temporary. Our bodies are not sinful or evil because they are of this material creation. However, if we fail to reckon ourselves 'crucified with Christ', then our bodies can become the vehicle by which the lower nature dominates us. If we allow

---

[58] James D. G. Dunn, Romans 1-8 (WBC), p. 387.

[59] C.E. B. Cranfield, Romans (ICC), p. 355.

[60] Michael Bird, Romans, p. 247.

[61] Richard Longenecker, Introducing Romans, p. 92.

[62] James D.G. Dunn, The Theology of Paul the Apostle, p. 475.

this to happen, then the works of the flesh as Paul defined in Galatians chapter 5 can have a detrimental effect upon our lives. As a result of our sin, self-deception begins to corrupt us, it darkens us and it deceives us.

Abiding in Christ for Spiritual Transformation

The struggle of the life of faith in this age is learning to allow the Spirit of the risen Christ to truly abide in us. We must daily make this choice to walk in the works of the flesh or yield to the Spirit. Abiding in Christ is a daily choice of humbly submitting to the cruciform life of faith. It is only from this place of humility that we can produce the fruit of the Spirit living in the power and wisdom of the cross. It's learning to live in the light of the age to come.

The problem is that we live in cracked clay jars. [63]The fragile vessel highlights divine power residing within human weakness. However, it's in understanding our frailty that helps us to be humble. Humility of heart bows down in worship recognizing we can't live this life alone. Jesus as the pattern Son showed us the way. Philippians 2:7 - 8 says Christ: "emptied himself, by taking the form of a servant, being born in the likeness of men. And being found in human form, he humbled himself by becoming obedient to the point of death, even death on a cross."

Jesus in the garden of Gethsemane prayed the prayer that we must daily pray. It is daily and even moment by moment being humble like Christ praying that we would walk in the will of the Father for our lives and not our own. Paul understood his frailty and we must understand ours. We don't focus on them, but we focus on the power of the cross which fills us with Christ wisdom and power to live a changed life. Paul told the Corinthians that "I discipline my body and keep it under control, lest after preaching to others I myself should be disqualified".

Paul understood his utter dependence on the Spirit to come alongside and help him during his journey. He knew that just as Jesus needed the power of the Spirit to fulfill his purpose, so do we. Paul in 2 Corinthians 3:5 - 6 shows he was just like you and me. He was not some demi-god, but a man who knew apart from Christ he was completely

---

[63] Murray Harris, The Second Epistle to the Corinthains, (NIGTC), p. 340.

lacking. He said, "not that we are sufficient in ourselves to claim anything as coming from us, but our sufficiency is from God, who has made us sufficient to be ministers of a new covenant, not of the letter but of the Spirit. For the letter kills, but the Spirit gives life".

Living Free From the Flesh: Overcoming Lust & Desire

We are never going to live in sinless perfection, but we can learn to live free from the flesh dominating our lives. James 1:14 talks about us being 'lured and enticed by our own lust' or as other translations say our own desire. It's not a Jezebel spirit that's the problem, it's your heart. You bow to the idols when the music plays because you make that choice. The Greek word for lust here is *epithumia*. It's important to take a look at this word because this word helps us to understand the need for healing and restoring our souls so that we don't bow to the flesh. *Epithumia* is translated lust. Let me show you how this word is used by the apostolic writers.

John in his first epistle 2:15-17 says, "Do not love the world or the things in the world. If anyone loves the world, the love of the Father is not in him. For all that is in the world—the desires of the flesh and the desires of the eyes and pride of life—is not from the Father, but is from the world. And the world is passing away along with its desires, but whoever does the will of God abides forever." Some have defined this as the deadly sins of pride, sexual immorality and the love of money.

The lust of the flesh, lust of the eyes and pride of life are not necessarily always depraved and immoral. The religious legalist takes many different forms and may display refined character, but their deeds nonetheless are inconsistent with the love of the Father. Jesus called the Pharisees who appeared righteous before men sons of the devil. It's what Paul called the false gospel of legalism in the book of Galatians.

Paul used this word *epithumia* throughout his epistles. We see the usage of this word in Galatians 5:16 where he tells us to, "walk by the Spirit, and you will not gratify the desires of the flesh. For the desires of the flesh are against the Spirit, and the desires of the Spirit are against the flesh, for these are opposed to each other, to keep you from doing the things you want to do." He then clearly defines the works of the flesh in verses 20 through 21. He says if you are doing these things then you are living in the flesh and not living by the Spirit.

"The works of the flesh are evident: sexual immorality, impurity, sensuality, idolatry, sorcery, enmity, strife, jealousy, fits of anger, rivalries, dissensions, divisions, envy, drunkenness, orgies, and things like these. I warn you, as I warned you before, that those who do such things will not inherit the kingdom of God." In the Foundation Publications School of Discipleship: Lesson 10 Part 2 'A Lifestyle of Repentance' I clearly define each of the works of the flesh. I encourage you to look at that if you want some clarification and more detailed definition on the works of the flesh.

Peter 1:13 - 15 tells us to be "sober-minded, set your hope fully on the grace that will be brought to you at the revelation of Jesus Christ. As obedient children, do not be conformed to the *passions* of your former ignorance, but as he who called you is holy, you also be holy in all your conduct" (emphasis mine). He then compares us to the temple of God built on the foundation of Christ and every member being a priest before God having a responsibility to live lives dedicated to the cruciform life of sacrifice.

In I Peter2:9-12 he says we are:

> "a chosen race, a royal priesthood, a holy nation, a people for his own possession, that you may proclaim the excellencies of him who called you out of darkness into his marvelous light. Once you were not a people, but now you are God's people; once you had not received mercy, but now you have received mercy. Beloved, I urge you as sojourners and exiles to abstain from the *passions* of the flesh, which wage war against your soul. Keep your conduct among the Gentiles honorable, so that when they speak against you as evildoers, they may see your good deeds and glorify God on the day of visitation" (emphasis mine).

The word *passions* in both texts are the Greek word *epithumia* and it says they wage war against your soul. It's this daily battle that we face. If we do not engage in this daily battle by obeying Jesus' command to live the cruciform life of faith and just go with the flow of our passions, then we begin to walk in self-deception.

John, Paul, Peter and Jude all used this Greek word *epithumia*. *Epithumia* is translated lusts and passions of the flesh being defined as the active and individual desire resulting in *pathos*. Now the word *Pathos* is a Greek word meaning the diseased condition of the soul out of which lust springs.

Paul, in clarifying sexual purity to the Thessalonians, used these two words together. In 1 Thessalonians 4:3 - 5 he says, "this is the will of God, your sanctification: that you abstain from sexual immorality; that each one of you know how to control his own body in holiness and honor, not in the **passion** (*pathos*) **of lust** (*epithumia*) like the Gentiles who do not know God (emphasis mine)"

It's why Paul could say all have sinned and fall short of the glory of God because apart from God none are righteous. It's an impossible task for the unbeliever to live a holy life. It's only possible for the child of God who learns to yield his or her life to the ability of the Spirit to live lives dedicated to holiness. Let me say that again because I find it amazing that so many Christians sit around judging unbelievers. It's an impossible task for the unbeliever to live a holy life. Yes, they live in the passion of lust because they do not know God. It's what sinners do, they sin, stop being surprised by it!

In contrast Paul was very clear to the one who has put their faith in Christ about the will of God concerning our sanctification. It's only possible for the child of God who learns to yield his or her life to the ability of the Spirit and dedicated to the cross that's going to be able to live a sanctified life.

Healing and Restoration of the Soulish Realm

You see, we all have areas in our soulish realm that have been damaged by our individual sin and the sin inflicted upon us by others. If these areas go without being healed and restored, then when the right circumstances arise, we will be led away by them and taken captive. Take for instance a young girl or boy who may have been damaged in their souls through the molestation of a relative or stranger. When that child reaches puberty and the right circumstances arise, that child will have a much stronger bent towards sexual sin, because of the diseased condition within the soul.

A person who was raised in a home with arguing and yelling is going to have a stronger bent towards outbursts of anger. It is statistically proven that those who grow up in the home of an alcoholic will have a higher likelihood of also becoming one. Not every person will have the same damage or disease within their souls, however, every soul born into Adam's race has been affected.

None of us has escaped the effects of sin. Let me say this for those in the back of the room. You don't have an addiction problem, and you probably don't have a demon problem. You have a sin problem. The works of the flesh are destroying your life because of the diseased condition of your soul therefore you can't control yourself.

The devil isn't making you do it. Demons can get involved with your lifestyle of fleshly living because they feed on the dust of your flesh, but you are willingly doing it and the only way to break the power of sin is through death. It's the answer Paul gave us in Galatians chapter 2 verse 20 when he said, "I have been crucified with Christ. It is no longer I who live, but Christ who lives in me. And the life I now live in the flesh I live by faith in the Son of God, who loved me and gave himself for me."

The journey of faith is learning to live a life in union with God. It's not a one-time process or a transaction like going to the car dealership to buy a new car or going to the front of some church and saying a prayer or taking communion. Faith and our salvation are a walk, it's a process and a lifetime commitment of learning how to grow into who we have become in Christ.

Transformed by Grace: The Journey of Faith & Salvation

You become a new person when you accept Christ into your heart, but we grow from faith to faith progressing in our salvation. However, the growth only happens as we learn to yield our lives to the river of God's grace. It's learning to become a habitation of God's Spirit in the midst of a world that is walking in an opposite direction.

You are saved by acknowledging Christ's redemptive work on our behalf which means you have been justified in Christ. You must also daily take up your cross and grow in the knowledge of Christ which means you are being sanctified. One day you will take off this mortal body and put on immortality which means you will be glorified with a new resurrection body like his.

We are in this world, but we live by a different Spirit. We are to live by the Spirit flowing from the throne of grace. It's learning to daily yield to the grace of God by faith working through love. It's only by our complete surrender to the cruciform way of life that we can be overcomers instead of being overcome by the trials of this life. Jesus nor his apostles taught us to have an attitude of escapism. We are not to seek to escape this material creation, but Jesus taught us to pray that his kingdom would come on earth as it is in heaven.

Embracing the Living Waters of the Spirit

The scriptures don't teach that our ultimate destination is some spiritual intangible place called heaven. Yes, to be absent from this body or to die means you will be taken immediately into the presence of the Lord as taught by Paul in II Corinthians 5:8. So yes, heaven is a real place and if you die before Christ returns you go there. However, scriptures teach that the kingdom of heaven came to earth through the man Christ Jesus, and it is going to fully consume this creation when he returns. Until Christ returns, we are merely getting a taste of the age to come in this present creation (Heb. 6:4) and as Peter said in 1 Peter 2:11 that we are "sojourners and exiles" in this present evil age.

Jesus himself said that we can come to him and drink in the living waters of the Spirit now in this age and it is a result of his first coming as God in human flesh. God stepped into time to redeem and to reconcile. He initiated the restoration of all things spoken of through the Hebrew prophets. In Christ we can partake of His resurrection power now. Yes, it's just a down payment, it's just a taste and simply a glimpse of what's to come, but it's the first fruit of a glory that will transform this present creation.

It doesn't mean the road is always a smooth road or that there are no struggles, pain and sacrifice. It's called the good fight of faith for a reason. Faith is about putting into practice and living out the redemptive work of Christ enduring to the end. Redemption is a process, just like God delivered the children of Israel from Pharaoh's armies and Egypt's power; he has delivered us from the 'god of this age' and his worldly system. The children of Israel didn't inherit everything all at once. They had to go through the wilderness and then eventually conquer the promised land of their inheritance.

In Deuteronomy 8:2 it says that the Lord led Israel into the wilderness for forty years so that he might humble them and test them, so they could see their hearts allowing God to change them. The wilderness is the training ground for genuine discipleship and spiritual growth. [64]Jesus relives Israel's wilderness testing but succeeds where Israel

---

[64] R.T. France, The Gospel of Matthew, (NICNT), p. 131.

failed. He overcame the devil, the world, sin and death (Heb. 2:14-15). We are followers of the risen Christ and it's in our wilderness places that God will show you that he is the Lord who provides, guides, saves, heals and delivers us along life's journey. It doesn't mean we will always be free from pain, suffering, heartache and have everything we want. [65]Suffering is not abnormal in Christian existence but intrinsic to it. It's a place where your faith grows as you learn to lean on the compassionate salvation that God has provided through Christ Jesus.

Salvation is a journey and a process of restoring our spirit, souls and ultimately our bodies into the image and likeness of Christ. [66]Salvation in Paul includes justification, sanctification, and final glorification. We have been delivered by the cross, but we are also being changed by the grace poured out through the cross. Grace is not merely forgiveness but must lead to transformation. [67]The goal of salvation is conformity to the crucified and risen Christ.

The Power of the Cross: The Sacrificial Life Of Faith

The walk of faith is 24/7; there is no part time gospel. The gospel consumes our lives like the sacrifice upon the altar, and we must give our whole hearts to God (Rom. 12:2). As we lay our hearts open before God, Paul said in Romans 1:6 that within the gospel is the "power of God for salvation to everyone who believes". So, within 'the word of the cross' is the power to be justified, reconciled, forgiven, sanctified and to have eternal life. Paul said that from the cross flows the wisdom and power to live in this life as a child of God.

As I've already said, salvation is both instant and progressive. What I mean is that just as a baby is born into the world through birth, so the believer is brought into the kingdom of God through new birth. We are born into the family, but we must mature in our faith. I John 2:12 talks about children, young men and fathers. John says, "I am writing to you, little children, because your sins are forgiven for his name's sake. I am writing to you, fathers, because you know him who is from the beginning. I am writing to you, young men, because you have overcome the evil one."

---

[65] Ben Witherington III, The Acts of the Apostles, p. 463.

[66] Thomas Schreiner, Paul: Apostle of God's Glory in Christ, (IVP), p. 221.

[67] Michael Gorman, Cruciformity, p. 45.

If you look at this text, you see a progression that we go through in our faith. Children understand forgiveness of sins. It is the foundation of our faith, and our feet must be securely established in the cross. Young men learn to overcome through the word of God abiding strongly in their hearts. Fathers are those who have matured in their faith because they are firmly grounded in their identity of forgiveness through Christ and have learned to consistently overcome the evil one. Fathers are not trying to be something because they know him, who is from the beginning and have come to the place where they are helping others learn how to practice their faith.

The Cruciform Life: Surrendering to God's Grace

If our lives are not wholly dedicated and surrendered to the Spirit which is being consecrated to God, then we will gravitate to the lower nature living our lives independent of Christ. It's why Jesus taught us to pray that his kingdom would come on earth as it is in heaven. [68]The Lord's Prayer invites believers to embody the coming kingdom in present obedience. It's why he told us that we must daily take up our cross and follow him. Cruciformity is participation of ongoing self-denial and identification with the resurrected Christ.

Yes, Christ is ultimately going to restore this present creation with fire (II Peter 3:5-7), but until then we are the earth he wants to restore. Man was made from the dust of the ground and our bodies are merely clay jars. The walk of faith in this life is about daily surrendering to the grace of God in humility. [69]Transformation is progressive and effected by the Spirit. It's about learning to live the cruciform life.

Paul clearly articulates the struggle in Romans chapter 7 and then in Galatians chapter 5 where he contrasts the works of the flesh with the fruit of the Spirit. [70]The conflict between flesh and Spirit defines Christian existence until the consumption. As believers we are not powerless, but we do have to make daily choices because divine enablement does not eliminate human responsibility.

Paul in Romans 8:4-8 gives us the solution saying: "the righteous requirement of the law might be fulfilled in us, who walk not according

---

[68] N.T. Wright, Jesus and the Victory of God, p. 289.
[69] Murray Harris, The Second Epistle to the Corinthians, p. 317.
[70] Thomas Schreiner, Galatians, (ZECNT), p. 336.

to the flesh, but according to the Spirit. For those who live according to the flesh set their minds on the things of the flesh, but those who live according to the Spirit set their minds on the things of the Spirit. For to set the mind on the flesh is death, but to set the mind on the Spirit is life and peace. For the mind that is set on the flesh is hostile to God, for it does not submit to God's law; indeed, it cannot. Those who are in the flesh cannot please God."

The Cross is the Healing Power of Emotional Wounds

Our souls can be damaged as we walk along life's journey groping around in this present darkness. The soul is where most of us have emotional wounds. Yes, all of us have been affected by Adam's sin, the sin inflicted upon us by others and our own sinful desires which all result in emotional wounds. If we don't bring these wounds to the cross then the wounds of the soul can affect our daily walk of faith, keeping the Holy Spirit from fully flowing through our hearts.

The soul is what I call the interface of our inner man. Computers are something that most of us understand in today's culture so let me explain the interface to you because I think it will help you understand. The definition of interface is where two systems interact and come together. Let me use your cell phone as an example because it is a computer where you get information from. If you're like me then you've probably dropped your cell phone before. If you don't have a cover then you may have broken your screen. The screen is the interface that the computer is connected to and outputs information for you. If the screen is cracked, then it's hard to get that information and that's what happens to our souls.

The soul is like our phone screen; it's an interface that displays to the world what's in our hearts because speech and action reveal the inner disposition (Luke 6:45). When you are born from above, all the power is within your heart, but your souls are still damaged. The Spirit of Christ lives in you, but your soul needs repair or restoration. Regeneration is the implanting of new spiritual life, but sanctification is the progressive renewal of the whole person. The soul gets clogged up with garbage through life's journey and it can block the flow of the river of God's grace from freely flowing in your hearts.

It's the living powerful word of God anointed with the Spirit that can clean, heal and restore our soul's. [71]The salvation of the soul refers to the ongoing deliverance of believers from sin's corrupting power. We need this daily restoration so that the soul can interface correctly with our spirits, made in the image of God so that the outflow of grace can be displayed to this world. It's why we need to daily seek God's heart through prayer and study of the scriptures. We need to daily reflect on the word of God which the Bible calls meditation and confession. It's as we allow God's word and Spirit to have a place in our hearts that we experience its power to produce faith which restores our souls.

It's why it's so important to daily take up our cross humbly submitting to the washing of the word. We must daily seek to be filled with the Spirit to repair damage to our souls and allow him to restore the interface of our hearts. It's why the Psalmist prayed, "create in me a clean heart, O God". I find this is the main reason so many believers are still dominated by the lower nature and living duplicitous lives being self-deceived. It is because they refuse to allow God to repair and restore the soulish areas of the heart so therefore, they live in the works of the flesh.

If you don't daily humbly submit, then you will be taken down paths of darkness being easily deceived. It's what James was saying in 4:5 - 8 that God: "yearns jealously over the spirit that he has made to dwell in us'? But he gives more grace. Therefore it says, "God opposes the proud but gives grace to the humble." Submit yourselves therefore to God. Resist the devil, and he will flee from you. Draw near to God, and he will draw near to you. Cleanse your hands, you sinners, and purify your hearts, you double-minded."

The Importance of Daily Surrender to God's Grace

If you don't learn to daily take up your cross and in humility surrender to God's grace, then the damaged areas of your soul will cause you to turn away from God. Just like Adam and Eve did after eating from the tree of the knowledge of good and evil. It's because of our pride and refusal to simply be humble enough to repent by yielding to the grace of God that we live duplicitous lives of deception.

The Holy Spirit convicts us trying to draw us back to the

---

[71] Douglas J. Moo, The Letter of James, (PNTC), p. 86.

humility of the cross, but many times we reject his loving call to repentance. It's because we have begun to deceive ourselves by refusing to live in the light of what God says so in essence, we become our own god living in the shadows of idolatry.

Paul in I Timothy 2:4 says God "desires all people to be saved and to come to the knowledge of the truth." I want to focus on this word knowledge. In this scripture the Greek word used for knowledge in this text is e*pignosis*. According to the Vine's Expository Dictionary the word is not used in the gospels or the book of Acts. However, Paul uses this word 15 times, Peter uses the word 4 times and it's used once in the book of Hebrews. We are going to be looking at some of these texts which will give us a fuller understanding so that we can live in the 'knowledge of the truth' staying free from self-deception.

Epignōsis is a strengthened or intensified form of "*gnōsis*" and both are translated as the one English word knowledge. *Epignōsis* conveys the thought of a knowledge which is fuller, larger and more thorough than *gnōsis*. It also conveys the idea of a more intimate and personal relationship than the simple term *gnōsis*. Before we get into understanding *epignōsis* in the next chapter we are going to look at this word *gnōsis* which is where the term Gnosticism comes from and the heretical teaching which many of the apostolic writers confronted.

CHAPTER 5

POST MODERNISM AND GNOSTICISM

"I am afraid that as the serpent deceived Eve by his cunning, your thoughts will be led astray from a sincere and pure devotion to Christ."

~ II Corinthains 11:3 ~

Gnosticism is not a word or a term that you hear a lot about today. It represents a form of spirituality that is prevalent in Postmodern society and plays a significant role in American culture. Now there are a lot of variations of Gnosticism. It is a term developed by scholars to understand certain groups, who were independent of each other and wouldn't even have recognized the term. The English poet, philosopher, and theologian Henry More first introduced the term "Gnosticism" in 1669. He was introduced to the term reaching the church father Irenaeus of Lyons (125 – 202 AD) in his treatise Against Heresies where he mentions the 'Gnostic heresy' and criticizes those who claim to possess 'knowledge (*gnōsis*) falsely so called'.

The Diverse Origins of Gnosticism

Gnosticism was not and is still not an organized religion or a coherent fixed set of beliefs. It was a complex mass of interrelated religious ideas. Gnosticism has no creed, and each person seeks their own personal truth with many paths leading back to the One that the Greeks called *Plêrôma*. [72]There was no single religion called 'Gnosticism.' Rather, there were a variety of movements and mythologies that scholars have grouped together under the label.

The Gnostic Heresy is more like a virus than an organized religious system. As a virus it latches on to its host and completely infects the host. It takes on the structure of the host mimicking the ideas and taking on the language. [73]Gnostic teachers borrowed language and forms from Jewish and Christian traditions while radically transforming

---

[72] Michael A. Williams, Rethinking "Gnosticism", p. 265.
[73] Elaine Pagels, The Gnostic Gospels, p. 20.

their meanings. It's the tree of the knowledge of good and evil producing a multitude of deceptions. [74]Some Gnostic groups adopted asceticism, other libertine tendencies; both stemmed from a radical dualism.

Gnosticism has had a much greater impact upon American culture than most realize. It was Carl Jung born in 1895 who mainstreamed Gnostic ideas couched in the pseudo-science of modern Psychology. Carl Jung, one of the fathers of modern Psychology was greatly influenced and inspired by Gnostic ideas. [75]He says, "from the beginning I felt the kinship with Gnostic thought." [76]Jung's psychology stands in a direct line of descent from ancient Gnosticim. No, I'm not against Psychiatrist, Psychologist or Counseling. However, we should be aware that many of the concepts, ideas and theories are anti-christ.

The moral relativism that was released upon America through the sexual revolution is rooted in Carl Jung's psychological work. Leaders of the 1960's hippie movement like Timothy Leary, a Harvard Professor of Psychology, were heavily influenced by his teaching. One could say without overstatement that Carl Jung is the spiritual father of Neo-Gnosticism and the New Age Movement. [77]Dr. Jeffery Satinover comments that "one of the most powerful modern forms of Gnosticism is without question Jungian psychology". [78]Jung regarded himself as a kind of prophet reviving ancient Gnostic religions in psychological form.

The Rise of Modern Gnosticism in American Culture

In the late 1980's and early 1990's New Age Religion became all the rage and made its way into mainstream American culture. It was originally looked on by most as a bunch of crazy Loonie rich Hollywood elites. The actress Shirley McClain wrote a book which detailed her search for truth outside of organized religion. Oprah Winfrey interviewed her on her show and before you knew it the alternative path of postmodern religion took root in America.

Today Gnostic ideas have made their way into most American

[74] Kurt Rudoph, Gnosis, p. 253.
[75] Carl Jung, Memories, Dreams, Reflections, p. 200.
[76] Stephan Hoeller, Jung and the Lost Gospels, p. 3.
[77] Jeffery Satinover, Homosexuality and the Politics of Truth, p. 191.
[78] Richard Noll, The Jung Cult, p. 9.

institutions, and has infected our culture through media, education, and politics. The ideas are prevalent in parts of the American Church. Obviously, the Progressive mainstream church has been completely captured and corrupted by this Postmodern heresy. We see a complete departure from the apostolic faith clearly laid forth in the New Testament. However, the Evangelical church which includes Pentecostals and Charismatics has been infected with this belief system.

Let me share a few statistics with you to demonstrate the point I am making. In 1990 the Pew research center said the US population was 85% identifying as Christians, but today in 2024 that number is around 60% and declining. To me the more troubling issue is what professing Christians believe and practice. George Barna the Christian sociologist did surveys in May of 2021 estimating that only around 9% of adult Christians believe the Bible to be accurate and reliable. Yes, I said 9% and it is this same 9% who take their faith seriously enough, to where it affects their day-to-day lives. It makes sense because if you don't believe the Bible is the word of God then it's not going to change your heart and way of life.

The Impact of the Gnostic Heresy on Christianity

Our Postmodern culture has been greatly influenced by Gnosticism. It has infected large portions of the church. Yes, we still have a lot of people who attend church meetings, but we must wake up to the fact that America is moving towards a post Christian society. You still have the name Christian in the titles of organizations and on the buildings, but many have departed from the faith of the Bible and are living lives of apostasy.

I am going to give you a few statistics concerning the beliefs among those who call themselves Evangelicals, which is someone who says the word of God should be taken as the final authority of our faith.

- Nearly 50% believe God learns and adapts to different circumstances, which means they believe God changes.
- 70% say that Jesus is created by God, which is a heresy denying the deity of Christ.
- 64% say that all religious faiths are of equal value.
- 66% say that 'having faith' matters more than which faith you

pursue.
- 57% believe in karma.
- 38% believe Jesus is a great teacher, but not God again denying the deity of Christ.
- 60% say the Holy Spirit is a force and a symbol of God's power or presence, but is not a living entity, which is denying the Trinity.
- 27% think the Holy Spirit can tell them to do something that the Bible teaches against.

If those statistics are anywhere close to accurate it should be cause for great concern. Its why Foundation Publications provides resources to make disciples who understand what the Bible teaches. If you have not gone through our free School of Discipleship visit www.foundationpub.org.

The Vital Importance of Sound Doctrine

Sound doctrine is extremely important because it is the basis of our faith and conduct. The church is to be a pillar and foundation of the truth found in Christ clearly articulated by the Hebrew prophets of the Old Testament and the apostolic writers of the New Testament. The dominant worldview in America today is not Biblical faith established in the sound truth of scripture. It is a blended belief system custom-made by each person and has a lot of resemblance to the ancient Gnostic heresy in which Postmodern spirituality is inspired by and founded upon.

To those of us who believe the Bible to be an accurate account of God's redemptive history in time we believe in the Genesis account of history:

- We believe that God created man in the garden of Eden in his image.
- We believe that man disobeyed and as a result was expelled.
- We believe that man because of sin was corrupted and lost the eternal glory of God. He forfeited his close communion with God when he partook of the tree of the knowledge of good and evil resulting in spiritual death which was followed by physical death.
- We believe that man in his fallen state is corrupted and not essentially good, but all have sinned falling short of the glory of God. As man was dispelled from the garden his heart did not turn in

humility and reliance back to the Creator.

- We believe the account of Genesis 6:5 - 6 which says: "The Lord saw that the wickedness of man was great in the earth and that every intention of the thoughts of his heart was only evil continually. And the Lord regretted that he had made man on the earth and it grieved him to his heart."

- We believe that God judged the inhabitants of the earth for their wickedness, and it was deluged with water causing every living thing to perish.

- We believe that God preserved the eight souls of Noah's family through his obedience to the covenant keeping Creator of heaven and earth. Hebrews 11:7 says: "by faith Noah, being warned by God concerning events as yet unseen, in reverent fear constructed an ark for the saving of his household. By this he condemned the world and became an heir of the righteousness that comes by faith."

The Tower of Babel: A Gnostic Perspective

The story of God's redemptive history in time brings us to the Tower of Babel in Genesis chapter 11. The origins of Gnosticism are very hard to trace, but the ideas seem to have originated before recorded human history being a result of Adam and Eve eating from the tree of the knowledge of good and evil. The Tower of Babel which was in the center of what became ancient Babylon, is recorded in the Bible as an attempt to reach heaven through man's collective self-effort escaping the evil world, an aspiration of the Gnostic heresy.

I don't want to extrapolate or assume too much about this portion of the Bible, but I do want to bring out a few key points. We see the origins of the city of Babylon in the book of Genesis and the book of Revelation talks of the city of Babylon which will affect all nations with its corruption prior to the second coming of Christ.

A theme that runs from the beginning of the Bible to its end is a major theme and therefore it should not be looked at as insignificant. Genesis 11:6 says: "they are one people, they have all one language and this is only the beginning of what they will do. And nothing that they propose to do will now be impossible for them." It doesn't implicitly say, but it seems as if they were using the creative power they possessed as image-bearers of God to act against God. It was man attempting to control, dominate and transcend the spiritual apart from the God who created all things. It sounds like the inspiration they had come from the serpent in the garden. Remember he said that by eating of the forbidden tree that the man and woman's eyes would be opened so that they would be like God.

The Tower of Babel: Transcending the Spiritual Realm

Babel means 'gate of god' and the Tower of Babel was about transcending this present material creation through secret knowledge. It was about man being in control of his own destiny and being a god. It was about man escaping this material creation through secret knowledge and hidden wisdom to the heavenly spiritual world. The prophet Isaiah talks of this Luciferic inspiration in chapter 14:13-14 saying: "I will ascend to heaven; above the stars of God I will set my throne on high; I will sit on the Mt. of assembly in the far reaches of the north; I will ascend above the heights of the clouds; I will make myself like the Most High."

It was the height of man rebelling against the God of creation and attempting to be the master of his own destiny. It was the collective pride of man coming together saying we will make our own way, forge our own path and create a world free from a God who rules over us. Remember the earth was destroyed by water and judged because of the wickedness of man's heart. It was men saying, 'we will live how we want'! We reject the restrictions and restraints placed upon the wickedness of our hearts. We will make our own pathway into the heavens. We will be free from the judgment of God by ascending and becoming gods controlling our own destiny.

It sounds like the famous song 'Imagine' written by John Lennon because it came from the same Luciferic inspiration. One world, joined together, rejecting the God of creation, but united together through some mystical experience taking one to the spiritual world of Nirvana. [79]The Tower of Babel represents humanity's attempt to achieve unity and greatness without God. When humans seek unity without truth, the result is coercion or confusion.

Gnosticism is a very fluid belief system without a real core to it,

---

[79] Os Guinness, The Global Public Square, (IVP), p. 33.

so it's easily merged resembling a virus that takes over its host. During the Second Temple Jewish time period right before the arrival of Christ Platonic ideas merged with Judaism, and it produced Jewish Mysticism. It was from here that the Jewish mystics emerged. [80]While there are similarities between certain Jewish apocalyptic ideas later Gnostic spirituality, the two are not identical. I do a detailed analysis of Second Temple Judaism and the epistle of Jude in by book "Contending For The Faith: A Historical Analysis of Jude" which thoroughly explains this subject.

As Christianity rapidly grew in the Roman Empire the ideas were already present due to the Grecian influence, so those ideas easily merged with Christianity, and by 200 AD you have Christian Gnosticism. It was this synchronized belief system that was one of the primary deceptions that the post apostolic writers and early church fathers confronted.

It's still one of the primary deceptions corrupting the foundations of our faith and eroding the pillars of truth on which the church is to be established. Deception is most powerful in the shadows and mixture. It's mixing in enough error with truth that causes the whole foundation to crack. The Babylonians understood Babel to mean 'gate of the god', the Hebrews understood it to mean 'mixed up and confused' which happens when we partake of the tree of the knowledge of good and evil. It produces and multiplies confusion throughout the earth which is what you see in Revelation chapter 17 and 18 concerning mystery Babylon. [81]Babylon represents the idolatrous world system organized in opposition to God.

The Gnostic Quest for Secret Knowledge

One of the modern organizations I think of is the World Council of Churches established by the United Nations in 1948. I'm not saying the World Council of Churches is Mystery Babylon, but it's a mixture of confusion and error. It's now no longer just about uniting Christians under one umbrella organization but merging Islam and all organized religions of the world brought together as one. In Revelation Babylon is referred to as a rebellious, insolent, covenant breaking whore and is an

---

[80] Alan Segal, Two Powers in Heaven, p. 9
[81] G.K. Beale, The Book of Revelation, (NIGTC), p. 867.

inversion of the humble, faithful covenant keeping Bride of Christ.

The basic premise of Gnosticism is that spiritual life is all about obtaining secret knowledge and hidden wisdom to free us from the prison of the material world. [82]Gnostic Christians claims to possess secret traditions from Jesus, which they regarded as superior to the public teaching of the church. There were and are still today many variations of Gnosticism, but in a nutshell, it is the belief that many roads of enlightenment lead back to the one true Light. Regarding creation, they believe an inferior evil god created the material world.

[83]A lot of Gnostic versions teach the inferior evil god is the Hebrew god which is associated with error, darkness and suffering. Now outside of this material world created by the evil god is 'One Supreme' cosmic entity called the *Plêrôma* by the Greeks. The 'One Supreme' cosmic entity exists in the spiritual world apart from and is not subject to the limitations of the material world. It's the creation story flipped on its head and it's an inversion of truth.

The Christian Gnostics of the infected the faith to supplant, undermine and replace it. The Christian Gnostics took the scriptures and twisted them to fit their ideas. [84]They taught that the 'One Supreme' cosmic entity was who sent Christ to earth in the form of a serpent to rescue Adam and Eve from the Garden of Eden. In other words, it was Christ who appeared to Eve and invited her to eat from the tree of the knowledge of good and evil. The evil Hebrew god who created the material world realized what was happening and threw Adam and Eve out of the Garden. [85]In some Gnostic myths the serpent becomes a symbol of the saving revealer.

Now to escape this evil physical world, created by an evil god and get back to the 'One Supreme' cosmic entity we must obtain the secret knowledge and hidden wisdom. Secret knowledge is the key to escaping the material evil world, raising us up into a place of spiritual divinity where we are absorbed back into the 'One Supreme' cosmic entity becoming a god ourselves.

---

[82] Elaine Pagels, The Gnostic Gospels, p. 20.
[83] Kurt Rudolph, Gnosis, p. 76.
[84] Ireanaeus, Against Heresies 1.30.7
[85] Bentley Layton, The Gnostic Scriptures, p. 67.

The Gnostic Heresy: Subverting the Redemptive Story with Mystical Insight

The Gnostic heresy took the redemptive story along with the gospel and subverted it using the same language. Satan is not a creator he is a liar, deceiver and twister of truth. He is a parasitical virus who uses Biblical scripture, terms and inverts them. Gnostic Christianity doesn't deal in concepts of sin and repentance, but with transformation and enlightenment. It teaches salvation based on knowing facts and having mystical insight therefore there are multiple paths back to the 'One Supreme'.

It's the spiritualism of Alcoholics Anonymous as the Big Book of A.A. says "We found that God does not make too hard terms with those who seek Him. To us, the Realm of the Spirit is broad, roomy, all inclusive; never exclusive or forbidding to those who earnestly seek. It is open, we believe, to all men. When, therefore, we speak to you of God, we mean your own conception of God."

It's a complete contradiction to the redemptive story that runs from Genesis to the book of Revelation as revealed by the Hebrew prophets and confirmed by the apostolic writers. Its why John opens his gospel telling the story of Christ from the view of the creation story and him being the Creator who became a real man that could trace his lineage back to David, Abraham and Adam.

The Gnostics taught that Jesus was not God manifested in human flesh and he did not rise from the dead in a resurrection body. The Gnostics taught a Jesus detached and untethered from the redemptive story grounded in the Hebrew prophets upon which the soil of our ancient faith originated. The Gnostics rejected the humanity of Jesus Christ since the 'One Supreme' cosmic entity could have nothing to do with matter therefore he could not have assumed a human body. They rejected Christ's incarnation, denied His crucifixion and claimed there was no bodily resurrection of Christ; thus, Gnosticism attacked the very heart of the gospel.

The Gnostic Jesus was a spiritualized Jesus, but not the Messiah declared by the Hebrew prophets and manifested in human flesh. The Gnostics recognized Jesus not as God in human flesh, but as an ascended master bringing the special *gnōsis* of salvation to humanity's imprisoned soul. He gave us this secret *gnōsis* and hidden wisdom so we could be set free from the material prison of our bodies by possessing this secret *gnōsis*.

The Belief in *Gnōsis* as Salvation

To the Gnostic, knowledge was everything and knowing was enough since *gnōsis* itself is the means of salvation. The spiritual world was the real world with most leaning towards varying forms of mysticism and a fascination with angels. It was the idea of escaping this evil material creation through secret *gnōsis* and spiritual experiences.

John, Paul, Peter, James and Jude all confronted aspects and the fruit of this false teaching in their epistles. The practical result of this heresy resulted in two extremes of human behavior. You had the legalists who would beat their bodies into submission and live ascetic lives detached as much as possible from the material world. All contact with the physical world should be reduced to an absolute minimum and you should not enjoy any bodily pleasures.

Paul goes into detail about this in Colossians saying in 2:23 that living this detached life has an "appearance of wisdom in promoting self-made religion and asceticism and severity to the body." It was strict adherence to ritualism as a pathway to the spiritual realm. [86]The Colossian heresy contained elements that later appeared in developed Gnosticism.

Paul in writing to Timothy addresses what he calls "the irreverent babble and contradictions of what is falsely called 'knowledge,' for by professing it some have swerved from the faith" which is a clear reference to the emerging Gnostic heresy in I and II Timothy. It was a false gospel based on a form of spiritual and ritualistic legalism. It had overlapping similarities to the Pharisaical legalism Paul addressed in his letter to the Galatians. I call these false ideas the 'gospel of legalism'.

You also had the opposite extreme of lawlessness, and it was those who permitted their physical passions to run whatever course they chose. Peter went into detail about this group in II Peter 2:18-19 saying that "they entice by sensual passions of the flesh those who are barely escaping from those who live in error. They promise them freedom, but they themselves are slaves of corruption." Those in this second group

---

[86] Douglas J. Moo, The Letters to the Colossians and Philemon, p. 45.

justified their lawless lifestyles with the erroneous notion that their evil bodies were destined for destruction anyway so what you do with your body doesn't matter. Morality was a matter of opinion therefore your personal conduct did not matter.

It is the false teaching that grace is a license to sin since it was their spirits, which they believed were good and would remain unharmed as long as they obtained the correct *gnōsis*. Having the secret keys to *gnōsis* and hidden wisdom is what matters, not godly conduct. John, Paul, Peter, Jude and even James confronted what I call this 'gospel of lawlessness'.

The Saving Power of *Epignōsis*: Understanding the True Knowledge of Christ

Gnōsis doesn't save us and I'm talking about even Biblical knowledge we get from the scriptures. The scriptures give us the knowledge that leads us to Christ, but it's Christ who saves, delivers, provides, heals and leads us. He is our all in all and we just humbly submit to his wisdom and power displayed through the cross.

In ending the last chapter, I told you there are two main Greek words translated into knowledge which are *gnōsis* and *epignōsis*. The *gnōsis* espoused by Gnostic spiritualism leads us into darkness, duplicity, slavery and deception. *Epignōsis* fills us with the power and wisdom of the cross. It's important that we understand the difference because they are worlds apart and our spiritual health depends on understanding the difference.

One of the scriptures that I mentioned in chapter 1 where Paul was talking about the last days is 2 Timothy 3:4 - 7. It talks of those who are "always learning and never able to arrive at a knowledge of the truth." The Gnostics were spiritual seekers of *gnōsis*, but the *gnōsis* they possessed did not lead to Christ. The word used for knowledge here in this text is *epignōsis* and it speaks of more than just knowing something but partnering with someone. It's the idea of abiding which is a more intimate and personal relationship. Now let's look at this word truth.

The Emphasis on Truth in the Gospel of John

Out of all the apostolic writers it was John who used this word 'truth' by far the most. Paul used the word 32 times, James 3 times, Peter 3 times, but John used the word 45 times. It was only John's gospel that recorded Jesus' interaction with Pilate where he posed the question: 'What is truth?'

The gospel of John opens showing us the origin of all things is God the Son by whom all things were created and is trying to embed upon our hearts that truth is only found in Him. John 1:4 - 5 says: "In him was life, and the life was the light of men. The light shines in the darkness, and the darkness has not overcome it." Vs 14 says, "the Word became flesh and dwelt among us, and we have seen his glory, glory as of the only Son from the Father, full of grace and truth."

John, through his writings, is attempting to show us that truth is not a concept, it's not just a good idea or some better way of living. It's not some illuminating mystical experience, but it's Jesus Christ, the very real God who created all things. Paul said it like this in 2 Corinthians 11:3: "I am afraid that as the serpent deceived Eve by his cunning, your thoughts will be led astray from a sincere and pure devotion to Christ". He then says in 2 Corinthians 4:2: "we have renounced disgraceful, underhanded ways. We refuse to practice deceit or to tamper with God's word."

Trust me I know what it's like to be led astray from a pure devotion to Christ and it happens so easily. Tampering with the word is taking it out of context and distorting it. The distortion of truth in our day abounds and many times it's subtle, deceitful, underhanded and disgraceful.

John, Paul, Peter, James, Jude and all the apostolic writers were not trying to teach us something new they were simply helping us understand our ancient faith revealed through the prophets. You hear warning, after warning to keep the faith and lay hold of the truth. 1 John 2:24 - 26 says: "Let what you heard from the beginning abide in you. If what you heard from the beginning abides in you, then you too will abide in the Son and in the Father. And this is the promise that he made to us—eternal life. I write these things to you about those who are trying to deceive you."

John was endeavoring to show us that truth is a person and when we accept the truth of Christ into our hearts, we are never going to be the same. He said to "as many as received him, to them he gave he the right to become children of God, even to them that believe on his name: who were born, not of blood, nor of the will of the flesh, nor of the will of man, but of God."

What you see throughout John's writing is that when you encounter the light you cannot remain in darkness and the truth exposes deception. If you have embraced Christ then the lies of the antichrist, false prophets, false teachers and false apostles are clearly seen.

Living Counter-Culturally as Believers in Christ

The Goodnews is that Creator took upon himself human flesh and came to us. He dwelt among us. [87]The Word did not merely appear to be human, he became flesh – fully entering the human sphere. He showed us the way when he "emptied himself, by taking the form of a servant, being born in the likeness of men. And being found in human form, he humbled himself by becoming obedient to the point of death, even death on a cross." We just have to humble ourselves by acknowledging the truth of the gospel which brings us into a partnership with him right now in this material creation.

Christ did not come to take us out of this creation, but he has begun the restoration of all things through his victory over death and Hades. Yes, we are pilgrims and aliens in this present evil age. Like Daniel we may live in Babylon, but we are refusing to live as Babylonians. We refuse to bow to their gods, and we refuse to worship the image of their idolatries. [88]Christians live as resident aliens whose allegiance belongs to another kingdom.

We have been saved by grace and given Spirit. Our lives are no longer to operate by the lust of the flesh, lust of the eyes or the pride of life because we know as 1 John 2:17 says: "the world is passing away along with its desires, but whoever does the will of God abides forever." [89]John does not condemn the created order but the rebellious system opposed to God. John wasn't saying the material creation was evil because we know that "God saw everything that he had made…was very good (Gen. 1:31)." What John was saying is that 'the god of this present evil age', Satan the serpent of old, has corrupted the heart of man like in the days of Noah.

The Goodnews of 'the word of the cross' is that God stepped

---

[87] D.A. Carson, The Gospel According to John, (PNTC), p. 127.
[88] Karen Jobes, 1 Peter (BECNT), p. 173.
[89] Colin Kruse, The Letter of John (PNTC), p. 94.

into his creation to redeem, justify, reconcile and restore his creation through the sacrificial Lamb of God. He has partnered with his body in the earth; His *ekklēsia* formed through the outpouring of the Holy Spirit and we are connected to his throne of grace.

Jesus taught us to pray that his kingdom would come on earth like it is in heaven. We are to persevere and remain faithful until he brings the fullness of his victory to this earth when he sits his feet upon the Mt. of Olives and throws Satan into the bottomless pit that he deserves. It's the Maranatha cry of our hearts.

The Redemptive Power of the Cross

The '*epignōsis* of the truth' is not mystical hidden secrets, but what Paul termed the 'word of the cross' in I Corinthians 1:18. Jesus is the pattern for our spiritual lives. As God manifested in human flesh he showed us the way. The 'word of the cross' is not just that Jesus died for our sins, but it's a comprehensive understanding of the gospel message centered in the Messiah who is the beginning and end of all things.

It's a focus on Christ birth, life, death, descent into hades, resurrection from the dead and ascension to the right hand of the Father. As a result of his ascension, he has poured out upon his church the Holy Spirit so that we can fulfill the mission that he started until his physical return to this earth wrapping up this age. It's this message that gives us a framework for understanding the truth which is found in Christ. It's this foundation upon which the body of Christ, his church is established.

If the church is to be a pillar and foundation for truth, then it must completely embrace the truth found in Christ. The gospel must be clearly and boldly declared in the power of the Holy Spirit as it was in the book of Acts.

If you believe the statistics that I quoted earlier from George Barna it's clear that this is not happening in the American Church, something has gone wrong, and the foundation has been eroded. The American Church needs major foundation repair. It must return to the simplicity of Christ and us crucified with him.

Paul opens his letter to the Ephesians and Colossians praying for them. Ephesians 1:16-18 he says: "I do not cease to give thanks for you, remembering you in my prayers, that the God of our Lord Jesus Christ, the Father of glory, may give you the Spirit of wisdom and of revelation in the knowledge (*epignōsis*) of him, having the eyes of your hearts enlightened (emphasis mine)."

In Colossians 1:9 - 10 he says: "we have not ceased to pray for you, asking that you may be filled with the knowledge *(epignōsis)* of his will in all spiritual wisdom and understanding, so as to walk in a manner worthy of the Lord, fully pleasing to him: bearing fruit in every good work and increasing in the knowledge *(epignōsis)* of God; being strengthened with all power (emphasis mine)."

Discovering God's Will and Truth Through Prayer

If you don't know how or what to pray, then take these prayers that Paul prayed and make them your prayers. I use these prayers all the time in my personal devotion because I want to be filled with the knowledge of his will. I want the eyes of my heart enlightened with the understanding of Christ's redemptive power and wisdom. The word Paul uses for knowledge here is not *gnōsis*, but *epignōsis*. Paul was praying that their hearts would be consumed with the Person of Christ and not just an idea, a concept or some mystical insight.

Do you want to know the will of God for your life? Do you want to be consumed with the love of God captivating all your heart, soul and strength? Do you want to live in the light of the truth and not the darkness of deception? Our goal is to grow up into Christ and fulfill the will of God for our lives. To do this we must be established in the *epignōsis* of the truth. In other places Paul called it 'the mystery'. Peter called it "the prophetic word more fully confirmed".

Paul in 1 Corinthians 4:1 - 2 describes himself as a steward. Paul said one should "regard us, as servants of Christ and stewards of the mysteries of God. Moreover, it is required of stewards that they be found faithful." Stewardship in this verse has nothing to do with being good with our money. It has everything to do with being faithful to God's mysteries revealed to Paul.

'The Mystery' in the Book of Romans

The word translated mystery doesn't mean mystery as we think of something mysterious, mystical, strange or some hidden *gnōsis*. It means something previously unrevealed. A secret and something kept hidden until the appointed time by God. Paul used the term to describe the gospel that had been revealed to him. [90]In Paul, a 'mystery' is not something mysterious, but something once hidden and now revealed in salvation history.

The book of Romans was a theological masterpiece that Paul wrote. He ends this book saying, "now to him who can strengthen you according to my gospel and the preaching of Jesus Christ according to the revelation of the mystery that was kept secret for long ages but has now been disclosed." Did you hear that? It says the mystery has been disclosed and made known. It's not hidden anymore! [91]The 'mystery' is God's redemptive plan, long concealed but now revealed in Christ. It's not something we can't understand or some secret *gnōsis* for the initiated, but the centrality of Christ which is the power and wisdom of our missional journey.

Now Paul, although he was a very well-educated man was able to make his message so simple that the uneducated could understand it. It's so simple that we stumble over it. In I Corinthians 1:24 he said "we preach that Christ was crucified, the Jews are offended, and the Gentiles say it's all nonsense. But to those called by God to salvation, both Jews and Gentiles, Christ is the power of God and the wisdom of God." The simplicity of Christ is a stumbling stone and at the same time the foundation that the whole household of faith is built upon. [92]The content of Paul's preaching was singular – Christ crucified.

On a personal level it's all about being born from above, becoming a new creation and allowing Christ in us to mature us so that our hearts are filled with his life-giving Spirit. [93]The new birth is the work of the Spirit that gives life from above. It's the only way to be free from self-deception. It's what Paul was praying for the church in Ephesus and Colosse to be filled with the *epignōsis* of Christ himself. Paul's *epignōsis* is relational and Christ – centered not elitist *gnōsis*.

It's not the Platonic Gnostic dualism of escaping the material world to get to the spirit world. It's that we have been crucified with Christ. We've died to this world through the body of Christ. It's eating his flesh and drinking in the blood of the New Covenant. It's our complete identification with his death, burial and resurrection. The truth

---

[90] G.K. Beale, A New Testament Biblical Theology, p. 193.

[91] Douglas J. Moo, The Epistle to the Romans, (NICNT), p. 936.

[92] Gordon D. Fee, The Frist Epistle to the Corinthians, (NICNT), p. 76.

[93] D.A. Carson, John (PNTC), p. 188.

is that through the *epignōsis* of Christ:

- We have the very same Spirit that raised Christ from the dead alive in our hearts.
- We are not trying to escape to heaven, but the very life of heaven, the powers of the age to come has come to reside in us.
- We are not gods, but we are children of the Father humbly dependent on his ability displayed on our behalf through the life of the Spirit.
- We have been placed into Christ.

Its why John opens his gospel showing us that Jesus is the Creator God, but he also affectionately calls those who receive him the children of God. It's what Paul was praying that we would truly understand and live as the children of God in this present evil age. We live in self-deception when we refuse to live up to our inheritance as those given the Spirit of God. Peter, James, Jude, John and Paul all clearly lay out the character traits of the sons of light.

Paul in Galatians 5:22 - 24 says those born of the Spirit produce good fruit and he then defines what that looks like which is: "love, joy, peace, patience, kindness, goodness, faithfulness, gentleness, self-control; against such things there is no law. And those who belong to Christ Jesus have crucified the flesh with its passions and desires." You can't do this on your own. It's why Jesus said: "unless a grain of wheat falls into the earth and dies, it remains alone; but if it dies, it bears much fruit."

Abiding in Christ: Love, Service, and Mission

Fruit is the defining factor because it's not something we can produce without abiding in Christ. We are not our own, we have been bought with a price to serve him who has been raised from the dead. Abiding in Christ and demonstrating his nature of love is the proof that we are his. To love God with all our hearts and love others sums up our mission. It's a simple message that all can understand living in the *epignōsis* of the truth.

Paul, in discussing the great divide between walking in the flesh and walking in the Spirit, says in Galatians 5:14 that: "the whole law is fulfilled in one word: 'You shall love your neighbor as yourself.'" Love is evidence of our relationship with God and has actionable results producing tangible fruit through the Spirit's participation in our lives. John in his first epistle 3:8 says, "let us not love in word or talk, but in deed and truth." It's what James was saying that our faith must have action and be living, or we are just deceiving ourselves.

Transformation from Children of Wrath to Children of Light

You know before we responded to the gospel and were given the Holy Spirit, we did not have this choice. Ephesians 2:2-3 says: "you once walked, following the course of this world, following the prince of the power of the air, the spirit that is now at work in the sons of disobedience— among whom we all once lived in the passions of our flesh, carrying out the desires of the body and the mind, and were by nature children of wrath, like the rest of mankind."

Sons of disobedience live sinful lifestyles because it's their nature and that's what they do. Paul in writing to the Corinthians said: "I wrote to you in my letter not to associate with sexually immoral people—not at all meaning the sexually immoral of this world, or the greedy and swindlers, or idolaters, since then you would need to go out of the world."

Christ has freed us from the power of sin, but we are not free to abuse others or take advantage of them. No, you don't have the freedom to go into sex clubs. If you are giving your money to a woman for sex don't say it's to help them out and feed their children. You're lying to yourself! If you are dancing on a pole to make your living, then don't call yourself a child of God. There is no such thing as strippers for Jesus. Just because you and your wife agree to swap sex partners does not make it ok. It's still adultery and sexual immorality.

Embracing Repentance: A Call to Examine Ourselves

Paul wasn't saying we have the freedom to live in sensuality, excessive greed and the corruption of our culture. He is saying those who call themselves children of God and are living such lifestyles what they need to: is examine themselves. It's what I'm asking you to do. It's what I've had to do many times during my journey of faith, which is to repent and turn away from the flesh. We can no longer stand in the valley of decision. We are either going to eat the flesh and drink the blood of Christ or we are going to fall away into apostasy.

The gravitational pull between walking in the flesh and living in the Spirit can only be resolved by the humility of the cross. I can't cast the flesh out of you, but you can turn away from the works of the flesh. It's what true repentance is all about which is acknowledging the truth found only in complete submission to Christ.

James 1:21 tells us the way we learn to walk with God and live in the truth is the pathway of humility. Humility is the key to transformation. The arrogant and self-sufficient stumble over the simplicity of the cornerstone groping around in darkness as they trip over the truth and live in self-deception. It's why they are deceived because their pride refuses to acknowledge the foolishness of the cross.

Humility teaches us how to change from the inside out. It is performed as we are filled with the Spirit, and we receive with meekness the engrafted word of God which can save or deliver the soul. We must have a desire to hear, listen to and respond to the word of God in humility of heart. It is only the message of the cross that has the power to change us because we are incapable of changing ourselves. True and lasting change can only happen in our hearts; by allowing the truth of the foundation of Christ to live within us.

The Foundation of Faith: Mercy and Judgment

I want to end this reminding you of Isaiah 28:16 -17 where the prophet says: "I am the one who has laid as a foundation in Zion, a stone, a tested stone, a precious cornerstone, of a sure foundation: 'Whoever believes will not be in haste.' And I will make justice the line and righteousness the plumb line; and hail will sweep away the refuge of lies." The end of this age is about sweeping away the refuge of lies that have covered the foundation. It's the place that mercy and judgment kiss together.

If we don't make the very foundation of our faith a living reality in our hearts, then we are found to be false witnesses to the truth. Are we going to be wheat that bows in humility or the prideful arrogant tares living under a refuge of self-deceptive lies? I'm going to end this lesson having you read the book of Hebrews and let this speak for itself.

Hebrews 10:19 - 31 says: "therefore, brothers, since we have confidence to enter the holy places by the blood of Jesus, by the new and living way that he opened for us through the curtain, that is, through his flesh, and since we have a great priest over the house of God, let us draw near with a true heart in full assurance of faith, with our hearts sprinkled clean from an evil conscience and our bodies washed with pure water.

Let us hold fast the confession of our hope without wavering, for he who promised is faithful. And let us consider how to stir up one another to love and good works, not neglecting to meet together, as is the habit of some, but encouraging one another, and all the more as you see the Day drawing near.

For if we go on sinning deliberately after receiving the knowledge of the truth, there no longer remains a sacrifice for sins, but a fearful expectation of judgment and a fury of fire that will consume the adversaries. Anyone who has set aside the law of Moses dies without mercy on the evidence of two or three witnesses. How much worse punishment, do you think, will be deserved by the one who has trampled underfoot the Son of God, and has profaned the blood of the covenant by which he was sanctified, and has outraged the Spirit of grace? For we know him who said, "Vengeance is mine; I will repay." And again, "The Lord will judge his people." It is a fearful thing to fall into the hands of the living God."

CHAPTER 6

THE ELEMENTAL SPIRITS OF THE WORLD

"See to it that no one takes you captive by philosophy and empty deceit, according to human tradition, according to the elemental spirits of the world, and not according to Christ."

~ Colossians 2:8 ~

The book of Philippians is one of Paul's most personal epistles written from a prison cell to a church with whom he had an intimate relationship and with whom he shared a participation in the gospel. The second chapter of this book not only lays out the redemptive work of Christ when God became man laying down his life on our behalf, but it also clearly portrays that our lives are to demonstrate the cruciform way of life. We are to follow in his footsteps and live our lives by the example that he demonstrated.

Embracing Humility and Servanthood in Christ

Chapter three starts out talking about the 'gospel of legalism', He tells them in verse 2 to: "Look out for the dogs, look out for the evildoers, look out for those who mutilate the flesh." Paul tells us in verses 3 thru 5 to: "Do nothing from selfish ambition or conceit, but in humility count others more significant than yourselves. Let each of you look not only to his own interests, but also to the interests of others. Have this mind among yourselves, which is yours in Christ Jesus…who emptied himself, by taking the form of a servant."

The dogs, evildoers and those who mutilate the flesh are all the same group. It's those who Paul addressed in Galatians 1:7 whom he said: "trouble you and want to distort the gospel of Christ." In II Corinthians 11:20 he called them "deceitful workers" who try to dominate you and manipulate you for gain:

- It's those who use you to make themselves feel important and exalt themselves over you.
- It is those who are skillful at twisting the word of God and use fear to

keep you in a place of submission under them.

- It is those who deceptively control people so that they can profit monetarily and sometimes sexually from their submission.
- It is a narcissistic personality that loves to dominate and excerpt power to satisfy personal needs.

Paul ends Philippians 3:18-19 saying that: "many, of whom I have often told you and now tell you even with tears, walk as enemies of the cross of Christ. Their end is destruction, their god is their belly and they glory in their shame, with minds set on earthly things."

It's the same language that Paul ends the book of Romans by saying in chapter 16:17-18 to: "watch out for those who cause divisions and create obstacles contrary to the doctrine that you have been taught; avoid them. For such persons do not serve our Lord Christ, but their own appetites, and by smooth talk and flattery they deceive the hearts of the naive."

The Deceptive Trap of Legalism

What I want to help you understand in this chapter is the false 'gospel of legalism'. It is one of the two main enemies of the cross of Christ which the apostolic writers confronted, opposed and condemned.

The Bible opens with two trees in the Garden of Eden. The book of Revelation ends with a tree bringing healing to the nations. In the middle of the Bible, we have a tree that separates time and testaments. It is where the God who created all things stepped into time opening the doorway to the age to come. It is through the tree of the cross that the restoration of all things has begun.

Trees are mentioned in the Bible more than any living thing other than God and people. A tree marks the spot of many major events in the redemptive story of history. The fall of man, the judgment of the flood, the Abrahamic covenant and the downfall of Nebuchadnezzar just to name a few. A lot of things can be said about trees from the scriptures.

Two things I want to bring out are the fruit a tree produces, and the underlying root system hidden to the eye. Jesus talked about both the fruit and the root. John the Baptists, the one who was sent in the spirit and power of Elijah to turn the nation of Israel to repentance said in Matthew 3:10, "the axe is laid to the root of the trees. Every tree therefore that does not bear good fruit is cut down and thrown into the fire."

Always Examine the Fruit Before You Eat

In chapter 7 of Matthew Jesus tells us how to detect false prophets who deceptively disguise themselves. He says in verse 18 thru 20 that: "A healthy tree cannot bear bad fruit, nor can a diseased tree bear good fruit. Every tree that does not bear good fruit is cut down and thrown into the fire. Thus you will recognize them by their fruits." Root systems are hidden from the natural eye, but bad fruit is very distinguishable and impossible to hide over time.

An honest observation of the American Church can conclude that there is some bad and rotten fruit. If you see bad fruit, then there are problems with the root system. It's why Paul always focused on foundations. Jesus was warning us about those who twist truth to take advantage. Don't get hung up on the term 'false prophets' because Jesus was simply talking about anyone who alters the foundation of his words which he goes on to talk about in verses 24 thru 27 of this same chapter.

Twisting the truth alters the grace of God and when you alter the original design of God's truth then we can find ourselves no longer rooted in Christ. Just as with Eve the serpent alters God's word using deception to take captive souls. It's why we always need to examine our lives and make sure that we do not allow ourselves to move away from Christ who is the truth. We drift because we have become untethered from the cross.

It happens if we embrace a refuge of twisted scripture. Just as in the days of Jeremiah there are prophets who give "vain hopes. They speak visions of their own minds, not from the mouth of the Lord" (Jeremiah 23:16). Pride has filled their hearts, and they are no longer messengers of the cross grounding the people in Christ the foundation but are leading those with itching ears into ditches of extremism.

Paul in 2 Timothy 4:3-4 tells us about these days when he says: "people will not endure sound teaching, but having itching ears they will accumulate for themselves teachers to suit their own passions and will turn away from listening to the truth and wander off into myths." The two false ideas I am hoping to lay an ax to the root of are legalism and lawlessness. Legalism and lawlessness lead you into ditches taking you off the secure pathway of sound doctrine and the focus of living the cruciform life of faith.

Jesus and the apostolic writers warned us of wolves in sheep's clothing disguising themselves. One of the main traits of a wolf will be pride and arrogance. Pride blinds, deceiving and leads to narcissistic behavior. A wolf coerces, controls and dominates to take advantage. A spiritual wolf seeks to separate its prey from the safety of sound doctrine pushing you into extremes so they can take advantage. I am not saying that someone who has some incorrect understanding of scripture is a wolf. The way I am using the term in this book is primarily about spiritual abuse. I am addressing those who use the Bible and spiritual experiences to control, manipulative and gain advantage over others.

Remember there is nothing new under the sun, it's the same old story over and over. The motivation is always the same for power, money and sexual exploitation. It may not be all three at once, but sometimes it is. I don't think you need me to point out the multitude of modern-day examples. Paul said almost the same thing that Jesus said in Acts 20:29 - 30: "after my departure fierce wolves will come in among you, not sparing the flock; and from among your own selves will arise men speaking twisted things, to draw away the disciples after themselves."

A wolf doesn't keep it in the center focusing on the sound doctrine of Jesus and the cross, but they draw disciples after themselves twisting the scriptures. Sound doctrine produces healthy living, and the fruit will be living lives that demonstrate the new life produced through the cruciform life of Christ in us. The two ditches of extremism I hope to help you avoid come from the same root system. The one tree which is the tree of the knowledge of good and evil produces the fruit of legalism and lawlessness.

The False Gospels of Legalism and Lawlessness

What I am attempting to do is show you that these two false gospels spring from the same root system. Legalism and lawlessness are the two main lies attempting to corrupt the foundation of the church. I will show you that it's only by staying completely grounded in the root system of the tree of the cross that we can experience true freedom found in the grace of God. We must hold our feet to the fire of the cross allowing the imprint of the cruciform life to be the only pathway for our feet.

Let's look at the 'gospel of legalism' because the deception of legalism has an appearance of good. It appears respectable, clean, polished and proper. Religious legalism has the appearance of being good to the natural observer.

The New Testament starts out attesting to the fact that religion is inadequate to change the human heart. In the scripture I just previously quoted, John the Baptist, the prophet who came in the spirit and power of Elijah was sent to prepare Israel for the coming Messiah. He said, "bear fruit in keeping with repentance. And do not presume to say to yourselves, 'We have Abraham as our father,' for I tell you, God is able from these stones to raise up children for Abraham'". He was saying you can't hide in your heritage and traditions as if that alone makes you a child of God.

John the Baptist and Jesus: Challenging Legalism

John the Baptist and Jesus turned the gospel of legalism on its heads. The legalists misinterpret the heart of God and create a system which they think is protecting the glory of God, but it destroys it. The religious leaders of Jesus' days were the Pharisees and historians estimate they had developed a system of 613 laws adding to the Mosaic Law.

The Pharisees had produced a heartless, cold and arrogant brand of legalism. Jesus compared it to bondage and the servitude of slavery saying in Luke 11:46 that they: "load people with burdens hard to bear" and they did not care but enjoyed it because they were the big fish on top of the spiritual food chain getting to reap the benefits.

The gospel of legalism produced by the Pharisees can be summed up in Matthew 15 and Mark 7 which both tell the same story. The scribes and the Pharisees had major issues about Jesus and his disciples not following their traditional methods of washing their hands before they ate. The issue was not cleaning hands. It was because they were not following the ritualistic traditions the Pharisees had developed over the years attempting to interpret and live out the Mosaic law.

The power the Pharisees had over the people was because the people obeyed their rules. The Sadducees were the real power brokers in Israel because Rome had granted them the political power to control the Temple. The historian Josephus described them as secular and not interested in Judaism as a faith. He described them as not believing in a God who directed the affairs of men, but they believed man was left to his own devices to figure things out. I call them practical atheists who used the Jewish religion and Temple as a means of power.

The Pharisees didn't have any real power, so they had to use the power of persuasion to manipulate and control the people. The Pharisees controlled the people through their religious teaching because they sat in the seat of Moses interpreting the Law teaching the nation of Israel. If people did not follow their traditions, then the very system by which they maintained their power would be undermined.

The Pharisees had become blinded and deceived by their own legalistic system. Jesus called them blind guides. The Pharisees had taken the Mosaic Law and drove it into the ditch of legalistic extremism. It became stuck in the deep ruts of bondage. It was a road that led them and others away from God, but they had come to believe their own lies. The legalistic system produced by the Pharisees no longer resembled the Mosaic covenant law. It had become a shelter of falsehoods where they hid the wickedness of their hearts. Jesus quoted the prophet Isaiah 29:13 saying: "This people honors me with their lips, but their heart is far from me; in vain do they worship me, teaching as doctrines the commandments of men."

Jesus was clear in his response to the Pharisees that the root of the problem was not the Mosaic law, but their hearts and the system they had built to retain their power, prestige and dominance over the people. Matthew 15:10-20 Jesus said: "Hear and understand: it is not what goes into the mouth that defiles a person, but what comes out of the mouth; this defiles a person." Then the disciples came and said to him, "Do you know that the Pharisees were offended when they heard this saying?"

Jesus "answered, 'Every plant that my heavenly Father has not planted will be rooted up. Let them alone; they are blind guides. And if the blind lead the blind, both will fall into a pit.' But Peter said to him, "Explain the parable to us." And he said, "Are you also still without understanding? Do you not see that whatever goes into the mouth passes into the stomach and is expelled? But what comes out of the mouth proceeds from the heart, and this defiles a person. For out of the heart come evil thoughts, murder, adultery, sexual immorality, theft, false witness, slander. These are what defile a person. But to eat with unwashed hands does not defile anyone." Paul defined these activities as the works of the flesh in Galatians chapter 5.

Hypocrisy is the Result of Legalism

The gospel of legalism produces hypocrisy because that's all it can produce, it's the fruit that springs from the root of the tree. To be a hypocrite is simply to be an actor. In the 23rd chapter of Matthew Jesus takes his prophetic ax out and chops down the tree of legalism showing it to be hypocritical deception. The fruit of any legalistic system, no matter how spiritual it may present itself, always produces religious actors which are wolves in sheep's clothing.

Jesus showed us that wolf packs are not content to just corrupt themselves, but they are driven by the desire to dominate others and it's then that they become abusive. Jesus said to them that: "you travel across sea and land to make a single proselyte, and when he becomes a proselyte, you make him twice as much a child of hell as yourselves (Matt. 23:15)."

The religious hypocrite needs an audience to feed their desires to control the lives of others. Here are a few things Jesus said about this system of religion in Matthew chapter 23. Jesus pointed these traits out to us so that we could identify false spiritual systems and abusive spiritual leaders. If you see these traits pay attention. The Pharisees were skilled legalists using the word of God for the purpose of power. Jesus said they:

- Preach, but do not practice what they preach.
- Lay out demands, rules and insist on others to follow their guidelines to control them.
- Do what they do to be seen as the holy man or woman of God.
- Love to be honored and esteemed by others for their dedication to the system along with their religious fervor.
- You must call them by their title because it is their identity which gives them a feeling of importance, superiority and authority over you. The title is not the issue, it's the attitude of the heart.
- They are very eager to find others who will submit to their system and replicate the system.
- They have a strong focus on sacrificial giving to support the system and use financial strings to manipulate.

- They demand blind obedience to the system and to their personal authority, refusing to be questioned.

The Pharisees believed that they were not just the chosen seed of Abraham, but that their system was protecting the Abrahamic covenant. I want to finish up talking about the Pharisees and the greed attached to their system. Religion doesn't change a greedy heart. It masks greed, but greed has a way of breaking through the veneer of religion. The root system of religion is greed, power and control.

The Pharisees were masters at using their religious position to fill their pockets and built a system that was filled with greed because wherever you have hypocritical religion one of the fruits is greed. The Pharisees used their religious position to get money and called it the blessing of God.

The True Intent of the Abrahamic Covenant

To the Pharisees, being wealthy was a sign of God's approval. In other words, "I gain wealth because I'm so righteous that God is blessing me therefore you need to listen to me if you too want to be blessed." John the Baptist, Jesus' and the apostolic testimony of scripture demonstrated sacrifice, worship from the heart, obedience, surrender to the provision of God and living lives of contentment. The fruit of a true servant is humility, transparency and sacrificial love. The fruit of a wolf is greed, power and control.

Paul like John the Baptist and Jesus turned the legalist on their heads and showed us the true intent of the Abrahamic covenant. Paul in Galatians 3:14 says the 'blessing of Abraham' is not riches, prosperity, power, ruling over others and dominating their lives. It's what the legalists thought they had a right to do.

Paul shows us the fulfillment of the Abrahamic covenant in the New Testament. He defined what the Law and Prophets said concerning the blessing of Abraham. He says it is "the promised Spirit through faith". Let me say this again for those in the back of the room who hold to this false American prosperity doctrine. The blessing of Abraham is the New Covenant of the Spirit and it's not more complicated than that.

Go read the context of Galatians chapter 3 because it's not the health and wealth gospel. Just as [94]Thomas Schreiner says, "the blessing of Abraham is interpreted as the reception of the Spirit not material prosperity but eschatological salvation." Taking the word of God out of context and making merchandise out of it is a dangerous path to go down.

Yes, God wants to prosper us. The Greek word prosper used in 3 John 2 where John says, "that you may prosper and be in good health" is *euodoo*. The Strong's Exhaustive Concordance of the Bible gives this definition: "to help on the road, to succeed in reaching and to have a prosperous journey." [95]John's wish reflects well-being in a holistic sense, not a promise of wealth. It simply means that yes as any good father, Father God wants to provide for us along our journey of faith.

The Messianic age has come in the power of the Holy Spirit and fire to deal with the evil heart of greed exposing the whitewashed facade of hypocrisy. Jesus is our pattern and no he was not rich in the context of American prosperity. Jesus had enough to accomplish the will of God during his 3 ½ years of earthly ministry, but there is no evidence he had great wealth. One of many scriptures' that are twisted is in 2 Corinthians 8:9 where Paul says: "you know the grace of our Lord Jesus Christ, that though he was rich, yet for your sake he became poor, so that you by his poverty might become rich."

The text here in 2 Corinthians has nothing to do with becoming rich in the sense of American prosperity. It's that the very God of heaven humbled himself by becoming a man. It's that through Christ's crucifixion, resurrection, ascension and outpouring of the Spirit we can receive the riches of heaven. Yes, the entire context of chapter 8 and 9 is about giving and helping others, but what Paul is saying in this text is that Jesus' willingness to lay down his life is our example of how to give.

I'm not saying there is anything wrong with having money or even having great wealth. What I am saying is that we cannot twist the scriptures and make them say things they don't say. Jesus warned us to not let money become an idol in our hearts (Mark 6:24) and Paul gave us that same message (I Timothy 6:10). Money is not the problem. The issue lies with the heart and what we give our hearts too. Wisdom is the key to successful living, and we are called to be wise in all facets of our lives.

---

[94] Thomas Schreiner, Galatians, (ZECNT), p. 207.
[95] Daniel Akin, 1, 2, 3 John (NAC), p. 240.

The Birth of the Church: A Fulfillment of Prophecies

On the day of Pentecost when the church was born through the outpouring of the Spirit. It was born from the soil and roots of the ancient faith which the prophets predicted over thousands of years. Our faith sprang from the loins of the Abrahamic covenant promised through the seed of the woman. It started on the threshing floor of the Jewish temple born in the soil of the Law and the Prophets.

The Jerusalem council did not happen until approximately 20 years after the resurrection of Christ. The church was called 'the way' and was looked upon as a crazy sect of Judaism that followed a Jewish insurrectionist crucified by the Romans but believed to be a risen king of the Jews.

The apostolic writers brought clarity, insight and understanding on how the God who stepped into time as a man came to fulfill the Abrahamic covenant. It is through his resurrection from the dead that he fills those who believed with the power of the Spirit. The gospel produces the fruit of the kingdom in the heart of those grounded in the root system of the tree of the cross.

I love to read the gospels because it is the redemptive story being told by the one who wrote the story. Jesus and his words are amazing, many times mysterious and hard to understand. His own disciples had to ask him to repeat, explain and expound on what he really meant. The apostolic writers help us to interpret many of the things that Jesus taught and I'm thankful for their insight. Paul who wrote two thirds of the New Testament epistles was given special insight into what he called 'the mystery' and even went so far as to call it his gospel in Romans 16:25.

The Remarkable Credentials of Paul the Pharisee

Paul as a leader of the Pharisees was at the top of the food chain of the gospel of legalism when he was blinded by the risen Christ on the way to Damascus. I don't think him being blinded by the glory of God was insignificant because he had spent his life up until that time blinded and deceived by Pharisaical legalism.

Paul was not just any Pharisee, but he lists his credentials in Philippians 3:5 - 6 saying: "circumcised on the eighth day, of the people of Israel, of the tribe of Benjamin, a Hebrew of Hebrews; as to the law, a

Pharisee; as to zeal, a persecutor of the church; as to righteousness under the law, blameless."

Paul took the gospel of legalism seriously and his whole life was dedicated to protecting the system until God began to captivate his heart. A lot of speculation has been written as to if Paul had ever seen or been around Jesus' ministry. No historical evidence nor any scriptures indicate Paul and Jesus encountered one another prior to the Damascus Road experience. We do know that many of the Pharisees were coming to faith during the time of Christ ministry and after his resurrection. Paul was a man on a mission to crush the sect called 'the way' and we first hear about him in Acts chapter 7.

In this chapter Stephen was brought before the high priest for preaching about the resurrected Christ. He gave one of the most amazing sermons recorded in the Bible detailing the purpose of God through Israel and fulfilled in Christ. The glory of God was on Stephen as he preached under the power of the Holy Spirit.

Acts chapter 7:55 - 58 says Stephen: "full of the Holy Spirit, gazed into heaven and saw the glory of God, and Jesus standing at the right hand of God. And he said, "Behold, I see the heavens opened and the Son of Man standing at the right hand of God." But they cried out with a loud voice and stopped their ears and rushed together at him. Then they cast him out of the city and stoned him. And the witnesses laid down their garments at the feet of a young man named Saul."

Paul, who was called Saul at the time, encountered this experience up close and it is my theory that his heart was pricked by the Holy Spirit. He was the Sheriff on the scene and by laying down his garments he was giving his seal of approval for this stoning of Stephen as blasphemy against the legalistic system he was defending.

I've seen this in my own lie that in my darkness and deception the Holy Spirit was tripping me up trying to get me to change my ways. The anointing of Stephen's preaching had knocked cracks in the veneer of Paul's deception, and we see in the next chapter that he was transformed by the resurrected Christ with the rest being history. He was then commissioned as an apostle of Christ to the Gentiles.

Paul was the perfect vehicle to destroy the gospel of legalism, and he wielded his sword with effectiveness. It was his familiarity with this legalistic system that helped him to expose, uncover and root out this false gospel. It was the epistle of Galatians, Romans and the book of Hebrews that really helped me understand the transition from the Mosaic law to the gospel of grace. We don't know the author of Hebrews, but it is my opinion that Barnabas was the author.

Why Paul is Unlikely to be the Author of Hebrews

The book of Hebrews is the only book in the New Testament where the author did not identify himself. According to Tertullian of Carthage (160 – 225 AD), the first Latin father, the epistle to the Hebrews was written by Barnabas and I agree for a few reasons. It does not seem to be Paul because speech and writing patterns have distinctive signatures that each person develops. Hebrews just doesn't have Paul's writing patterns although it does seem that he had influence upon its author.

The author had a relationship with Timothy, one of Paul's closest associates, so that puts Paul close to the author (Heb. 13:23). Hebrews was written by someone who was very familiar with Mosaic law. Barnabas was a Levite (Acts 4:36) so that made him very familiar with the temple, priesthood and sacrifice system. It was someone who clearly understood the purpose of the coming of Christ who fulfilled the Mosaic law establishing a new temple and sacrifice system founded in the risen king priest Jesus Christ

It's the book of Galatians more than any other epistle that puts a stake in the heart of Pharisaical legalism that was trying to stay attached to the newly formed faith. The place of Mosaic law then and now is one of the greatest debates in the church dividing believers in warring camps. The book of Acts sets the stage for the book of Galatians.

- **Acts 9** Paul gets transformed and starts preaching in Damascus. A plot to kill him is found out so he escapes, and Barnabas takes him to Jerusalem introducing him to the apostles then again due to his preaching; his life is threatened so he goes to his hometown of Tarsus.
- **Acts 10** opens with Peter receiving a vision and is then taken to Cornelius's home who was a Roman soldier and Gentile. He preaches the gospel for the first time to a group of Gentiles. The Holy Spirit fills the Gentiles. The Gentiles began speaking in tongues having been filled with the Spirit, so Peter baptized them into water seeing that God bore witness to their conversion of faith.

The first Gentile church was started.

- **Acts 11** Peter reports back to Jerusalem. The Jerusalem church had been scattered due to persecution after Stephen's powerful preaching. It then says just north in the city of Antioch a great many came to the Lord through the preaching of those who were scattered so Barnabas was sent to check out the reports. Barnabas confirmed the reports and saw a need to establish new believers, so it says that he sent for Paul. It says Barnabas and Paul stayed there for a year teaching and making disciples.
- **Acts 12** opens with James, the brother of John, being beheaded, then Peter being put in prison and shortly thereafter released by an angelic visitation. Acts 13 opens with Barnabas and Paul being commissioned by a group of prophets in Antioch and sent on their first apostolic mission. It was during this time that they planted churches in southern Galatia. The great transition from the exclusive gospel to the Jewish community centered in Jerusalem was about to be overtaken with Paul's revelation of 'the mystery' and his apostolic mission to the Gentiles. Antioch became one of the first apostolic hubs to reach the Gentiles with the gospel.
- **Acts 14** tells of Barnabas and Paul's journey. Then **Acts 15** opens with the great debate when: "some men came down from Judea and were teaching the brothers, "Unless you are circumcised according to the custom of Moses, you cannot be saved." Basically, they were saying Gentiles must become Jews to truly be followers of the Jewish Messiah.

You see, many of the Jewish believers in Jerusalem never stopped worshiping in the Temple, keeping the Mosaic law and still thought Gentiles were second class citizens in the kingdom of God. It was this group that taught the Mosaic Law was still in effect and to be a true believer in Christ you had to come under the requirements of the Mosaic Law with circumcision as the sign of covenant obedience. Acts 15:5 says it was those who "belonged to the party of the Pharisees" who came to the province of Galatia bringing what Paul called a false gospel to the churches he and Barnabas had planted.

Warning Against Distorting the Gospel

Paul's letter to the Galatians opens saying in 1:6-8: "I am

astonished that you are so quickly deserting him who called you in the grace of Christ and are turning to a different gospel—not that there is another one, but there are some who trouble you and want to distort the gospel of Christ. But even if we or an angel from heaven should preach to you a gospel contrary to the one we preached to you, let him be accursed."

Paul was perplexed that the Galatians were so fickle and easily persuaded to disregard what he had taught them concerning the grace of God lived out through the cruciform life of faith. Paul called these Pharisaical interlopers' false brethren in Galatians 2:4-5 who he said were trying to bring them under a false system and bring them into slavery.

Paul warned Titus about this group telling him in Titus 1: 9-11 to: "give instruction in sound doctrine and also to rebuke those who contradict it. For there are many who are insubordinate, empty talkers and deceivers, especially those of the circumcision party. They must be silenced, since they are upsetting whole families by teaching for shameful gain what they ought not to teach."

Paul gave similar instruction to Timothy telling him in Timothy 1: 3 - 7 to: "remain at Ephesus so that you may charge certain persons not to teach any different doctrine, nor to devote themselves to myths and endless genealogies, which promote speculations rather than the stewardship from God that is by faith. The aim of our charge is love that issues from a pure heart and a good conscience and a sincere faith. Certain persons, by swerving from these, have wandered away into vain discussion, desiring to be teachers of the law, without understanding either what they are saying or the things about which they make confident assertions."

Narcissistic Prideful Legalists and Groupthink

The false teachers Paul was addressing were not just trying to bring them back under slavery to the Mosaic law, but to their system and their false authority. It's this same group Paul addresses in II Corinthians 11:3 - 4 saying: "I am afraid that as the serpent deceived Eve by his cunning, your thoughts will be led astray from a sincere and pure devotion to Christ. For if someone comes and proclaims another Jesus than the one we proclaimed, or if you receive a different spirit from the one you received, or if you accept a different gospel from the one you accepted, you put up with it readily enough."

He was addressing false apostles preaching a false doctrine for the purpose of creating a system that others had to submit to so they could be under what Paul with tongue in cheek called 'super apostles'. Paul said do not yield in submission to them even for a moment so that the truth of the gospel might be preserved.

False systems designed to control, manipulate and put fear in the hearts of people to submit are powerful tools. We see how powerful they are that even one of the pillars of the church could be swayed. In Galatians 2:11 - 13 Paul had to confront Peter who had been swayed by this deceptive error.

Paul in Galatians 3:1 says "O foolish Galatians! Who has bewitched you?" Legalism is about control and Paul equated it with a spell that blinded them from the crucified Christ. Self-control is a fruit of the Spirit, but control is witchcraft and is one of the works of the flesh. Witchcraft in its simplest form is simply trying to manipulate, dominate and control you through the power of persuasion.

Paul said when Peter: "came to Antioch, I opposed him to his face, because he stood condemned. For before certain men came from James, he was eating with the Gentiles; but when they came, he drew back and separated himself, fearing the circumcision party. And the rest of the Jews acted hypocritically along with him, so that even Barnabas was led astray by their hypocrisy." False deceptive doctrines gain their power through Groupthink.

Groupthink is a powerful tool when wielded in the hands of a narcissistic prideful leader who sets themselves up as the authority and voice of God. It is so powerful that even people who should know better are persuaded through fear of rejection and reprisal. Paul warned Titus in 1:10 - 11 about those who are: "empty talkers and deceivers, especially those of the circumcision party…teaching for shameful gain what they ought not to teach." Again, narcissistic prideful leaders are always motivated by power and profit. They can only produce the fruit that is in the root system of their hearts.

The Mosaic Law Is Fulfilled In Christ

It is through Paul's epistles, especially Galatians and Romans that we come to understand the Mosaic Law has not been set aside. It has been consumed with the bright light of the knowledge of the glory of

God in the face of Jesus Christ. We now understand the words of Christ when he said:

- "Do not think that I have come to abolish the Law or the Prophets; I have not come to abolish them but to fulfill them." Matthew 5:17
- "Until heaven and earth pass away, not an iota, not a dot, will pass from the Law until all is accomplished." Matthew 5:18
- "Everything written about me in the Law of Moses and the Prophets and the Psalms must be fulfilled." Luke 24:44

The words of Christ are why Paul could so confidently say in Galatians 5:14 that: "the whole law is fulfilled in one word: You shall love your neighbor as yourself." If you love your neighbor, you are not going to steal from them or commit adultery with their spouse. It is clear from the words of Jesus and Paul that we are no longer subject to the ritualism of the Mosaic Law. It is clearly addressed in Galatians, Romans and the book of Hebrews. In the New Covenant the standard bearer is not the Law and the Prophets, but the law of the Spirit of life found in Christ the surer word of prophecy fulfilling all that is written by the very Word made flesh.

The One New Man: Unity in Christ for Jews and Gentiles

Jews and Gentiles have been brought under the law of Christ creating what Paul called the one new man, the body of Christ in the earth. Ephesians 2:13 - 16 tells us that we have: "been brought near by the blood of Christ. For he himself is our peace, who has made us both one" that is Jew and Gentile.

It says that Christ "has broken down in his flesh the dividing wall of hostility by abolishing the law of commandments expressed in ordinances, that he might create in himself one new man in place of the two, so making peace, and might reconcile us both to God in one body through the cross."

Paul in Ephesians 3:4 - 6 talks of his: "insight into the mystery of Christ, which was not made known to the sons of men in other generations as it has now been revealed to his holy apostles and prophets by the Spirit. This mystery is that the Gentiles are fellow heirs, members of the same body, and partakers of the promise in Christ Jesus through the gospel."

The gospel of legalism is a false gospel. It is divisive to the body of Christ. It is harmful and it is used to create dominating, controlling systems for personal gain and power. It causes the foundation of Christ to be covered with a refuge of false regulations and manmade rules severing you from the root of the freedom found in the cross.

The book of Hebrews clearly articulates that we are under a new law, which is the law of the Spirit of life found in Christ. Our worship is in a new temple, the body of Christ and we are all now part of a new priesthood offering up the sacrifices of a New Covenant. It shows us that we have been brought into the king priest ministry of Christ who is sitting at the right hand of the Father ruling from heaven until he comes back to rule on earth.

The Crucial Role of the Holy Spirit in Redemption

The author of Hebrews says in 10:29 that when we turn back to the Mosaic law or any other system seeking to be justified, then we are: trampling "underfoot the Son of God." rejecting "the blood of the covenant by which" we have been sanctified and we are outraging "the Spirit of grace."

It's what Jesus called blaspheming the Holy Spirit in Luke 12:10. It is the Holy Spirit who points us to the blood of the cross as the only means of our redemption, our only mediator and if we reject the blood of the covenant, it has eternal consequences. Our freedom from sin and death is only found in the tree of the cross. The Holy Spirit is always pointing us to Christ who has come in the flesh to redeem, restore and reconcile us back to God the Father.

If we turn to the Mosaic law to be justified, or any other manmade system then we are building back the walls of separation. Paul was addressing narcissistic wolves who had set themselves up as the new mediators between God and man. It was turning the Galatians from the crucified and risen Christ to a rule-based religion centered on submitting to them. Paul called it a false gospel of legalism.

Confronting Gnosticism: Paul's Battle in Colossians

It's in the book of Colossians that Paul addressed another form of legalism based on Jewish Mysticism. Colossians is the companion epistle to Ephesians even as Romans is to Galatians. It was written in the same period and sent by the same messenger Tychius. The central theme of Colossians is Paul unveiling the mystery of Christ, while that of Ephesians is Paul unveiling the mystery of the church.

The legalism Paul is challenging in the book of Colossians is much more elusive, mystical, equally exclusive and harmful. In Colossians Paul is dealing with a specific type of Jewish Mysticism. Paul seemed to be addressing something similar in Titus 1:14 when he wrote about those who devote themselves to "Jewish myths and the commands of people who turn away from the truth." It's the same thing he warned Timothy about, who was overseeing the church in Ephesus.

It was a form of spiritualism that was very mystical, espousing enlightened ideas of hidden *gnōsis* and wisdom. The group that Paul was addressing had set themselves up as enlightened mediators to the spiritual world. The mystical spiritualism that Paul was confronting were those who went into detail about the spirit world, giving great attention to angels and mystical visions.

It seemed to promote extreme dedication to the Jewish calendar making it into a mystical time clock that you could use to discern the times. It used the Jewish calendar much in the same way astrologists use the calendar to determine your destiny. Everything was a hidden mystery that only the initiated understood and everyone else was living in darkness without this hidden *gnōsis*, but if you would submit to them, you too could become an elite spiritual warrior.

The Perils of Strict Spiritual Ritualism

Paul in Colossians was confronting a false spirituality that put a strong emphasis on a strict adherence to religious ritualism. It was a rigorous form of abstinence. It is based on the belief that by rejecting the desires of the flesh and trying to control them through religious ritualism you can bring yourself into a higher spiritual state.

Paul seems to be addressing a very similar mindset in 1 Timothy 4:1 - 3 when he says: "the Spirit expressly says that in later times some will depart from the faith by devoting themselves to deceitful spirits and teachings of demons, through the insincerity of liars whose consciences are seared, who forbid marriage and require abstinence from foods that God created to be received with thanksgiving by those who believe and know the truth." It's the only place Paul uses the actual term 'teaching of demons' or some translations say 'doctrine of demons'.

Let's look at this text in Colossians and see what Paul was saying to the church in Colossae and how we can apply that to us today. In Colossians 2:8 Paul starts describing this false spiritualism based around mystical legalism warning them to let: "no one take you captive by philosophy and empty deceit, according to human tradition, according to the *elemental spirits* of the world, and not according to Christ. (emphasis mine)."

Paul talks about this philosophy in 1 Timothy 6:20 - 21 telling Timothy to: "avoid the irreverent babble and contradictions of what is falsely called knowledge." Yes, knowledge in this text that is the Greek word *gnōsis*. Paul goes on to say "for by professing it some have swerved from the faith." The word deceive is the Greek word *planao* and means to wander. Deception causes you to swerve and wander away from sound doctrine into the ditch of extremism.

Regarding empty deceit Paul said it this way in Ephesians 5:6 to: "let no one deceive you with empty words." The empty or useless words that will not profit your spiritual growth in Christ is what Paul called human traditions based on 'elemental spirits' of the world.

Deciphering the Meaning of '*Stoicheion*'

Let's see if we can figure out what Paul wants us to understand about the '**elemental spirits**' of the world. You will see that some translations call it 'elemental principles'. In the Greek there is just one word, *stoicheion* which is sometimes translated 'elemental spirits' in Colossians. In Galatians it's translated as 'elemental principles'. In the book of Hebrews, it's translated as 'first principles'.

The Greek word *stoicheion* is used in Hebrews 5:12 when the author says: "by this time you ought to be teachers, you need someone to teach you again the basic principles of the oracles of God. You need milk, not solid food."

The 'basic principles' or some translations call them 'first principles' are the A,B,C's of our faith. We know that because he goes right into describing what he is talking about. Hebrews 6:1 - 2 says: "not laying again a foundation of repentance from dead works and of faith toward God, and doctrine of baptisms, the laying on of hands, the resurrection of the dead and eternal judgment." It's what I teach in the first section of the Foundation Publications School of Discipleship. You can find that at www.FoundationPub.org, lessons 1 thru 22.

Peter also used this word in his second epistle when describing the second coming of Christ in fiery judgment. 2 Peter 3:9 - 10 Peter says: "The Lord is not slow to fulfill his promise as some count slowness, but is patient toward you, not wishing that any should perish, but that all should reach repentance. But the day of the Lord will come like a thief and then the heavens will pass away with a roar and the **heavenly bodies** will be burned up and dissolved and the earth and the works that are done on it will be exposed (Emphasis mine)."

In other translations 'heavenly bodies' is translated 'elements' the same Greek word *stoicheion*. Peter just spoke of God using water to judge and to cleanse the earth of unrighteousness during the days of Noah. The 'elements' seem to refer to God's beginning. The A,B,C's of God creating the heavens and the earth described in the first two books of Genesis.

The Lexical Aids To The New Testament says the usage of the word in this context is the elements or first principles of matter. It's atoms which are the A, B, C's of matter. Atoms are the building block holding all things together in this present creation.

At Christ's second coming everything is going to change in the same way it did in the days of Noah except this time the fire of God will be the agent of judgment and transformation. It seems that God's fire is going to change things on a molecular level which will transform us from mortal to immortal through the resurrection power of Christ.

Paul seems to refer to something similar happening at the second coming of Christ in Romans 8:21 - 23: "the creation itself will be set free from its bondage to corruption and obtain the freedom of the glory of the children of God. For we know that the whole creation has been groaning together in the pains of childbirth until now. And not only the creation, but we ourselves, who have the first fruits of the Spirit, groan inwardly as we wait eagerly for adoption as sons, the redemption of our bodies."

At Christ second coming the fire of God is going to burn up or transform the 'elements' of creation. We along with creation at that time will be resurrected and changed. Hebrews chapter 12 talks of this same transformation ending the chapter saying, "our God is a consuming fire."

It's why Paul called the resurrection a mystery. In 1 Corinthians 15:50 - 53 Paul says, "I tell you this brother's flesh and blood cannot inherit the kingdom of God, nor does the perishable inherit the imperishable. Behold! I tell you a mystery. We shall not all sleep, but we shall all be changed, in a moment, in the twinkling of an eye, at the last trumpet." It's the final stage of our redemption and the fullness of our salvation.

The word *stoicheion* is used 2 other times in the New Testament and they are found in the book of Galatians and Colossians. In Galatians chapter 3 Paul is dealing with the Mosaic Law that was given to him on Mt. Sinai. It was the covenant that was made with Israel to be a kingdom of priests and a holy nation.

God spoke to Moses on Mt Sinai. Exodus 19:16 - 19 says that when God came down to meet with Moses: "there were thunders, lightnings, a thick cloud on the mountain and a very loud trumpet blast, so that all the people in the camp trembled...Now Mt. Sinai was wrapped in smoke because the Lord had descended on it in fire. The smoke of it went up like the smoke of a furnace, and the whole mountain trembled greatly. And the sound of the trumpet grew louder and louder."

In Galatians 3:19 Paul says that the law was "ordained through angels." Stephen in Acts 7:53 as he is preaching his last message to his Jewish audience before he was stoned says: "you who received the law as ordained by angels."

The word **ordained** in both texts is the same Greek word. The Greek Lexical Aid to the New Testament comments on this word saying the Mosaic law was given in the midst of thick dark clouds, blazing fire and winds. It's not saying the Mosaic Law was given by angels but **witnessed** by angels as described in Hebrews chapter 12 which basically repeats Exodus chapter 19. The angelic host who witnessed the giving of the Mosaic Law was the dark clouds, blazing fire and winds. It was the author of Hebrews who in 1:7 compares angels to 'winds and a flame of fire.'

The author of Hebrews starts his epistle going out of his way to make the point that Christ is the eternal God who created all things and is therefore superior to angels which he clearly lays out in 1:4 - 14. In chapter 1 and chapter 2 the author speaks of the supremacy of Christ to both the Mosaic law and to angels.

Hebrews 2:1-3 starts out saying: "we must pay much closer attention to what we have heard, lest we drift away from it." The author is referring to what he just talked about in chapter 1 concerning the supremacy of Christ and him being superior to Moses and the Mosaic Law which was given in the midst of angelic activity on Mt. Sinai.

F.F. Bruce says, "the law was given to bring sin to light". The Mosaic law defines sin. It clearly says don't steal, don't lie, don't commit adultery etc. The Mosaic law reveals the wickedness in man's heart. The law was not meant to free us from sin, but to show us how sinful we are.

Paul called the Mosaic law, "the ministry of death, carved in letters on stone" in 2 Corinthians 3:7. It caused the children of Israel to cower in fear when it was given because the intent was to show us our sin and lead us to repentance. However, it was inadequate to truly change the heart because that could only be done by the life-giving power of the Spirit.

The author of Hebrews is making a similar argument that Paul is making in II Corinthians and it's also the argument he is making in the book of Galatians and Romans. It's that the crucified and risen Christ is the new and living way superior to the Mosaic law which was temporary until the Messianic age of Christ. As believers in the Messiah, we are not to live lives under the veil of the law because it is not capable of changing our hearts.

Hebrews chapter 2 is teaching us the same thing that Paul was teaching us in Philippians chapter 2 concerning God becoming man through Christ the Messiah. Verses 7 thru 8 says: Jesus "emptied himself, by taking the form of a servant, being born in the likeness of men. And being found in human form, he humbled himself by becoming obedient to the point of death, even death on a cross."

Hebrews chapter 2 starts out talking about Christ's ministry of signs, wonders and various miracles he performed during his 3 ½ years of ministry through the power of the Holy Spirit. He then says in verse 9 thru 10 that "for a little while he was made lower than the angels, namely Jesus, crowned with glory and honor because of the suffering of death, so that by the grace of God he might taste death for everyone."

The Role of Man and Angels in This Age

In these scriptures we can see that man is lower than angels in this age because we are mortal which means we are subject to death. Jesus said in the coming resurrection we will not be subject to death and will be like angels. Matthew 22:30 Jesus said that in the coming resurrection of the dead we will "neither marry nor are given in marriage but are like angels in heaven."

Paul in I Corinthians 6:3 says that in the coming age we will judge angels, but in this age until Christ returns man is lower than the angels. In this present age man is but mortal and subject to death. However, in the age of resurrection we will rule with Christ and be over angels. However, that will not be until: "the Lord Jesus is revealed from heaven with his mighty angels in flaming fire, inflicting vengeance on those who do not know God" according to 2 Thessalonians 1:7 - 8.

Jesus the eternal Son stepped into time to bring the kingdom of heaven to earth to help aid and deliver humanity. He came to deliver us from a fallen angel, Lucifer, Satan, the serpent of old the devil. The author of Hebrews says Jesus became flesh and blood sharing our humanity feeling our frailty. In Hebrews 2:14 - 15 it tells us that Jesus became a man so: "that through death he might destroy the one who has the power of death, that is, the devil and deliver all those who through fear of death were subject to lifelong slavery."

At the moment when God stepped into time becoming a man, he was made lower than the angels so that he could justify, redeem, restore and reconcile man back to God. However, in Christ's resurrection and ascension he is now our Mediator. The resurrected Jesus is sitting on the throne with angels subject to him as the first man to be raised from the dead, the last Adam (I Corinthains 15:45).

Paul shows us in Ephesians 1:20 - 23 that Jesus has been raised from the dead and seated at the right hand of power in the heavenly places as scripture says, "far above all rule and authority and power and dominion, and above every name that is named, not only in this age, but also in the one to come."

The Mosaic law is no longer our mediator and angels are not supposed to be mediators between us and God either. Jesus is the only mediator between man and God. It's not a holy man or holy woman. It's not the Mosaic Law and it's not angels. As 1 Timothy 2:5 so clearly says: "there is one God, and there is one mediator between God and men, the man Christ Jesus."

The Speculation Surrounding Principalities and Powers

If you study the Bible, you will come to find out that it really does not give us a lot of details about angel's along with their hierarchical structure nor Satan. Angels are mentioned around 273 times in the Bible, but we are only given the names of 3 angels which are Gabriel, Michael and Lucifer. Paul tells us in Ephesians 6:12 that: "we do not wrestle against flesh and blood, but against the rulers, against the authorities, against the cosmic powers over this present darkness, against the spiritual forces of evil in the heavenly places." We don't have a lot of specific details about this unseen spiritual world.

The Bible does not give us a lot of details about this subject. However, you do have those who go into detail and give a tremendous amount of time along with speculation to the unseen spiritual world. You have those who tout varying methods of spiritual warfare from spiritual mapping, apostolic decrees, to commanding angels and the list goes on.

Yes, I believe in angels and that they are presently active in the affairs of man, but I can't find a scripture in the New Testament that says angels are our mediators or teach us how to interpret scripture? The Holy Spirit is our teacher, but angels are never said to be our teachers or mediators. Angels come to understand the gospel through the *ekklēsia*. Paul said in Ephesians 3:10: "that through the church the manifold wisdom of God might now be made known to the rulers and authorities in the heavenly places."

Peter says something similar in I Peter1:12 when talking about when the Hebrew prophets being moved by the Spirit prophesied of the coming Messiah. "It was revealed to them that they were serving not themselves but you, in the things that have now been announced to you through those who preached the good news to you by the Holy Spirit sent from heaven, things into which angels long to look." Angels do not teach us, but they learn from us according to these two texts.

You have a multitude of books along with sermons concerning the mystery that surrounds angels and Satan. Two of the favorite pet principalities that are talked about among the spiritual warrior gurus are the Leviathan spirit and the Jezebel spirit. I'm not even going to get into the details of what I consider very speculative teachings.

Leviathan is mentioned twice in the Bible in two very obscure passages however, it never mentions a Leviathan spirit. Yes, I believe in spiritual warfare, but I don't believe in making things up and saying things the Bible doesn't say. Yes, Jezebel was a wicked figure in the Bible, but show me where it talks about a Jezebel spirit?

Witchcraft, sexual immorality and sensuality are called by Paul works of the flesh in Galatians 5:19-20. Now do demons get involved in the works of the flesh? I think it's safe to say that they can and do, but Paul never talked about a Jezebel spirit. A false doctrine happens when we start making the Bible fit our speculation and pet ideas. In the Foundations Publication School of Discipleship, we have two lessons that cover this subject. If you want more information to study on this subject Lesson 41 and 42 called Spiritual Warfare will help you out on this topic.

Peter ends his second epistle talking about those who twist the scriptures to fit their ideas. Some of these so-called prophets take dream's that they've had and make doctrines from their dreams. Darren, don't you believe we have prophets today. Yes, I do, and I believe we have false ones too. False ones speculate on things that are not clearly revealed in scripture and teach vain imaginations produced through the vanity of their own hearts. Trust me, I would rather not address this topic, but it's a widespread cancer that is shipwrecking many people's faith.

Paul told us not to speculate in I Timothy 1:4. Speculation causes you to create a teaching about things the Bible does not give real clear understanding on. It will cause us to swerve and wander into vain discussions. 1 Timothy 1:7 talks of those who make confident assertions about things the Bible does not make clear. It's one thing to look at an obscure passage of scripture and ask questions. It is a whole different issue when people start giving a 'thus saith the Lord' on an obscure text. It's the same thing that happens when you start taking multiple texts out of context then bring them together making confident assertions.

I've found those who focus on false ideas of spiritual warfare tend to live in a constant state of unrest, confusion and lack peace. Yes, we are in a spiritual battle as we walk through this evil age, but nowhere in scripture are we told that we possess the authority to pull down principalities and powers of darkness. It's simply not in the Bible as authority given to believers.

Jesus has given us authority to cast demons out of individuals, but Satan along with his hierarchical structure will not be dismantled and destroyed until the second coming of Christ. He will fully displace the unseen spiritual powers that rule this present evil age and only at his return. Our mission is to pray and proclaim the mystery of Christ setting captives free. I've seen sincere believers spend a lot of wasted time in the fantasy world of speculation.

The Power of Prayer and Proclaiming the Gospel: Misconceptions on Spiritual Warfare

The linchpin of this false idea concerning pulling down principalities is built around II Corinthians 10:4 - 5. Go read the entire chapter for context. You will see the scripture is not Paul telling us to bind dark spiritual forces and then to give apostolic decrees to displace the Leviathan or Jezebel spirits controlling churches, cities or regions.

Paul is talking about confronting false ideas that have created a stronghold in people's minds opposing the freedom we have through the cross and "bringing every thought captive to the obedience of Christ." It's called prayer and proclaiming the gospel under the power of the Holy Spirit. It's what we are to be focused upon which is the Great Commission Christ has given the church and demonstrated through the book of Acts.

Angels are not to be our primary focus. I refer to the subject of angels and the spiritual world as the back story. Yes, angels and spiritual forces of evil in heavenly places are both very real and involved in the affairs of man, but they are not the main focus of the redemptive story.

The apostolic writers make a point in wanting us to know what we need to know about angelic activity. However, neither angels which are the agents of God nor the agents of Satan are given a main role. It's when we bring them to the front and center that we run into the potential to be led astray. Shining the light on angels and making them the main focus is a pathway to the spirit of error. That's when we get into problems swerving over into the ditch of extremism and deception.

'Stoicheion' in Galatians and Colossians

Let's go back and look at the last three times the Greek word *stoicheion* is used. It is translated as 'elemental things' in Galatians and 'elemental spirits' in Colossians. In Galatians Paul uses this word two times in Galatians chapter 4.

In chapter 3 Paul is comparing faith in Christ to the faith Abraham possessed before the giving of the Mosaic Law on Mt. Sinai. Verses 7 thru 9 say: "Know then that it is those of faith who are the sons of Abraham. And the Scripture, foreseeing that God would justify the Gentiles by faith, preached the gospel beforehand to Abraham, saying, 'In you shall all the nations be blessed.' So then, those who are of faith are blessed along with Abraham, the man of faith." He contrasts relying on the works of the law which results in sin, failure and a curse; to justification by faith and how we receive the blessing of the Spirit.

He ends chapter 3 saying: "Now before faith came, we were held captive under the law, imprisoned until the coming faith would be revealed. So then, the law was our guardian until Christ came, in order that we might be justified by faith. But now that faith has come, we are no longer under a guardian, for in Christ Jesus you are all sons of God, through faith. For as many of you as were baptized into Christ have put on Christ. There is neither Jew nor Greek, there is neither slave nor free, there is no male and female, for you are all one in Christ Jesus. And if you are Christ's, then you are Abraham's offspring, heirs according to promise."

The Law as a Tutor: Leading up to Christ

Chapter 4 opens by talking about the Mosaic law being like a tutor designed to protect the promise. The word tutor is the Greek word *paidagogos* from which the English word pedagogue comes from. In the ancient world, the pedagogue or tutor was one who had charge of the underage heir. The heir was in line to get the entire inheritance, but he had to be trained before it was given.

It was the tutors responsibility to keep the heir out of trouble and protect him until he reached manhood so he could receive his inheritance. Until he matured, he was no different than a household slave even though he was to be heir to the inheritance.

The Mosaic law was restrictive, telling us what we could not do, and Paul compared it to a tutor, some translations say manager or gatekeeper. Analogies are always limited, but Paul defined his analogy of the Mosaic law as being a tutor saying in Galatians 4:1 that the law made us like slaves and could not give us freedom.

Paul then says in verse 3: "In the same way we also, when we were children, were enslaved to the '*elementary principles*' of the world" (emphasis mine). It's the same Greek word *stoicheion*. Paul then uses *stoicheion* again in this same chapter. Paul just tells them that Christ the Messiah had come in the fullness of time. He says in Christ we are no longer under the tutor of the law and subject to slavery.

Galatians 4:6 - 10 says: "And because you are sons, God has sent the Spirit of his Son into our hearts, crying, 'Abba! Father!' So you are no longer a slave, but a son, and if a son, then an heir through God. Formerly, when you did not know God, you were enslaved to those that by nature are not gods. But now that you have come to know God, or rather to be known by God, how can you turn back again to the weak and worthless *elementary principles* of the world, whose slaves you want to be once more? You observe days and months and seasons and years! (emphasis mine)"

Here is what Paul is saying and it will help us understand his usage of this word *stoicheion* in Colossians. In Galatians Paul is telling them in 4:8 that "formerly when you did not know God, you were enslaved to those who by nature are not gods." He was reminding the Galatians like he did to the Corinthians that the gods they used to be enslaved to were not gods at all, but demons.

Paul in warning the Corinthians to not turn back to idolatry says in 1 Corinthians 10:14-21 to: "flee from idolatry....Consider the people of Israel: are not those who eat the sacrifices participants in the altar? What do I imply then? That food offered to idols is anything, or that an idol is anything? No, I imply that what pagans sacrifice they offer to demons and not to God. I do not want you to be participants with demons. You cannot drink the cup of the Lord and the cup of demons."

Paul in Galatians 4:8 is comparing them turning away from the crucified Christ and now turning to the Mosaic law to be justified is just like turning back to idolatry. Observing days, months, seasons and years; Paul is referring to the Jewish calendar and the Jewish feasts upon which the law was based. It's falling from grace! Submitting to the false gospel of legalism is a departure from the faith laid down by the apostles and Paul compared it to their former slavery to demons.

Paul was telling the Gentiles in Galatia that the Jews were subject to slavery under the Mosaic law, but the Gentile pagans were subject to slavery to demons attached to the 'elemental spirits' (*stoicheion*) of the world. The only solution for both Jew and Gentile is the tree of the cross. If you go study the books of Hebrews and Romans you will see the same message which is that as believers in Christ, we are no longer under the ritualism of the Mosaic law based on the Jewish feasts centered around days, months, seasons and years.

We have covered all the other times this Greek word *stoicheion* has been used. Let's now look at Paul's usage of it in addressing the heresy in Colossae. I'm only going to look at portions of Colossians chapter 2 in discussing this subject. I'm going to start with verse 20 and 21 where Paul said: "If with Christ you died to the '***elemental spirits***' of the world, why, as if you were still alive in the world, do you submit to regulations—"Do not handle, Do not taste, Do not touch" (referring to things that all perish as they are used)—according to human precepts and teachings?"

The Mystical Spiritualism Addressed in Colosse

As I said earlier, the legalism Paul confronted in the book of Colossians is much more elusive, mystical, equally exclusive and harmful. In Colossians Paul is dealing with a specific type of Jewish Gnosticism. As I also said earlier Paul seemed to be addressing something similar in Titus 1:14 when he wrote about those who devote themselves to "Jewish myths and the commands of people who turn away from the truth."

In Paul's first letter to Timothy 1:3 - 4 he tells him to: "remain at Ephesus so that you may charge certain persons not to teach any different doctrine, nor to devote themselves to myths and endless genealogies, which promote speculations." Paul never addressed this in his letter to the Ephesians church, but Colossians was a sister letter so it would have been read to the larger community in that area.

Paul was addressing a form of spiritualism that was very mystical, espousing enlightened ideas of hidden *gnōsis* and wisdom. Here are some of the traits of this false spirituality:

- It went into detail about the spirit world and gave an inordinate amount of attention to angels along with mystical visions.
- Angels were given a mediatorial role in revealing the hidden *gnōsis* and mysteries of God.
- It taught the scriptures had hidden mysteries that only the initiated understood and everyone else was living in darkness without this

hidden *gnōsis*.

* It promoted extreme dedication to the Jewish calendar making it into a mystical time clock that you could use to discern the times. Using it in the same way astrologists use the calendar to determine your destiny.

Paul called this type of false spirituality being subject to the *stoicheion*. Instead of being crucified with Christ and being dead to this world. It's being focused upon and influenced by the 'elemental spirits of the world' which are demons. It's making this mystical world of the spiritual front and center instead of part of the background. It's making a fascination with angels, visions and ritualistic spiritual experiences the center of our faith. It's practicing ritualistic fasting to enter secret portals of heaven. It's focusing on dates, times and using the Jewish calendar as a sort of Ouija board to discern the times.

I'm not against fasting it's a spiritual discipline taught in the Bible which I practice. What Paul is addressing is a false spirituality that sees fasting as a ritualistic tool to get access to the spiritual world. Fasting is giving up primarily food for a season of time so that you can focus on prayer, study of the word of God and it's about denying ourselves. We are not trying to get to God by fasting, but we are simply humbling ourselves before God and reminding ourselves of all that he has done for us through Christ. The asceticism that Paul is addressing is using fasting to access the spiritual world through ritualistic practices. It's adding to the cross.

Paul was warning the Colossians not to give an inordinate amount of time, fascination and attention to angels. Angels had a place in the giving of the Mosaic law. It was a multitude of angels that produced fire, smoke and a tempest around Mt. Sinai when God came down to speak to Moses giving him the law. Angels were active in the Old Testament and showed themselves when Jesus came into the world. We know angels ministered to Jesus. Angels are seen assisting in the mission of the *ekklēsiu* in the book of Acts. Angels are part of the redemptive story from Genesis to Revelation, but they are not the central focus.

What Paul is addressing in Colossians chapter 2 is a false form of spirituality that sees angels as performing a mediatorial role between man and God. It's the teaching that angels are spirit guides. It's New Age Gnosticism and not the Bible although it may use the Bible.

Remember Satan disguises himself as an angel of light, but he always twists scriptures. It is making angels and the spiritual world the main thing which leads to deception. It's like pointing your car headlights at an animal and then following it into a ditch. It's the Gnostic heresy that the apostolic writers were confronting.

Angels in the Jewish Book of Enoch

The Jewish Book of Enoch teaches a false idea that everything has its angel: [96]the stars have their angels; each of the four seasons has its angel; [97]each of the 12 months of the year has its angel and each of the 364-day calendar of the year has its angel. In addition, it was the idea that angels give secret *gnōsis* along with wisdom providing a role in helping us to understand and approach God.

Paul said in combination to this fascination with angels are those who go into detail about visions. He said these visions give them puffed up imaginations. I am one who believes in the manifestations of the Spirit and prophecy. I believe the Holy Spirit leads us, speaks to us and teaches us, but it all points towards Christ. In Colossians Paul was dealing with a false spiritualism and mysticism that was leading people away from Christ. It was fanaticism that focused on the mystical, spiritual world and it produced this false reality detached from the soundness of truth. It was spiritually that saw the word of the cross as insufficient.

The Galatians were seduced to turn to the Mosaic law adding to the cross. The Colossians were seduced to turn to spiritual mysticism adding to the cross. It added angelic visitations and spiritual visions. Today you hear those who are always talking about out of body experiences, spirit travel and the hidden *gnōsis* to become an elite spiritual warrior of the last days.

It's those who are always talking about some mysterious dream or vision they had instead of the word of God and sound doctrine. You have some who make regular trips to heaven and angels stand at their beds almost nightly while Jesus appears to them regularly. It all sounds so spiritual and deep. It's through these mystical experiences that they

---

[96] George W.E. Nickelsburg, 1 Enoch 1: A Commentary on the book of 1 Enoch, p. 297

[97] James C. VanderKam, Calendars in the Dead Sea Scrolls, p. 57.

set themselves up as spiritual guides leading you into this spiritual realm. I've heard some say that they can even teach you how to go to heaven.

I believe prophets are one of the five gifts Christ gave to his church and are for today. I was in the Prophetic Movement for the first 25 years of my walk with God. I speak as an insider and with a heavy heart because I know many who just want to sincerely know God in a deep intimate way. However, as an insider I am giving a warning because many have gone into the same ditch of mysticism that Paul was addressing here in Colossians chapter 2.

I lived in that ditch for many years, so I understand how it's very easy to get into it. It's easy to get lost in the fantasy land of mysticism and the first step to escape is realizing it's a fantasy land. It leads you away from the simplicity of the cross.

What Paul is addressing in Colossians is a false spirituality that makes these mystical experiences the main thing where everything is spiritualized. Mystic spiritualism is a demonic parasite that uses scripture and sounds very spiritual, but always out of context. It twists the truth and mixes in enough error so that the truth is perverted. It's no longer preaching Christ crucified centered upon the gospel. It takes your eyes off the head of the church causing you to focus on spiritual sounding fantasies which lead to extremism.

The Dangers of Distorting Truth and Distracting from the Gospel

Paul was warning the Colossians and us today not to get caught up in this fantasy world of mystical illusion. Paul said in Colossians 2:19 that when you start making these experiences the main thing that you become severed from Christ the head. Instead of growing in the *epignōsis* of Christ and maturing in your faith it is leading you away from him. It's why we are exhorted to test the spirits because deceptive spirits take us away from a life devoted to soundness of truth found in Christ (I John 4:1).

I know a segment of the church who see themselves as this elite group of last day warriors who are pulling down principalities through their elite spiritual insight and authority. It's those who say they can make apostolic decrees and angels will follow their orders. Yes, they say they possess this power that even Christ did not use, but they seem arrogant enough to think they can command angels.

Yes, that's right there are zero scriptures of Christ or his apostles commanding angels. It's a teaching based on speculation not clear apostolic teaching found in the Bible. All these so-called apostles and prophets teach something none of the actual apostles taught. That should say everything!

You will hear them tell stories of angels who visit them and give them hidden mysteries and insight into the spiritual battle plans of the last days. It's these elite spiritual warriors who have been given governmental authority to bring healing to the nations. I tell you what it is: a whole load of puffed up, deceptive and delusional pride. It's the fantasy land of mysticism. You might as well be watching a Marvel Movie.

In Colossians Paul was addressing this false Gnostic idea of secret mysteries and hidden wisdom that only the elite warriors of light could lead you into. Today we are told all we must do is listen to these elite spiritual warriors because they possess the hidden insight into the true mysteries of Christ. It's only through their inside story that you can truly know God as you should. Paul cautioned us to let no one control you, manipulate you and deceive you with messages from angels or visions from their puffed-up minds.

Please listen to me carefully. If you hear this nonsense, do not give it a place in your lives because it is poisonous fruit. An overemphasis of the spiritual realm making it the main thing instead of the crucified and risen Christ is one of the main pathways to deception.

The Deceptive Origins of Islam and Mormonism: Angelic Revelations and False Spiritual Ideas

Do you know that the two greatest false spiritual ideas in the earth today were given through the message of an angel! Islam and Mormonism both originated through an angelic revelation creating puffed up imaginations of deception. You need to think about that truth before listening to some so-called apostle or prophet that starts teaching you about the revelation they got from an angel.

We are told to test every spirit. We are told to judge prophecy and to discern all things because there are people who will use their fanciful speculations to control, dominate and use you. You will know them by their fruit because the root of deception is always pride mixed with greed and the lust to satisfy some ungodly desire. It may take some time, but the truth always has a way of making it out into the light.

The Legalism of Ritualistic Gnostic Practices

Paul was referencing the ritualistic practices of abstaining from certain foods and following regimented forms of ritualistic regulations to attain spiritual enlightenment. The Essenes, a strict form of Jewish Mysticism, could touch neither oil, nor meat, nor wine. Sabbath-keeping was strictly followed. The historian Josephus said they avoided the pleasures of the body; they prohibited marriage and took vows of poverty. It seems Paul was referring to this when writing to Timothy when talking about the teaching of demons. It's here in Colossians 2:23 when he said this type of spirituality has an: "appearance of wisdom in promoting self-made religion and asceticism and severity to the body, but they are of no value in stopping the indulgence of the flesh."

It's trying to live holy through secret *gnōsis* and it's impossible. It leads to frustration and living in what I call the cycle of dead works. (In Lesson 7: The Cycle of Dead Works of the Foundations Publication School Of Discipleship I fully cover the topic of repentance from dead works.) Now prayer and fasting should be part of our lifestyle of discipleship. Denying a flesh ruled life happens when you are filled with the Spirit. Asceticism is based on working your way to enter the spiritual world through ritualism and is adding to what Christ has already accomplished for us through the cross.

If you accept these false teachings, they begin to put a veil over your understanding and perverts the image of Christ. It's what Paul told the Galatians that they had been bewitched. The Galatians had been seduced and persuaded by false teachers telling them that they needed to add to what Christ had already done through the tree of the cross. Paul said they were nullifying the grace of God in Galatians 2:21. In Galatians 5:4 he tells them that as a result they had "been severed from Christ, you who are seeking to be justified by law; you have fallen from grace."

It's a very similar message that Paul gave to the Colossians. What you think is making you a spiritual superstar results in bondage. If you allow this false spirituality to take root in your life it will cause you to no longer hold fast to Christ your mediator, head and high priest. The world of mysticism leads you to put your trust in ritualism, angels, visions and hidden *gnōsis* while rejecting the simplicity of Christ. Sound doctrine produces sound living, but false doctrines produce deception, confusion, twisted thinking and division.

The Destructive Impact of Legalistic Control

The fruit of legalism whether that is Pharisaical legalism or mystical legalism is described by Paul in Galatians chapter 5 when he talks of the works of the flesh. I break down the works of the flesh into 3 categories. Hedonism, Emotionalism and Legalism. The fruit of legalism is disputes, dissensions and heresies. (In Lesson 10 Part 2: A Lifestyle Of Repentance of the Foundations Publication School Of Discipleship I fully cover the topic of the works of the flesh.)

Have you ever noticed that those who think they are super spiritual are always at war with someone? It's either fighting the devil or one of his agents on the earth, but they are always in a state of war. It's because the legalistic works of the flesh couched in religious terminology produces this bad fruit.Disputes can be translated as selfish ambition. It's the type of thinking that always asks what's in it for me? Only doing things with the motive of gaining and getting the advantage from what you do. The Pharisees were skilled legalists and used their man-made moral codes to gain advantage, power and get profit. It's using others to get what you want or using religion to get an advantage over others.

Selfish ambition can be understood as a motivation to elevate oneself or to put one's own interests before another's. Selfish ambition can be putting down others so that you can be lifted up. Have you ever been around that person who is always putting someone else down to try to gain advantage? How about church groups always putting down other groups as not spiritual so that you will join their special highly spiritual group. It is a self above others approach, which is the opposite of humility.

The next word is dissensions. Dissensions literally means division or sedition. It has to do with those who are actively trying to cause separation between individuals or groups of people. It's more than just having a common disagreement or differing viewpoint, but it's when an individual or a group of people are pursuing a goal to cause division. It's an arrogant, unyielding attitude that will divide over trivial issues because one does not get their own way.

Pride is at the root of division in the same way Satan, through pride went his own way and took a 1/3 of the angels with him. A lot of people look at this as that one person who is always creating chaos in the church, and you do have those. It can also be seen when a pack of wolves closes ranks to try to protect the pack and their false system. We see pictures of the lone wolf, but wolves are normally pack animals.

The Truth Behind 'Don't Touch God's Anointed'

Have you ever heard the term 'don't touch God's anointed'? You will hear certain groups use this term within systems that promote the teaching of spiritual covering, culture of honor, covenant keeping and the armor bearers which are those who serve the anointed leader. You have variations of this perverted teaching on spiritual authority and I'm going to fully address this in later lessons.

The key text that is used is in Psalm 105:15: "Touch not my anointed ones, do my prophets no harm!" However, in the context of that Psalm it is not referring to any one person, but to the whole nation of Israel whom we're all anointed as a kingdom of priests. Psalm 105 was David's spiritual song that he sang when bringing the ark of the Lord to Jerusalem for the first time as recorded in, I Chronicles chapter 16. I encourage you to go read both of those chapters for yourself.

One of the other texts is taken from 1 Samuel 24:6 when David said: "The Lord forbid that I should do this thing to my lord, the Lord's anointed, to put out my hand against him, seeing he is the Lord's anointed." In context David had been anointed king by the prophet Samuel, but Saul was still king and pursuing David to kill him. David was hiding in a cave with his men, and he had the opportunity to kill Saul, but he didn't.

David didn't kill Saul, but he did call him out on his injustice and perversity in persecuting him without cause (I Samuel 26:9 – 10). David confronted Saul just in the same way that Paul stood up to Peter in Antioch confronting him about the error of his ways.

If a spiritual leader uses these texts to insulate themselves from correction, legitimate criticism and feedback. It should be a blaring red flag waving in the wind. Prophets or any spiritual leader are not infallible but should be tested. Every leader has blind spots and when he or she thinks they are infallible that's when they wind up in a ditch.

Spiritual leaders should display humility. Humility is being able to listen to others. It's being humble enough to know that you are not always right. It's knowing that you are just a small part of the whole. Paul commended the Bereans because they "received the word with all eagerness, examining the Scriptures daily to see if these things were so" (Acts 17:10-15). What were they doing? Checking to make sure what Paul was saying was correct. Paul said test all things. John told us to test the spirits, and we have a responsibility to hold one another accountable. We all have the propensity to fall into error because we are all just mortal. It's why humility of the heart is so important.

It's the holy man myth to elevate someone to the place of an infallible oracle. If your authority, prophecy and doctrine are not able to be challenged then I would say you probably need to examine yourself. If you can't handle being challenged and examined, then according to I Timothy 3 and other scriptures you should not have a place of leadership. Pride is what causes dissension in the body of Christ not legitimate questioning and accountability.

Heresies: Divisive Opinions and Arrogant Attitudes

The last word in this list of the works of the flesh is heresies which means groups who divisively express their opinions creating factions. We think today of heresies in terms of wrong ideas and teachings. It is, but the word carries an emphasis on wrongfully dividing over opinions and speculations. Heresies can be thought of as hardened dissensions. There is all the difference in the world between believing that we are right and believing that everyone else is wrong. It is an arrogant attitude which believes the way we think is the only way to think and not giving room for any differing opinion.

It's not standing on clearly stated doctrinal positions, but it's taking obscure scriptural stances and making them non-negotiable. It's the attitude that says: it's my way or the highway and it creates a faction. Paul was dealing with this exact attitude when writing to the church in Galatia which had started listening to the heretical legalism that certain men started preaching contrary to the central message of the cross.

We have the same legalists today who want to turn believers away from focusing upon the cross of Christ to outward ordinances, legalism, mystical experiences or a combination of both. It's simply false deceptive ideas that create factions because selfish ambitious people want to take you captive and control you. Legalism is living life by man-made moral codes that creates selfish ambition, dissensions and divisions. It causes you to create heresies.

CHAPTER 7

THE GOSPEL OF LAWLESSNESS:
A CALL TO EMBRACE THE CROSS

"because lawlessness will be increased, the love of
Many will grow cold."

~ Matthew 24:12 ~

In this chapter what I want to show you is the other side of the tree of the knowledge of good and evil. It's what I call the 'gospel of lawlessness'. It's the flip side of the tree, but it's still fed from the same root system. The gospel of lawlessness is one of the two main enemies of the cross of Christ which the apostolic writers confronted, opposed and condemned.

If you look at Jesus' prophetic prediction on the Mt. of Olives concerning the end of the age, he makes a statement. The statement is found in Matthew 24:12 where he predicts that: "because lawlessness will be increased, the love of many will grow cold." He says it right in the middle of wars, rumors of wars, famines, earthquakes, persecution and false prophets. [98]Lawlessness here denotes a repudiation of God's standards, resulting in the erosion of love.

Let's examine this word lawlessness. The Greek word for lawlessness is *anomia* and it simply means against law. Paul uses this word when talking about a final figure who appears right before Christ second coming whom he calls: the 'man of lawlessness' in II Thessalonians 2:3. It's the same figure that John refers to as the Antichrist in I John 2:18. [99]The defining trait of this figure is opposition to God's order and [100]authority because lawlessness characterizes the ultimate rebellion against God.

Instead of speculating about who this figure is and from where he will arise on the earth. I want to clearly show you that as John said:

---

[98] D.A. Carson, Matthew, (EBC), p. 565.
[99] Gene L. Green, The Letter to the Thessalonians, p. 322.
[100] Gordon D. Fee, Pauline Christology, p. 93.

'so now many antichrists have come." The Bible may not talk about a Leviathan spirit or a Jezebel spirit, but it does talk about the 'spirit of the antichrist' in I John 4:3 that is operating in the world. [101]The author affirms both a future figure and a present manifestation of antichrist in false teachers.

It is the 'spirit of antichrist' that operates as an enemy to the cross of Christ because one of its characteristics is denying the true preaching of the cross. 1 John 4:2 says: "by this you know the Spirit of God: every spirit that confesses that Jesus Christ has come in the flesh is from God and every spirit that does not confess Jesus is not from God." The spirit of antichrist is first and foremost a denial of the word of the cross. It's a denial of the love of the Father shown and demonstrated to us through the gift of the Son of God.

The Contrast Between Loving the World and Loving God in John's First Epistle

John makes a very profound statement in I John 2:15 that will give us some insight into understanding more fully what John was expressing through the thought 'that Jesus Christ has come in the flesh'. He said:

> "Do not love the world or the things in the world. If anyone loves the world, the love of the Father is not in him." *He then defines what loving the world means* in verses 16-17: "For all that is in the world—the desires of the flesh and the desires of the eyes and pride of life—is not from the Father but is from the world. And the world is passing away along with its desires, but whoever does the will of God abides forever."

[102]The 'world' in this context does not refer to the created order but to the realm of human life organized in rebellion against God. John throughout his epistle makes the contrast between loving the world and loving God making it clear that you can't do both at the same time. [103]John's point is not that believers withdraw from society, but that they

---

[101] Howard Marshall, The Epistles of John, (NICNT), p. 148.
[102] Colin Kruse, The Letters of John, (PNTC), p. 93, 95.
[103] Karen Jobes, 1, 2, 3, John (ZENCT), p. 125.

reject the system of values opposed to God [94]because the transient character of the world system stands in sharp contrast to the permanence of obedience to God.

I do think one mistake we've made in the American church is that we have made the gospel into something that is very cheap. What I mean is that it's been diluted, perverted and changed into something that has no power to bring forth the fruit of repentance. The sacrifice of Christ has been presented as something that cost nothing for us to take possession of when Christ and the apostolic authors all said it cost us our lives. We've made it palatable, packaged and able to be sold to the masses. It's profitable to be in the gospel business or at least it's profitable to be in the American gospel business.

It seems that John was addressing this idea that you can say you are a follower of Christ while at the same time you are denying the reality of how Jesus lived in the flesh as our prototype and how we are called to follow in his footsteps. The call to follow Jesus entails self-denial and submission to his lordship. No Jesus did not preach the American dream nor was he a Genie in the bottle. He is not the Jesus at the drive thru window that says you can have it your way. Americans are great at merchandising, marketing and packaging. Sadly, we have merchandised the gospel and its produced a very shallow superficial Christianity. I'm very concerned that far too many believers' lives have been built upon the sand of superficiality, hype and outright lawlessness.

We are no longer under the Mosaic law, but we are not without law which means that we can live without restrictions and live anyway we want. [104]The believer is no longer under the Mosaic law but remains under the lordship of Christ. Jesus and all the apostolic writers affirm this clearly established position which is you cannot say you are a child of God while you live like a child of the devil. [105]Persistent unrighteousness reveals one's true spiritual allegiance. John in his first epistle is trying to help us understand something about the very heart of the Father and what truly walking in the love of God means.

The Believer's Journey In This Present Evil Age

Paul, the author of Hebrews, Peter and Jude all likened the

---

[104] Thomas Schreiner, New Testament Theology, p. 684.
[105] I. Howard Marshall, The Epistles of John, p. 187.

believer in Christ comparing us to the nation of Israel who had been delivered from Pharaoh's power through the sacrificial blood of the Lamb. All of them likened the walk of faith to a walk and a journey through the wilderness of this evil age. All of them taught us that the only way to fulfill our journey would be to turn away from the evils of this age.

Paul in 1 Corinthians chapter 10 uses the whole chapter to explain this reality. In verse 6-8 he says: "Now these things took place as examples for us, that we might not desire evil as they did. Do not be idolaters as some of them were; as it is written, 'The people sat down to eat and drink and rose up to play.' We must not indulge in sexual immorality as some of them did." He continues giving us example after example of wandering away from the faith.

The author of Hebrews in chapter 3 talks about not letting the hardness of our hearts keep us from pushing forward into faith. Verses 12-14 the author prophetically compares Israel in the wilderness to the believer in Christ. Telling us to: "Take care, brothers, lest there be in any of you an evil, unbelieving heart, leading you to fall away from the living God. But exhort one another every day, as long as it is called "today," that none of you may be hardened by the deceitfulness of sin. For we have come to share in Christ, if indeed we hold our original confidence firm to the end."

Peter in the first two chapters of his first epistle uses the example of Israel journeying through the wilderness as to the believers' life journeying through this evil age. In 1 Peter 2:11-12 he says: "Beloved, I urge you as sojourners and exiles to abstain from the passions of the flesh, which wage war against your soul. Keep your conduct among the Gentiles honorable, so that when they speak against you as evildoers, they may see your good deeds and glorify God on the day of visitation."

All the apostolic writers are saying the same thing. It's one coherent message and it's what I call the chorus of the cross. It's yelling at us throughout the scriptures, but are we listening? It's in plain sight, but it is offensive to us because it costs. It costs us the passions and desires of our flesh. Like the children of Israel, we are not content with manna. Our souls long for the delicacies of Egypt. The author of Hebrews called it the deceitfulness of sin because we are only thinking of the pleasures of Egypt while we forget the bondage and servitude of sin.

The Cruciform Life Of Love

The heart of the New Covenant is about living, abiding and demonstrating the love of the Father through the cruciform life of following the pathway of the blood, water and Spirit of God. It's living a life intertwined with the life of the Spirit by daily eating the flesh and drinking in the blood of the covenant. [106]The new covenant promise centers on inner transformation by the Spirit. It's taking up our cross and following in the footsteps of our Lord who came as an actual man. God came in the flesh to show us the cruciform way of living.

It's taken me a lot of years to conclude what was always staring me in the face. It was yelling at me and trying to persuade me away from my own selfish ways. It was love that kept knocking on my door wanting into the deep recesses of my heart. I was afraid to open that door because I had been hurt so many times. It's what Jesus said: because lawlessness abounds the love of many would grow cold.

Lawlessness has a way of hardening our hearts and giving us calluses where we don't feel. We just don't care anymore, and we give up trying to live the cruciform way. We start to go with the flow of our own hearts that have been hardened with our own sinful desires. We give up and give in because we get tired of fighting the good fight of faith. It's what I talked to you about regarding the struggle we have with the flesh. Trust me, I understand because the struggle is real to live a godly life in this present age. I wish I had the magic wand to make you perfect and without sin, but there isn't one. We are going to struggle in this age with the flesh and the deceitfulness of sin. The problem is not the struggle, it's giving up and becoming one who practices lawlessness.

It's what John was saying in 1 John 3:4, "everyone who makes a practice of sinning also practices lawlessness; sin is lawlessness." It's quitting, turning back and giving your lives over to evil deeds. It's turning your back on the cross and going back to allowing the works of the flesh to dominate your life.

The Power of Love: Insights from John's Epistle

As we progress towards the end of the age hurricane force winds

---

[106] Thomas Schreiner, New Testament Theology, p. 597.

of lawlessness will be sweeping the earth. The solution is not going back to the Mosaic law and legalism nor turning to mysticism but being anchored in the love of God demonstrated to us when Jesus came in the flesh. John in his first epistle uses the word commandment and commandments 13 times. I think he is trying to teach us something important.

One of the most important rules of understanding scripture is to let the scriptures interpret themselves. Don't try and read into the text but allow the text to explain itself and allow other texts to help give you additional insight. What is John talking about in keeping the commandments? It seems that John is totally contradicting everything that Paul taught us regarding grace and everything I've said in the last two lessons. It is the argument that some make in rejecting Paul's teaching of grace. It's interesting that John never uses the terminology of grace in explaining the redemptive work of Christ in any of his epistles, but instead he chose to use the terminology of love and truth.

An interesting fact is that the only place John ever uses the word grace is when he opens his gospel expounding on the eternal Son who created all things and took upon himself human flesh. He uses the word grace 4 times in chapter one, and it is the only gospel that uses the word grace. Grace is not found in the Synoptic gospels, but only in John's. However, John never uses that word in his epistles when speaking about the redemptive work of the cross, but only love and truth.

Let's look at the opening of John's gospel. John 1:14 - 17:

> "the Word became flesh and dwelt among us and we have seen his glory, glory as of the only Son from the Father, full of *grace and truth*. John bore witness about him, and cried out, "This was he of whom I said, 'He who comes after me ranks before me, because he was before me.'" For from his fullness we have all received, *grace upon grace*. For the law was given through Moses; *grace and truth* came through Jesus Christ" (emphasis mine).

John's focus is on God becoming man and through the gift of Christ sacrificial life. The truth that was veiled or hidden under the Mosaic law has come in the person of the Messiah. The interesting thing about John's usage of the word grace is that he combines it with the word truth, and he is the only New Testament writer to do that.

- It's only John's gospel that records John the Baptist saying he saw "Jesus coming toward him, and said, "Behold, the Lamb of God, who takes away the sin of the world!"
- It's only John's gospel that tells the story of Nicodemus and our need to be born from above through the new birth of the Spirit.
- It's only in John's gospel that the woman at the well in Samaria is recorded where Jesus speaks of true worship of the Father in spirit and truth. It also speaks of the Spirit being a living well from within our hearts.
- It's only in John's gospel that Jesus and the Father are described as one and the same.
- It's only in John's gospel that the Spirit is spoken of in terms that can only be described as God. A whole chapter is dedicated to understanding the ministry of the Holy Spirit. The mystery of the Godhead is clearly spoken of in the gospel of John as no other book in the entire Bible.

In John's gospel Jesus describes his followers:

- As branches dependent on him the Vine.
- As sheep dependent on him the Good Shepherd.
- As hungry sojourners walking through the wilderness of this age dependent on him who is the Bread of life.

Jesus describes himself as the true light that shines in the darkness of this world showing us the narrow path of his way. He says that he is the way, the life and the truth which spoke of his body replacing the Temple given through the Mosaic law. Jesus spoke of truth found only in him that will set us free from the lies of the antichrist permeating this present world order. He declared himself to be the resurrection who gives us victory over death. He showed and demonstrated himself as the servant that lays down his life for us whom he calls friends.

The Significance of the Passover in John's Gospel

John's gospel focuses on the Passover in a way the Synoptic

gospels don't. John's gospel opens showing us the eternal Word, God the Son creating all things. John's gospel is endeavoring to tell us something concerning the importance of the cross. He whom Jesus knew closer than anyone else seems to focus on the Passover and how Jesus fulfilled it making it central to his entire message. [107]The Passover motif provides a theological framework for John's presentation of Jesus' ministry.

John is the only author to record Jesus and his disciples attending 3 Passover celebrations in Jerusalem during the time of his earthly ministry. [108]The book of John mentions at least three Passovers, thereby extending Jesus' ministry over several years and giving Passover theological prominence.

John chapter 2 he opens with his first recorded miracle of changing the water into wine at the wedding feast. It then takes us to Jesus cleansing the Temple at the beginning of his ministry during the feast of Passover. It's only here that the words of Jesus regarding his body being the new temple and replacing the Jewish Temple after his resurrection are recorded (John 2:19). [109]John's placement of the temple cleansing signals that Jesus replaces the temple as the locus of God's presence.

In John chapter 6 it was the crowds that were heading to Jerusalem to attend the feast of Passover that Jesus performed the miracle of feeding the multitude of people with the young boys 5 loaves and 2 fish. The Passover setting prepares readers to understand Jesus' discourse in sacrificial and Exodus imagery. [110]John presents Jesus as the fulfillment of Passover and temple imagery.

Jesus and his disciples were observant to the Mosaic law. Jesus throughout his earthly ministry was not lawless. He was the personification of the Law and the Prophet's being their fulfillment in human flesh. The Pharisees were always accusing him and his disciples of not following one of their rules, but they could never find him breaking the Mosaic law. [111]Jesus did not break the Mosaic law; conflicts arose over Pharisaic interpretations around their Oral Tradition.

In John chapter 12 thru the rest of his gospel, we see John

---

[107] Andreas Köstenberger, A Theology of John's Gospel and Letters, p. 105.
[108] D.A. Carson, The Gospel According to John, (PNTC), p. 177.
[109] Andreas Köstenberger, A Theology of John's Gospel and Letters, p. 106, 349.
[110] G.K. Beale, A New Testament Biblical Theology, p. 616.
[111] D.A. Carson, The Gospel According to John, (PNTC), p. 190, 623.

focuses on the last Passover. [101]The passion narrative of the cross forms the theological climax of John's gospel. John out of all the gospel accounts wanted to sear upon our hearts the centrality of God laying down his life and [102]the allusion is to the Passover lamb (Exodus 12:46). He wants to show us the love of the Father through the sacrificial death of the lamb of God and its centrality to the redemptive story.

John chapter 11 records the resurrection of Lazarus making a point to say in verse 5 that: "Jesus loved Martha and her sister and Lazarus." [112]John underscores Jesus' love to interpret the sign theologically. Chapter 12 opens recording that it was six days before the Passover and we see Mary in verse 3 take: "a pound of expensive ointment made from pure nard, and anointed the feet of Jesus and wiped his feet with her hair. The house was filled with the fragrance of the perfume." [113]The anointing anticipates Jesus' burial.

Mary's act was an extravagant display of love. It was a sacrificial act prophetically declaring the cross and resurrection, but it was foolishness to the earthly minded. Judas was offended by this demonstration of a heartburning with obedient love. Mary's act contrasts sharply with Judas' pragmatic objection. He was offended because he was filled with greed and a lust for power. Enemies of the cross reject the self-giving pattern of Christ. He had a veneer of religion, but he was an enemy of the cross because his heart had been hardened by sin, lawlessness and willful disobedience. He was one who operated by the spirit of antichrist.

What has been called Jesus' high priestly prayer was only recorded in John's gospel in the Garden of Gethsemane just before his crucifixion. It is during this episode that he calls Judas, the son of destruction. You will see that Jesus in his prophecy on the Mt of Olives recorded in Matthew 24:15 that he talks about the abomination of desolation. We also see Paul use this same terminology when saying in 2 Thessalonians 2:3 that: "unless the apostasy comes first, and the man of lawlessness is revealed, the son of destruction." Apostasy is falling away and turning your back on the cross. It's willful determination to be disobedient and live in a lawless attitude towards the sacrifice of Christ.

If you read through Jesus' high priestly prayer in John chapter 17 the one thing that occurs over and over is Jesus talking about obedience

---

[112] Craig Keener, The Gospel of John, (Vol. 2), p. 843.
[113] D.A. Carson, The Gospel According to John, (PNTC), p. 430.

to the will of the Father and staying true to his word. John's gospel records this prayer and not the shorter prayer found in the Synoptic gospels where Jesus prayed to the Father, "not my will, but thine be done." It was such an intense time of prayer for Jesus in the Garden of Gethsemane that drops of blood perspired from him. It was a complete surrender to the will of the Father, the purpose for which he came into the world which was to be the lamb of God who was slain. It was at this time during his complete surrender that Jesus told his disciples to: "watch and pray that you may not enter into temptation. The spirit indeed is willing, but the flesh is weak."

The Power of Love: The Cruciform Life of Love

Jesus demonstrated his love of the Father through his obedience to the will of the Father. It was Mary's love for Jesus that moved her to do what she did. Her heart had been so touched by the life of Jesus that she willingly sacrificed. It was love that moved her heart and it's only love that will give us the courage to be obedient in the face of death itself. Jesus ends his prayer in the garden talking about that kind of love. A love that overcomes this world established in the one sacrifice of the cross.

The word love appears 57 times in John's gospel more often than all the other three Synoptic gospels together. The word appears 46 times in his first epistle. You know when I was a young man I came to know the Bible very quickly. I have an aptitude for learning, so I consumed Biblical information. I retained a lot of knowledge, but as a result I had a lot of pride. In my quest for truth, I had become in a way blinded by the Bible. I had become a Pharisee, and I didn't even realize I was one.

Life has a way of breaking us, but more than that I do think God has a way of breaking those who love him. We don't always know what we need. I find sometimes we make wrong choices that lead us down paths that break us, but the Father will allow things in our lives to humble us and show us our utter need of him.

In the same way that the children of Israel were led in their journey through the wilderness in like manner our journey through this evil age will bring us to the place where we must cry out, not my will, but your will be done Father. It's the Father's love that leads us to the cross because it's in being crucified with Christ that we can only truly know the Father's heart of love. It's a place that understands the flesh is weak. It's a place where you learn to surrender to the cross which is the only place that true love is found. The Holy Spirit is always prompting us to choose the way of the cross. We don't always listen, but he never stops pointing us toward the narrow path of following in the footsteps of our Master so that our feet are established on the rock of our salvation and tethered to the life of His Spirit.

John was the only disciple that stood below the cross on the day Jesus' blood poured down as he watched with Jesus' mother Mary. He watched the sun darkened for three hours, he heard him cry out that last cry and he witnessed the earthquake. He is the only author to record these words written in John 19:34-37: "the soldiers pierced his side with a spear, and at once there came out blood and water. He who saw it has borne witness—his testimony is true, and he knows that he is telling the truth—that you also may believe. For these things took place that the Scripture might be fulfilled: 'Not one of his bones will be broken.' And again another Scripture says, 'They will look on him whom they have pierced.' The whole focus of John's gospel was to show that Jesus was the God who stepped out of eternity into our humanity becoming the Lamb who was slain before the foundations of the earth.

The Cross is the Central Theme of the New Temple

It is the stumbling stone of the cross that is the very cornerstone of the New Temple. The Old Covenant Temple veil was torn from top to bottom. [114]Access to God is secured through the sacrificial death of Christ. It is only through the body of our Lord's crucified flesh and poured out blood that we have direct access to the very heart of the Father. John in his first epistle is preaching the cross to us in the terminology of the love of the Father.

Paul spoke of the grace of God in the same way that John speaks of the love of God, but they are both preaching the central theme of all the Law and the Prophets pointed towards. [115]Grace is love that stoops and rescues. It's the consummation of the ages found in the Lamb of God and who is the Lion of the tribe of Judah at the same time. It's the mystery that has been revealed and it's the one that the enemy continues to try to cover with a refuge of lies.

[114] Peter O'Brien, The Letter to the Hebrews, (PNTC), p. 356.
[115] John Stott, The Message of the Ephesians, (BST), p. 52.

Just like the Mt. of Transfiguration left an imprint upon Peter's soul and as he wrote his first epistle he reflected upon that experience. The crucifixion left an imprint upon John's soul. John writes as an eyewitness shaped by the events of the cross. As I've spent time reading the book of I John I'm called to a full surrender to the cruciform way of living. I am shown how incapable I am of living this life of faith without fully surrendering to the love of God displayed through the blood, water and Spirit of the cruciform life of faith.

It seems that's the context of Romans 8:28 when Paul says: "we know that for those who love God all things work together for good, for those who are called according to his purpose." In context Paul is describing our frailty and inability to truly change ourselves. We cannot overcome the flesh through our own ability or with Biblical *gnōsis*. [116]Transformation is the Spirit's work, not human self-reform.

I've tried and I've tried as hard as I can. I've failed over and over and over. The best I could do was be a religious actor, a hypocrite. Paul is showing us that it's only by the Spirit's help that we can truly love God and love others. It's the same message that John is telling us, but it's just from a different perspective.

The Jewish Perspective in the Epistles of John, James, Peter, and Jude

John along with James, Peter and Jude all write their epistles from a Jewish perspective. James is almost wisdom literature. Peter in his first epistle uses a lot of Jewish typology, Jude's small epistle quotes Jewish apocalyptic literature from the book of Enoch along with II Peter who draws upon Jude's epistle. If you read John's first epistle it leaves you with a lot of questions and on the surface, it seems to contradict some of Paul's basic teaching on justification by faith in the same way that the book of James does. One of the main keys to understanding the book of I John is understanding the way he uses love and truth.

It's only John's gospel that records the words of Christ saying in John 13:34 - 35: "A new commandment I give to you, that you love one another: just as I have loved you, you also are to love one another. By this all people will know that you are my disciples, if you have love for

---

[116] Thomas Schreiner, Romans, p. 414.

one another." In his first epistle John mentions keeping this commandment repeatedly and uses it as a test for being a child of the Father. [117]The command is new not in that love was unknown in the Old Testament, but in that the standard is now Jesus' own love, displayed supremely in the cross.

John doesn't ever explicitly repeat the words of Christ in his epistle because it must have been something his readers easily understood. It's a message that they had heard before. John is just reinforcing the message over and over in differing ways to show the importance of staying true to the centrality of the cross.

John in his first epistle uses the word commandment 13 times. If you don't understand what he is talking about then you would think John is telling us to keep the Mosaic law to fight lawlessness. John is not telling us that at all! [118]The singular 'commandment' is fundamentally Christological and relational, not a reimposition of Mosaic law. What John is telling us is that love has been clearly portrayed to us through Christ laying down his life for us and if we have truly been changed by the blood, water and Spirit of the cross then we will follow his example of love. [119]The commandment in view is the command to love one another, grounded in the self-giving love of Christ.

John's first epistle like no other epistle in the Bible is the most closely aligned with the words of Christ. It's almost a reflection of Jesus' prayer in John chapter 17 referred to as the high priestly prayer the night before his crucifixion in the Garden of Gethsemane. Jesus clearly outlined the new commandment that John repeatedly refers to in his epistle. It's not the Mosaic law, but the law of love which can only be lived out in this body of flesh by the power of the Spirit.

John doesn't explicitly say it, but it's clearly implied that to truly follow Christ our lives must become a willing sacrifice of love. [120]Obedience flows from love, and love from the Spirit's transforming presence. If you look at the sum total of his writings, you understand that love is synonymous with sacrifice and it's out of sacrificial love that obedience to the Father flows like a river of grace and truth.

---

[117] D.A. Carson, The Gospel According to John, (PNTC), p. 484.

[118] Karen Jobes, 1, 2, 3 John (ZECNT), p. 146.

[119] Colin Kruse, The Letters of John (PNTC), p. 88.

[120] D.A. Carson, The Gospel According to John, (PNTC), p. 499.

The Power of Obedience and Sacrificial Love in Following Christ

The author of Hebrews has the same message in Hebrews 10:5 - 9 in saying that: "when Christ came into the world, he said, "sacrifices and offerings you have not desired, but a body have you prepared for me; in burnt offerings and sin offerings you have taken no pleasure. Then I said, 'Behold, I have come to do your will, O God, as it is written of me in the scroll of the book.'" When he said above, "You have neither desired nor taken pleasure in sacrifices and offerings and burnt offerings and sin offerings" (these are offered according to the law), then he added, "Behold, I have come to do your will." *He does away with the first in order to establish the second*." (emphasis mind).

The new commandment that John and Jesus talked about was obedience to the Father's heart demonstrated through surrendering their lives as a sacrifice of love. It's the same message that Paul is telling us in Romans chapter 12 about presenting our bodies as a living sacrifice so that we can accomplish the will of God and mature into Christ likeness. Paul uses the same terminology as in Hebrews regarding the Old Covenant sacrifices. Paul in Romans 12:1 says, "I appeal to you therefore, brothers, by the mercies of God, to present your bodies as a living sacrifice, holy and acceptable to God, which is your spiritual worship."

It's only the sacrificial love of God that has the power to keep us from being lawless, walking in darkness and living in the flesh. It's that Jesus as the sinless lamb of God was the sacrifice that saved us from the wrath of God so therefore, we are compelled to love God with our whole hearts and be obedient children. It's just what Paul said in Romans 6:17 that we are to be: "obedient from the heart to the standard of teaching to which you were committed." Sound doctrine produces sound living demonstrated through the love of God.

The gospel that Jesus and his apostle taught was not cheap, selfish and lawless. It was not focused on me, me and me. It was sacrificial and to make it anything other than that is to make yourself an enemy of the cross. It's what John was talking about when he talked about how many antichrists have gone out into the world. Denying Jesus came in the flesh is to deny the cross. To be antichrist is to be anti-cross. It's rejecting the cruciform life of faith and following a substitute gospel of legalism or lawlessness.

Overcoming Lawlessness and Embracing the Blood of the Cross: The Key to Victory

John defines sin as being lawless. In 1 John 3: 4-6 he says: "Everyone who makes a practice of sinning also practices lawlessness; sin is lawlessness. You know that he appeared in order to take away sins and in him there is no sin. No one who abides in him keeps on sinning; no one who keeps on sinning has either seen him or known him." [121]Lawlessness here is not simply infringement of the Mosaic law but a refusal to submit to God's will as revealed in Christ.

What John is conveying to us in his first epistle and in his gospel is that if we are washed in the blood, identified with Christ through baptism and born of the Spirit we are joined to him. [122]John binds together incarnation, atonement, and Spirit-witness in defining Christian identity. He is showing us that being born of the Spirit and being a child of the Father is a complete identification with Christ. He is saying that because of what Christ has done in us, then we are going to have a desire to fulfill the commandment. The commandment to love God with all our hearts and to love one another because being born of God entails a new pattern of life. [114]Obedience flows from new birth; it is the evidence, not the cause, of salvation.

If we continue to practice lawlessness with no conviction of the Holy Spirit John is telling us, then we are not confessing Jesus as having come in the flesh to die for our sins. He is saying the same thing that Paul said, which is we make ourselves enemies of the cross. He says exactly what James in his epistle says that when we turn to the flesh and make friends with the world then we make ourselves enemies of God.

Yes, there is a solution, but there is only one solution and it's the one the Holy Spirit continues to try to point us towards which is the blood of the cross. The blood of the cross is not cheap, it costs us, and the price is our fleshly desires. John the author of the book of Revelation says we can only overcome the antichrist by complete surrender to the risen Christ. Revelation 12:11 says: "they have conquered him by the

---

[121] Colin Kruse, The Letters of John, (PNTC), p. 122.
[122] Karen Jobes, 1, 2, 3 John, p. 206.

blood of the Lamb and by the word of their testimony, for they loved not their lives even unto death."

The gospel is that we die so that Christ may live his life through us. It's life for life and is not without sacrifice. [123]Union with Christ means participation in his death and resurrection life. The gospel that Jesus and his apostles taught is the New Covenant of Christ body and blood. It's about our identification where we no longer live, but our lives are to be a love offering back to him in complete surrender. [124]Christian experience is fundamentally sacrificial in response to mercy.

The gospel of lawlessness is a message that says you can be a follower of Christ while you reject the cross. It's one that says you can live however you want to live and obedience to the Father doesn't matter. It's one that says you don't have to live out the cruciform life of faith. It's anti-cross and John called it antichrist. [125]Enemies of the cross reject the cruciform pattern of Christ's life.

John doesn't speak duplicitously and there are no shadows in his speech. He doesn't give you the postmodern grayness, but he cut's deep into the heart of flesh with a sharp knife. If you refuse to turn away from a flesh ruled life of lawlessness and sin through the work of the cross, then you are living under the spirit of the antichrist.

It's Paul who really defines what a lawless life devoid of the Holy Spirit looks like in Galatians chapter 5:19-21 he tells them:

"For the desires of the flesh are against the Spirit, and the desires of the Spirit are against the flesh, for these are opposed to each other, to keep you from doing the things you want to do. But if you are led by the Spirit, you are not under the law. Now the works of the flesh are evident: sexual immorality, impurity, sensuality, idolatry, sorcery, enmity, strife, jealousy, fits of anger, rivalries, dissensions, divisions, envy, drunkenness, orgies, and things like these. I warn you, as I warned you before, that those who do such things will not inherit the kingdom of God."

All the apostolic writers rejected the gospel of lawlessness. The

[123] Thomas Schreiner, Galatians, (ZECNT), p. 180.
[124] Douglas J. Moo, Romans (NICNT), p. 748.
[125] Gordon D. Fee, Paul's Letter to the Philippians, (NICNT), p. 386.

grace message has become extremely popular in America today, but I find that message so many times presented in a way where it is separated from the truth of the gospel of Christ. Understanding grace must be combined with understanding truth or grace becomes a license to reject the cross. The result is believers who feel like they have a license to sin. You cannot separate the message of the cross from the message of grace or it will produce lawlessness.

Salvation Through *Gnōsis*

The Gnostic's taught a false grace that was based simply on *gnōsis* and required no repentance or change. They denied that Jesus came in the flesh. Yes, Gnostic's talked about Jesus. However, it wasn't the Jesus who came in the flesh and who died on the cross as the lamb of God demonstrating the love of the Father. [126]The fundamental problem in many Gnostic texts is ignorance, and salvation is achieved through knowledge. It wasn't the Jesus calling you to identify with his sacrificial love by laying down your life in covenant with him and turning away from sin. Gnostics frequently reinterpreted Jesus as a revealer of hidden wisdom rather than the atoning Lamb.

- It was a different Jesus who just brought you the *gnōsis* of freedom to become a better you.
- It was a different Jesus who teaches that you just need the secret *gnōsis* to a higher development of self.
- It wasn't a Jesus who put any demands on you to repent, change and to take up your cross to follow him because getting *gnōsis* was enough. To have *gnōsis* was salvation for the Gnostic.
- [127]*Gnōsis* meant insight into one's divine origin and salvation was self-knowledge.

If we dilute the message of the cross so that it does not offend sinful lifestyles, then it's no longer the message of the cross. I'm afraid that's what's happened in far too many churches in America, and we are now seeing the fruit. To be more acceptable we have turned away from

[126] Michael Williams, Rethinking 'Gnosticism', p. 36.
[127] Elaine Pagels, The Gnostic Gospels, p. 19.

the foolishness of the cross, but in so doing we have denied the very power and wisdom that can only be displayed through that message. As Jesus said we have lost our saltiness.

The Crucial Role of Sacrifice in Upholding Truth

How can the church be a pillar of truth when so many in the church no longer understand the sacrifice of the cross? In the desire to be free from the Mosaic law many have turned to a 'gospel lawlessness'. John was telling us in his epistle that the love of the Father demonstrated through Christ becoming man has tethered us to the demand of his love. The only way to overcome this world and the spirit of antichrist is through following in the footsteps of his lifestyle of sacrifice.

Paul called us living sacrifices (Romans 12:1). Peter likened us to priests who offer up spiritual sacrifices (I Peter 2:24). The author of Hebrews says we are to offer up sacrifices. No, not the sacrificial system of the Mosaic law. It's a new law, it's a new temple and it's a new priesthood established on the ultimate sacrifice of Christ. John is saying the same thing as all the other apostolic writers is that our lives are now joined to his resurrection life. (In Section II of the Foundations Publications School of Discipleship I do an extensive series of lessons taking you though the New Testament sacrifices.)

We demonstrate that our lives have been offered upon the altar of the cross by loving one another. Jesus walked among us and demonstrated the love of the Father in his obedience. As Paul said in Philippians 2:8 that Jesus: "being found in human form, he humbled himself by becoming obedient to the point of death, even death on a cross." [128]The cross is the ultimate expression of Christ's self-giving obedience.

Grace that is not understood in the work of the cross is not grace. Grace is about sacrifice. Paul, who could safely be called the apostle of grace, goes into a lengthy understanding of original sin, the Mosaic law, redemption through the work of the cross and faith towards God in the first 5 chapters of Romans. [129]Grace in Romans is inseparable from the atoning death of Christ.

He opens chapter 6 saying this: "What shall we say then? Are we

---

[128] Gordon D. Fee, Paul's Letter to the Philippians, (NICNT), p. 210.
[129] Douglas J. Moo, The Epistle to the Romans, (NICNT), p. 232.

to continue in sin that grace may abound? By no means! How can we who died to sin still live in it? Do you not know that all of us who have been baptized into Christ Jesus were baptized into his death? We were buried therefore with him by baptism into death, in order that, just as Christ was raised from the dead by the glory of the Father, we too might walk in newness of life." Grace produces allegiance and obedience – not autonomy.

Paul here in Romans is emphatically saying the exact same thing that John is saying, but instead of using the terminology of love; he is using the terminology of grace. However, they are both preaching the cross and us crucified with Christ. [130]Johannine and Pauline theology converge in their emphasis on participation in Christ along with obedience. He goes on to say in verses 15 - 16: "Are we to sin because we are not under law but under grace? By no means! Do you not know that if you present yourselves to anyone as obedient slaves, you are slaves of the one whom you obey, either of sin, which leads to death, or of obedience, which leads to righteousness?"

The Danger of the Gnostic Heresy in Contemporary Christianity

You see a version of the Gnostic heresy taught that since your spirit is saved through *gnōsis* it doesn't matter what you do with your body. Irenaeus in his Against Heresies 1.6.2 says, "they say actions are of no consequence since the spiritual person cannot be defiled." It's the idea that sin is just wrong thinking. All you must do is adjust your thinking, not your lifestyle. You can have anything you want in life.

The church in America has become much more Gnostic in its thinking than I think most of us have realized. I've watched this transformation happen. It's very concerning because I look at so much of the church and I'm grieved because it's scripture that is twisted, perverted and packaged into a popular message that can be sold for lots of money because it appeals to the flesh. The following are popular teachings:

- You can create your own good life by the power of your words.

---

[130] Richard Bauckham, The Theology of the Book of Revelation, p. 72.

- You are meant to have 'the good life' and all you must do is believe the right things. If you just confess the right faith words over and over, then you will manifest 'god' likeness.
- You have the power within yourself to determine your destiny. You are little anointed ones that can be just like Jesus.
- You can be whatever you set your mind and heart to do. Jesus suffered for you, and you don't have to suffer. Riches, health, power and anything you want can be yours because you are the seed of Abraham.

The only problem is none of the apostles taught the following statements and you must twist scripture to come up with those teachings. You can only teach those things when you take scripture out of its original context and paste them back together making a gospel void of the cruciform life of Christ. It's one of the many versions of the spirit of antichrist that John said had gone out into the world, but it seems to be America's most popular version.

The Dangers of Sensuality and False Teachings

Peter said it this way in his II Peter 2:1 - 3: "there will be false teachers among you, who will secretly bring in destructive heresies, even denying the Master who bought them, bringing upon themselves swift destruction. And many will follow their sensuality, and because of them the way of truth will be blasphemed. And in their greed they will exploit you with false words."

The word *sensuality* in this text doesn't mean sexual per say, but it means with no fear of God. It's pride which is the original sin and living a me centered life. It's living in a life of excess. It's living a life without restraint. It's living in the works of the flesh.

Pride causes you to be lawless and walk away from the cruciform way of living. Did you know greed is idolatry? Paul in Colossians 3:5 tells us to: "put to death therefore what is earthly in you: sexual immorality, impurity, passion, evil desire, and covetousness, which is idolatry."

Let me remind you of the words of Christ when he said in Mark 7:20 - 23: "What comes out of a person is what defiles him. For from within, out of the heart of man, come evil thoughts, sexual immorality, theft, murder, adultery, coveting, wickedness, deceit, sensuality, envy, slander, pride, foolishness. All these evil things come from within, and they defile a person." If we don't put to death what is earthly in us by daily surrendering to the cruciform life of love, then we will find ourselves living in lawlessness.

Could this be what Jesus meant when he said in the context of false prophets in Matthew 7:21 - 23: "Not everyone who says to me, 'Lord, Lord,' will enter the kingdom of heaven, but the one who does the will of my Father who is in heaven. On that day many will say to me, 'Lord, Lord, did we not prophesy in your name, and cast out demons in your name, and do many mighty works in your name?' And then will I declare to them, 'I never knew you; depart from me, you workers of lawlessness.'" What I am hoping to do is ask us all to examine ourselves and make sure that we are living our lives in the humility of the cross.

Speaking the Truth in Love: Understanding Jesus' Message on Judgment

We have become so conditioned in our culture to accept anything and it's simply unhealthy. It's funny the one scripture even those in the world know and quote is that Jesus said don't judge. I find those who live in lawlessness will pull that one out and tell us that we are being legalistic to judge them. It's based on a misinterpretation of Jesus word's to judge not in Matthew 7:1-5.

Jesus didn't say we can't discern which is what judgment is, but he said we better look at ourselves first. [131]The prohibition concerns a judgmental attitude, not the exercise of moral discernment. He was saying that our heart should be motivated with love to see the person helped and to protect others. It's making sure that what we are saying is not only accurate, but merciful and motivated by love. We have an obligation to speak the truth, but we need to speak the truth in love. Our speech must be seasoned with grace in the hope of healing, restoration and setting that which is out of order back in its proper place.

False spiritual leaders will say that anyone who challenges their false teaching is a Pharisee. Jesus was not telling us to not judge someone's teaching or prophecy because that would be utter foolishness.

---

[131] R.T. France, The Gospel of Matthew, (NICNT), p. 283.

He was saying the same thing that Paul was saying regarding partaking of the Lord's supper, which signifies the type of sacrificial life of faith and love we are to demonstrate if we must judge. [132]Discernment is a Christian obligation, especially regarding doctrine.

It's why Paul said that we need to examine ourselves first. We need to take a good long look in the mirror before we ever try to speak the truth and make sure it is done in love which is with a heart to restore. The goal is restoration, not humiliation. God's heart of love is redemption, restoration and reconciliation through the cross.

A Call to Contend for the Faith

I've struggled writing and speaking on this subject on the 'gospel of legalism' and the 'gospel of lawlessness' because it's challenging me. I can imagine as the apostolic fathers wrote they knew they were frail men, but they were compelled by love to speak the truth. Paul said I: "tell you even with tears," about those who "walk as enemies of the cross of Christ." I've felt those tears as I've written this book, and I really take no joy in pointing out these things that I'm pointing. I have four fingers pointing back at me and my sincere desire is that what I write will not only challenge me, but challenge others to finish their race.

I've felt my heart burn. I feel like I am making a defense of the cross and us crucified with him. It's a message that has burned within me for many years. I've not always lived as one who is crucified, but the Holy Spirit always brings me back to this place of surrender. I know that it's only as we learn to abide in this message that we can truly experience victory over the flesh.

I don't like it, but I feel like Jude who was compelled: "to write to you about our common salvation, I found it necessary to write appealing to you to contend for the faith that was once for all delivered to the saints. For certain people have crept in unnoticed who long ago were designated for this condemnation, ungodly people, who pervert the grace of our God into sensuality and deny our only Master and Lord, Jesus Christ."

We are living in those days. I wish it wasn't so, but as I look around at the church in America, I find myself troubled by so much of

---

[132] Colin Kruse, The Letters of John, (PNTC), p. 152.

what I see. The pathway I see ahead for those who follow Christ is a pathway that leads to surrender. It's only by surrendering to the pathway of suffering and sacrifice that John said we can overcome this world.

Signs of the Times: Lawlessness, Cold Love, and the Danger of False Teachings

One of the signs that Jesus gave us describing the times before his return is that lawlessness would be abounding. He said this lawlessness would cause the love of many to grow cold. Paul said in 2 Timothy 4:3 - 4 that the: "time is coming when people will not endure sound teaching, but having itching ears they will accumulate for themselves teachers to suit their own passions and will turn away from listening to the truth and wander off into myths."

John ends his epistle saying this in 1 John 5:21: "Little children, keep yourselves from idols." It's a very peculiar way to end. To me it's the summing up of all that he said, which is that if we subject ourselves to the spirit of the antichrist then we are living anti-cross. Our faith is about surrendering to the one sacrifice of Christ.

Idolatry is no longer living in the shadow of the cross but living in the shadows of whatever we refuse to surrender to him. Having money and being successful is not the problem, but money or success captivating our hearts is idolatry.

Whatever we allow to have a hold on our hearts divides our attention and Paul said that's where the serpent causes our hearts to be led astray from a sincere and pure devotion to Christ. James said it's when we become a friend of the world that our affections are divided, and we become an enemy of God.

The Gnostic heresy is an attempt to bypass the cross. It's rejecting the lamb of God as the main story and the centrality of the believers' lives. It's when we do not give Christ his rightful place in our hearts, and we are denying his lordship over our lives.

It's why John ended his epistle warning us to keep ourselves from idols. It's why I am urging you in an age where idolatry is the norm that we cannot let this present evil age quench the love of God in our hearts leading us into a lifestyle of lawlessness. It's my prayer that we all examine ourselves in the shadow of the cross. It's my prayer that our lives are being lived through the love of that one holy sacrifice.

166

CHAPTER 8

THE POWER OF SEXUAL IDOLATRY

"For this is the will of God, your sanctification: that you abstain from sexual immorality."

~ I Thessalonians 4:3 ~

In the introduction of this book, I will tell you about my journey of faith and how just after one year of getting delivered from a drug addicted lifestyle I became involved in a Charismatic cult in East Texas. I left disillusioned, confused and grasping to understand. I had become friends with a group of ministers from New York while there and they went back to New York. I was invited by them to go to Long Island and help them plant a church, so I needed to save up some money. I had moved back to Dallas after leaving East Texas and I spent the summer cleaning carpets since I had spent the last few years running a janitorial business.

I grew up in Dallas, so I was familiar with various parts of the city. I was sent out that morning in one of the cleaning vans to do a carpet job just northwest of downtown Dallas. I got off the highway and arrived at a high-rise apartment building. It was the summer of 1991, I was 22 years of age, and I was in good shape. I remember walking into the building and this guy seemed to be checking me out. I really didn't pay him any attention, but something just felt weird. We got up to the 5th floor of the building and a young guy opened the door, so we set up to clean.

I'm cleaning and as always, I'm observant so I'm looking at pictures in the apartment. I see two guys together in all these pictures and still not really thinking about anything. We finish cleaning and get out into the hallway. All I see is males. We get to the lobby again, all friendly males and again I feel like I'm getting checked out.

To me something felt strange, but it still hasn't clicked. We packed up and I pull out of the apartment complex. I drive down the road and get to a T in the road with a red light. I'm sitting at the red light when I look up right in front of me is this hot pink modern looking building that says Metropolitan Community Church. At that moment it clicked, and I realized exactly where I was in the middle of one of the biggest same sex districts of Dallas.

Embracing Alternative Sexual Lifestyles: A Controversial Debate in Christianity

I tell this story because in 1991 the sight was like spotting a rare unicorn. Metropolitan Community Church was a forerunner of what is now a large part of the church in America where alternative sexual lifestyles are not just tolerated but celebrated. I could go down a lot of rabbit holes on this subject and volumes of books have been written on both sides of what has become one of the greatest debates of our times.

The question is can you reject the created order and be a faithful believer in Christ? Can you live in, accept, affirm and celebrate alternative sexual lifestyles while saying you are a follower of Christ? The question is important because our sexuality is something that is sacredly tied to the very depths of our hearts and the most intimate parts of our identity.

What I am hoping to do is share my journey of learning how to live in the truth of the love of God that has been demonstrated to us through the redemptive work of the cross. We are seeing in these times the shifting with the sand of every wind of doctrine. We are witnessing the twisting of scriptures and the craftiness of men's deceitful schemes in open view. It's confusing to a lot of people. We've all watched those who we thought were solid believers walk away from and even denouncing the faith.

What I am hoping to do is help you be grounded in some of the eternal truths by which I've learned to live my life in a world going the opposite direction. I'm going to let scriptures speak for themselves because the vast amounts of scriptures speak very clearly on this subject concerning our sexuality.

Let's start the conversation by talking about something we all share alike which is pain. The pain of sexual abuse is one of the deepest scars that any individual will ever have to endure. I wish it was something rare, but all of us know someone or maybe we have been sexually abused by a family member, a member of the clergy, some other authority figure or we endured a violent sexual incident.

The trauma left upon the soul is something only God can heal. I know because it happened to me. I never believed in repressed memories unconsciously blocked because they are associated with trauma that is too severe to be kept in conscious memory. I always thought it was something a therapist induced, and people just needed a scapegoat to feel better about themselves. Well, I was 33 years old and had been teaching in discipleship schools, a team member on church plants, pastoring churches and on the mission field for over 10 years. I had been active in ministry with a master's degree in theology and had already written 2 books.

I did not get married until the age of 26 and I was delivered from drugs at the age of 19. I spent 7 years of my life single, and I did not date. I just pursued God and focused all my attention on him. I lived a life free from sexual immorality. I had my struggles, but overall, I lived pursuing God with all my heart. I found victory in Christ because I embraced the cross. Did I still have to struggle with lust? Of course, but I always imagined getting married one day and it would put that to rest.

Well, I was married, but I still struggled with lust and then came the age of the internet. I was 33 and had just left a ministry experience that was unhealthy. I was beaten up, defeated and burned out. As a young teenager I had a problem with porn, and I was sexually awkward. I knew I had a problem but didn't understand myself. Well at 33 I got on the internet which was new at the time and found some porn. In a short time, I couldn't control myself. My wife at the time discovered what I was doing. I remember it like it was yesterday, but as I sat at that kitchen table confessing my sin at that moment my mind was flooded with a memory of being sexually abused by a family member at the age of 9.

I never believed in repressed memories until it was mine. I tell this story with one hope in mind and that is to help anyone struggling with sexual sin to know that there is healing in the cross. I'm not talking to you about something that is theoretical. What I discovered was that in my pain I had to make a choice.

I had to choose to turn to the healing found in the cross or to a life of lawlessness choosing my own way. It's the choice all of us must make at some point. We must bring our sexuality to the cross or we are going to turn away from the God who took upon himself human flesh. Yes, it's going to be a struggle, but the life of faith is about struggle and that's why it's called the good fight of faith. Eternity is worth the struggle so we must learn to put to death the deeds of the flesh and allow the blood, water and Spirit of God to heal the wounds of our hearts.

The founder of Metropolitan Community Church Troy Perry has a very painful story. His father was a criminal who died when he was 11. He was then abused by his stepfather and dropped out of school by the age of 15 and became a licensed Baptist preacher. He had same sex attractions but married the daughter of his spiritual mentor and pastor. The pastor told him it would resolve his sexual dysfunction. He ended up moving to Los Angeles to pastor a Pentecostal church when his wife discovered a book, he had about same sex attraction. He eventually divorced and was excommunicated from ministry.

After leaving the Pentecostal church he attempted suicide then in 1968 he started the first Metropolitan Community Church. Today there are 222 churches, and it is considered a mainline Protestant church having the Nicene Creed as its statement of faith. Troy Perry is the pioneer of gay theology and has been celebrated by Presidents of the United States and Fortune 500 corporate leaders.

The Danger of Embracing Gnostic Heresy and the Impact of the Sexual Revolution

It seems to me that Perry took his pain and instead of turning to the cross he made a left turn into twisting scripture. He embraced the Gnostic heresy that says *gnōsis* is the key to salvation and we must learn to embrace our true inner self. Gnosticism teaches that male and female sexual distinctions are of the material creation. What really matters is what's in your heart which is your true inner self. Perry embraced that heresy and as a leader the path he chose has affected many people.

I think most of us have heard the boiling frog analogy. It describes a frog being slowly boiled alive. The premise is that if a frog is put suddenly into boiling water, it would jump out. However, if the frog is put in water it enjoys and then you slowly raise the temperature then the frog will not perceive the danger. The frog will be cooked while it enjoys the ride slowly roasting to its ultimate death. I do think the analogy is quite accurate when comparing it to how the Sexual Revolution has transformed American culture along with the church.

The Sexual Revolution of the 1960's has transformed the soul of America and there is no putting the Genie back in the bottle. As I look around the landscape of the church it has had an undeniable and detrimental effect upon far too many.

I don't think I have to point out the obvious because the number of high-profile Christian leaders in all Christian traditions across America have not just fallen into sexual sin, but many have made public pronouncements of their rejection of the core tenets of the faith. We have even seen some move over to a doctrine of inclusion when it comes to same sex attraction as accepted conduct for those who profess faith in Christ.

It started in the 1960's, but since the Digital Revolution our direct access to what can only be described as Sexual Idolatry has laid bare the heart of wickedness. The heat has been turned up to a hard boil and you will not be able to sit on the fence regarding sexuality. You will have to make a clear choice on the issue of sexual orientation and sexual sin. It will be one of the dividing factors separating the wheat from the tares.

Choosing Christ Over Apostasy

I believe the apostolic fathers had depth, width and breadth, but they were also simple. The gospel is simple enough for any man, woman or child to understand. John especially was clear, decisive and cut right to the point. It was Christ or antichrist, light or darkness, truth or deception, denying Jesus in the flesh or partaking of Christ in the flesh. What I hear today in the church so many times is the confusion of Babylon. Endless speculation and endless debate over issues that are clear if you take the word of God as actually saying what it clearly says.

We now stand in the valley of decision! It's only the cross that cuts through the chaos. The choice before us is embracing the cruciform way of following Christ or the apostasy of postmodern sexuality. Pride is the original sin and from which all rebellion against morality exists. The flesh is chaos, rotting flesh, vultures of demonic activity, death and the absence of God. Jesus likened the days of his return as like the days of Noah and the days of Lot where both periods were judged for their rejection of the covenant keeping God who restrains our conduct.

The Babylon spoken of in Revelation 17 and 18 by John is described as overflowing with sexual immorality. It gives us a vivid description of the inhabitants of the earth becoming drunk on the wine of that perversion. It talks of her being a dwelling place for demons, unclean spirits and detestable things. It is a description of open brazen displays of sexual immorality flooding the earth. It says that all nations will drink the wine of the passion of her sexual immorality. The Protestant Reformers interpreted this text as Babylon being the Catholic Church and yes, they were correct for their times.

Revelation 17:6 says that Babylon is drunk with the blood of the saints, the blood of the martyrs of Jesus. I'm not interpreting this text, but I am using it to show that the lawlessness of sexual immorality is one of the main things we must all come to terms with if we want to continue in the faith. It is one of those main central issues that oppose the blood of the cross. How you stand on this issue will determine if you embrace the message of the cross or if you will become an enemy of the cross.

What we are witnessing today in the church is nothing short of apostasy. Is this the great apostasy spoken of by Paul in II Thessalonians 2:3? I personally don't think so, but it's an apostasy that is undeniable as you look at the landscape of the American church. It's shaking the foundations of the church in America, and everyone is going to have to answer for themselves when Jesus asks them: "Who do you say that I Am?"

Is he the Jesus who condones, embraces and celebrates same sex attraction? It's no longer just same sex attraction. At the writing of this book, we are now up to LGBTQIA2S+. Honesty, I'm not even sure what that means except confusion. It's because Gnostic spiritually is a gospel of lawlessness where anything goes and confusion reigns. You have no end to the depravity and imagination of a heart given over to idolatry.

The end of the age is about harvest: wheat and tares coming to full maturity simultaneously (Matt. 13:30). I understand it shakes and challenges some people's 'once saved always saved' theology. No, the term 'once saved always saved' is not in the Bible and the apostolic fathers never used it. I think scripture teaches that if you choose to walk away and deny the cross that the Spirit will contend with you, but he will not nor can he override your will. Our salvation is secure in the power and wisdom of the cross. No one can separate us from the love of God, but we can deny him, and it's called apostasy.

The Battle Against Idolatry in John's First Epistle

The little statement that John ended his first epistle on has always intrigued me. John ends his letter saying in 1 John 5:21: "Little children, keep yourselves from idols." He writes this whole epistle seemingly saying nothing about idolatry and then ends with this admonition. Could it be that John's epistle is all about combating idolatry in the life of the believer and he ends with an obvious statement?

I think we many times look at idolatry as a problem with the ancients and not something modern man really has to deal with. I mean modern man is much too sophisticated to bow down to some lifeless idol, right? We are much too enlightened and educated to think in such outdated ways, but [133]idolatry is trusting in anything other than God for ultimate security. Actually, I really identify with Paul when he is walking through the city of Athens in Acts chapter 17. It says in verse 16 that: "his spirit was provoked within him as he saw that the city was full of idols." It doesn't take discernment to look around modern American culture to see that our land is full of idols. However, one of the main idol's that can be streamed instantly to us all is sexual images of all sorts. Yes, sexual sin is idolatry.

The gospel of sexual immorality is nothing new. In our days however, we are being confronted by sins of the heart, mind and bodies in ways that have never been imagined in human history. Just as in the days of Noah the lawlessness of man is great in the earth and the thoughts of his heart are only evil. Sexuality goes to the very heart of who we are and who we are has everything to do with worship.

Paul starts the book of Romans giving a clarion call of the heart of the gospel. Chapter 1:16 - 17 he says: "I am not ashamed of the gospel, for it is the power of God for salvation to everyone who believes, to the Jew first and also to the Greek. For in it the righteousness of God is revealed beginning and ending in faith, as it is written, 'The righteous shall live by faith'."

A Journey of Our Ancient Faith In Hebrews 11

The author of Hebrews in chapter 11 has given us one of the best historical views of our ancient faith. He takes us through a list starting with Abel's blood sacrifice and the patriarchs who all demonstrated through their lives that they chose to worship the one true living God in the midst of great wickedness, idolatry and hostility.

The author of Hebrews says that we are rewarded for our faith. God will walk with us during our journey in this life providing for us

---

[133] G.K. Beale, We Become What We Worship, p. 35.

along our way, but our ultimate reward awaits the resurrection from the dead at the judgment seat of Christ. Read the whole chapter and it will show you what faith looks like. Volumes of books have been written about this chapter. Rightfully so because it is packed with a variety of examples of what it means to be a person of faith living in a surrounding culture that seeks to quench the fire of God from your heart. I want to share with you a text that has helped me tremendously in my journey.

Hebrews 11:25 - 26 says this about Moses who had to make a choice between the lust of the flesh, the lust of the eyes and the pride of life or the way of the cross. It says that he chose: "rather to be mistreated with the people of God than to enjoy the fleeting pleasures of sin. He considered the reproach of Christ greater wealth than the treasures of Egypt, for he was looking to the reward." Moses had to make a choice between the false spirituality of Egypt, or the cruciform life of faith found in the lamb of God. Moses choice to obey the call to follow resulted in the deliverance of the Hebrew nation through the display of power demonstrated through the Passover story.

God's Wrath Revealed in the Book of Romans

Paul in Romans chapter 1 goes from talking about the power of the gospel and faith to a text in verse 18 that will most likely be debated about until the return of Christ. He says: "for the wrath of God is revealed from heaven against all ungodliness and unrighteousness of men, who by their unrighteousness suppress the truth." To go from the power of the gospel and us being saved by faith then right into this statement seems abrupt and out of place. It seems to me he is making the same kind of contrast that John made in his first epistle.

What we have tried to do in our postmodern mindset is always find a way out. We prefer nuance because quite honestly, I would agree that in a lot of arenas finding middle ground is necessary. I worked in corporate America for 20 years and the only way you get things done in the corporate world is learning to compromise. Corporate America could very accurately be called Babylon in so many ways. Just like Daniel, we need the wisdom of the cross so that we can get things done and many times that will mean compromising or finding middle ground.

Paul taught us that we live in this world, but we are not to live by the spirit of this world. Living by the spirit of the world is not finding middle ground to get things done. Living by the spirit of this world *is compromising the moral standards clearly laid out in the word of God and sexual sin is clearly shown to be against God.* Daniel lived in Babylon, but he did not bow to their idols. He did not compromise the clear moral standards of scripture.

I'm not saying we need a scripture for every decision we make or everything that we do. To think that way is simply religious and quite ridiculous. The Bible does not tell us everything about how to live this life, but it clearly says that God's will is that we abstain from sexual immorality (I Thess. 4:3-8).

Religion adds to the Bible like the Pharisees: we make up rules, ways of thinking and man-made standards. We say this is the way to live if you really want to know God and do what is right. Just follow our way because we've figured it all out. Jesus nor did the apostolic fathers leave us a 10-step program to follow on how to live this life of faith.

Jesus came to deal with our hearts. Remember he said, "out of the heart come evil thoughts, murder, adultery, sexual immorality, theft, false witness, slander. These are what defile a person. But to eat with unwashed hands does not defile anyone." Jesus went straight to the root of the problem which is worship because man has a vacuum in his heart that is going to be filled with something.

Paul in Romans chapter 1 hits us right in the heart and strikes right at the feet of our idols. The error described in Romans 1 is not the neglect of worship, but the exchange of worship. It's exchanging and rejecting the created order. It's rejecting the God who created male and female. To reject that order is to reject the God who created all things.

It's not an ideal you have to impose on others. Paul was writing to the church in Rome. It was a city where sexual immorality ran rampant and same sex relationships was an excepted norm. Paul wasn't calling on the government to impose restrictions; he was calling on believers to reject sexual idolatry. [134]Idolatry and sexual immorality are inseparably linked in Paul's argument.

If the worship of God is abandoned, the result is not a state of 'no worship', but of 'false worship'. Idolatry destroys human dignity and freedom, and it ushers people directly into the experience of the wrath of God. False worship results in ungodliness and God's active opposition against the suppression of the truth.

It's not my intent to fully deal with this text, but I want to bring

---

[134] Thomas Schreiner, Romans (NICNT), p. 92.

out a few things to help you understand that when you embrace the gospel of lawlessness then you make yourself an enemy of the cross. In Romans 1:25 it says when we do this, we: "exchange the truth about God for a lie and we worship, and we serve the creature rather than the Creator."

Understanding the Heart of Idolatry

A lot in the church have focused on same sex attraction as being the main point of this text in Romans chapter 1. In their inquisition against one specific form of idolatry they miss the idols in their own lives. It's what Jesus was saying when he said you are trying to take a splinter out of other people's eyes while you're blind to the idols of your own heart. Paul is not making an argument against one form of sin or type of lawless act. He is simply showing us that when we refuse to give God his rightful place in our hearts then our hearts are going to be filled with the spirit of lawlessness.

If you read the whole text, same sex attraction is just a small portion and only one of the many sins of the heart listed in Romans 1:28-32. Paul also lists envy, murder, strife, deceit, hatred, gossips, slanderers as some of the many lawless acts of those who are not loving God and loving others. All these sins show us that we are practicing lawlessness, living in the works of the flesh and in opposition to the Spirit. The list is very similar to the sins that Jesus said comes out of the heart defiling a person and Paul gave us in Galatians 5:19-21.

Sexual immorality is a form of worship and Paul equates it with idolatry. Worship goes to the heart of who we are being created in the image of God. Man was designed to be a dwelling place of the Creator with the imprint of his nature embedded upon our hearts. Our sexuality lies at the core of our hearts and sexual activity is one of the most intimate acts that we can do in this life.

Sexual idolatry makes fewer moral demands than God and promises us much more freedom. It's living a life with no restraints on our sexual desires and exchanging a focus to creation instead of our hearts focused on the Creator. Inner motivation and affections make their impact on outward attitudes and actions that come from the heart. The freedom that idols offer is in fact nothing other than slavery.

Peter said it this way in II Peter 2:19 that: "They promise them freedom, but they themselves are slaves of corruption. For whatever overcomes a person, to that he is enslaved." Paul said it this way in Romans 6:16 "Do you not know that if you present yourselves to anyone as obedient slaves, you are slaves of the one whom you obey, either of sin, which leads to death, or of obedience, which leads to righteousness?"

The Dangers of Putting Sex on Par with Basic Necessities in a Postmodern World

The body has the natural needs of food and water, or we die. Our postmodern world, just like service to ancient idols, has put sex on par with food and water as a necessity to live. To do that is to put sex in a place it was never intended. It's when we refuse to acknowledge God giving him his rightful place in our hearts that we become our own god. The result of being our own god leads to sexual immorality because we do whatever our lawless hearts want to do. It's a heart void of self-control. Practicing sexual immorality is a demonstration that we are not abiding in the Spirit because one of the fruits of the Spirit is self-control.

Sexual immorality is intertwined with the redemptive story from Genesis to Revelation because it's something we all face in varying ways. Rahab the harlot, Tamar who played the harlot, Bathsheba the bathing beauty, Jacob visited prostitutes, David committed adultery, and Solomon had a major problem with his sexuality. All of these individuals are a part of the lineage of Christ. To me that speaks to the reality that God knows our frailty regarding our sexuality, and he is interested in helping us find our way.

Sexuality is at the heart of being human. The body and sex are not evil, but our hearts if not dedicated to the cross and surrendered to the Spirit can be. The redemptive story and the very lineage of the Messiah is telling us something about a merciful God who understands our weakness. The same God who created all things is also a redeemer, our restorer and ultimately took upon himself human flesh to reconcile our hearts back to his covenant of love.

In Acts chapter 15 when discussing the issue of Gentiles living under the law of Moses an agreement was made. Acts 15:19 - 20 it says that: "we should not trouble those of the Gentiles who turn to God but should write to them to abstain from the things polluted by idols, and from sexual immorality and from what has been strangled, and from blood."

Paul confirms his stance on sexual immorality and goes so far as to say in 1 Thessalonians 4:3 - 5 that: "this is the will of God, your sanctification: that you abstain from sexual immorality; that each one of you know how to control his own body in holiness and honor, not in the passion of lust like the Gentiles who do not know God." Paul and the other apostolic authors are clear and uphold the moral standards of a sexuality that stands in stark contrast to the lax sexual appetites run wild in a society that has rejected God.

I've had to grapple, struggle and put my sexuality in its proper place in my life. The scriptures clearly teach us that one of the fruits of a life lived in union with Christ is self-control. I'm not going to tell you that it's without struggle. However, once you understand that's it's God's will to live your life free from sexual sin dominating your life, at that point you begin to surrender. It's only in totally dedicating your life to the cross and giving the members of your body to be governed by the Spirit that you can live in freedom.

Exploring Paul's First Letter to the Corinthians: Addressing Key Issues in the Church

Let's look at Paul's first letter to the Corinthians. Paul addressed **four main issues** in the church that was in the city of Corinth:

- **The first** one was that they had become too focused on the cult of personality which he addresses in chapters 1 through 4.
- **The second** one had to do with how to live sexually pure in an idolatrous society that gave license to sexual immorality in chapters 6 through 10.
- **The third** one was how to practice our faith in a way that promotes equality among all the members of the body no matter socioeconomic status or gender as discussed in chapter 12. Head coverings for wives in chapter 11 was a specific cultural context for Corinth and not a universal standard.
- **The fourth** issue he stressed was the need to practice our faith in a way that brings edification and structure while giving a place to the liberty of the Spirit in chapters 11 through 14. He ends in chapter 15 addressing the fundamental doctrine of resurrection from the dead.

I want to look at some of the things he says centered around idolatry and sexual immorality. Paul starts chapter 5 discussing a dysfunctional sexual situation in one of the families of this community. He tells them they need to address it because it is causing disruption. In addition, it's demonstrating an inaccurate representation of the redemption found in Christ to unbelievers.

Paul ends the chapter instructing us to not judge unbelievers for their sexual sin, greed, idolatry, drunkenness and dishonesty. At the same time, he tells us that we need to hold one another in the body of Christ accountable to the standard of living the cruciform life.

In chapter 6 Paul continues his discussion using similar terminology as he did to the Galatians. He tells us in 1 Corinthians in 6:9: "Do not be deceived: neither the sexually immoral, nor idolaters, nor adulterers, nor men who practice homosexuality" will inherit the kingdom of God. It's in chapter 10 where Paul continues his focus on sexual sin tying it in with worship and idolatry.

He opens chapter 10 using Israel being delivered from the power of this worldly system through the cross and our identification with the cruciform life being understood in the doctrine of baptisms. He then goes into a dialogue showing us examples of how we must not allow evil desires to overtake us, keeping us from fulfilling our journey of faith.

The Dangers of Indulging in Immorality

1 Corinthians 10:7-8 says: "Do not be idolaters as some of them were; as it is written, "The people sat down to eat and drink and rose up to play." We must not indulge in sexual immorality as some of them did." The term "play" here, as The Expositor's Bible Commentary brings out, means "drunken, immoral orgies and sexual play." They ate the food sacrificed to the golden calf and then many indulged in a sexual orgy in accordance with the pagan cult practices of Egypt. It's just one of many examples the New Testament gives us.

If you examine the Bible, you will see that food and sex are inextricably tied together. The book of Proverbs often draws a parallel between gluttony and sexual immorality, presenting both as manifestations of unrestrained desire (Prov 23:1–3; 23:20–21; 5:3–5). Bruce Waltke comments saying, "the sage portrays both overeating and sexual immorality as failures of disciplined desire."

Let's look at Abraham's oldest son Esau who sold his birthright to his brother Jacob for a bowl of lentil stew because he cared more for instant gratification than the promises of God. [135]Esau represents the person who exchanges enduring inheritance for momentary satisfaction. In Hebrews 12:16 when the author mentions this story, it is interesting how he comments about Esau and the context in which it was written. In mentioning him, the author then exhorts us to not be "sexually immoral or unholy like Esau, who sold his own birthright for a single meal". Illicit sexual activity is a pathway to spiritual darkness.

All sexual activity outside of the covenant of marriage between a man and woman is fornication. The Bible many times calls it sexual immorality which is an all-encompassing term. Jewish and early Christian sources consistently understood *porneia* to include all sexual relations outside of marriage. Sexual activity demands covenant responsibility because it's the way God designed it from the beginning.

The New Testament only speaks of one covenant made through the body and blood of Christ. It's to be our primary focus as those who have been purchased by his blood, sanctified through baptismal identification and empowered by his Spirit to live a life in union with him. [136]Christ's self-offering establishes the definitive covenant relationship between God and his people.

The Covenant of Marriage in the New Testament: Union with Christ Over Roles and Responsibilities

The New Testament speaks of marriage in the terms of a covenant although the actual word covenant is not used. It is however, clearly implied in Christ and Paul's usage of the imagery in comparing marriage between the husband and wife. Jesus in Matthew 19:4-5 uses the Genesis account to describe marriage between husband and wife saying they are no longer two but one flesh. He ends verse 6 saying "What therefore God has joined together, let not man separate."

Paul compares marriage to our union with Christ in Ephesians 5:31-32. Marriage is the husband and wife in union under Christ the

---

[135] David DeSilva, Perseverance in Gratitude, p. 469.
[136] Peter O'Brien, Hebrews, p. 322.

head. I lean stronger towards an egalitarian view of marriage since the original creation was not about an over/under, structure, but the union of the two becoming one.

The man and woman were in the garden both naked and were not ashamed. The sexual union between husband and wife is much more than just procreation, it's about intimacy. The design is Trinitarian. God, husband, wife = oneness. The mystery of marriage which Paul called it in Ephesians chapter 5 used the Genesis text and likened the union between husband and wife as a picture of Christ in union with his body.

To me the goal of a healthy marriage is two becoming one under Christ the head. The focus is union not roles and responsibilities. The Bible does not tell us that the wife is to rule the kitchen while the husband is to be served. It does not tell us that the husband is supposed to be the sole provider, and the wife is to be home raising children. A certain 1950's American culture tells us that. If that's how you want to live, I think that's fine, but don't tell me it's because the Bible teaches this idea.

The Bible does not teach this 1950's perfect idea of American culture and its simply an American myth. The Bible does not teach a wife cannot work outside of the home. Just because you are convicted of a certain way to live your life don't judge others if they don't hold to your personal convictions. The New Testament is about the freedom of the Spirit within the law of love. It's not about conformity to religious systems made by man.

Married couples should have the freedom and uniqueness to work out the details of how they are going to live in partnership with one another. To make people fit into some kind of clearly defined roles is what the Pharisees did, and it restricts the creativity of the Spirit in a couple's lives.

Marriage is not commanded in the Bible and it's not for everyone. Paul said marriage is a choice and if you choose that path then you are brought into a union with your spouse where Christ is to be the center. Paul said in I Corinthains 7:8-9 that: "it is good…to remain single, as I am". But if "you cannot exercise self-control," you "should marry. For it is better to marry than to burn with passion."

Paul taught that if you do choose to marry then it has its own set of problems. No one is supposed to live in the middle of marriage partners. No, not ministers, not fathers or mothers and not kids. No one, but Christ because he alone can help a couple finish the good work of being one flesh that he started in their relationship. To become one flesh is going to take two people laying down their lives for one another. The only way to truly do it is both following the command of Jesus to take up their crosses first and foremost following him.

The Significance of Fellowship in Christian Faith

If you look in I Corinthians chapter 10 as Paul discusses food, idolatry and sexual immorality he is communicating in terms of union. If you look at verses 14 - 33, he gets really clear on these subjects and shows us why it's so serious. Verses 14 - 21 Paul says: "my beloved, flee from idolatry. I speak as to sensible people; judge for yourselves what I say. The cup of blessing that we bless, is it not a participation in the blood of Christ?

The bread that we break, is it not a participation in the body of Christ? Because there is one bread, we who are many are one body, for we all partake of the one bread. Consider the people of Israel: are not those who eat the sacrifices participants in the altar? What do I imply then? That food offered to idols is anything, or that an idol is anything? No, I imply that what pagans sacrifice they offer to demons and not to God. I do not want you to be participants with demons. You cannot drink the cup of the Lord and the cup of demons. You cannot partake of the table of the Lord and the table of demons." There is no middle ground when it comes to sexual purity.

A lot of implications can be drawn from this text. The first one is fellowship because our faith was founded on the fellowship of Christ and one another. As believers we share together in the one sacrifice of Christ through his body and blood. We have been brought into union with Christ and by participation with the same altar we have been brought into union with one another. I think that's what John was talking about in his first epistle as he emphasized love and truth. John used different terminology than Paul, but he was saying the same things. All the apostolic writers gave us this exact same message which is you cannot be a friend of the world while saying you are in union with God. It's impossible!

Paul said in 1 Corinthians 6:12-13 that: "I will not be dominated by anything. "Food is meant for the stomach and the stomach for food"—and God will destroy both one and the other. The body is not meant for sexual immorality, but for the Lord, and the Lord for the body." He then once again puts sexuality in the context of worship, union and identification in verses 16 - 20. Sex is much more than a physical act. It's a spiritual one that penetrates not just the body, but the heart. [137]Sex is never merely physical; it creates a one-flesh relationship.

The Spiritual Impact of Sexual Sin

Paul is using this exact same imagery in I Corinthians chapter 6 warning us against sexual immorality because it does not bring us into the freedom of the Spirit, but the bondage of a flesh ruled life. Paul in verse 17 says: "he who is joined to the Lord becomes one spirit with him. Flee from sexual immorality. Every other sin a person commits is outside the body, but the sexually immoral person sins against his own body. Or do you not know that your body is a temple of the Holy Spirit within you, whom you have from God? You are not your own, for you were bought with a price. So glorify God in your body."

Sexual sin is about worship, and we cannot worship at the altar of sexual immorality while we say we are partaking of Christ. The only way to do that is to live in the false illusions of lies which is idolatry. Sexual sin opens your life up to spiritual darkness. The Bible equates sexual sin with idolatry which the Bible clearly articulates from the book of Genesis to Revelation.

Paul ends the book of I Corinthians talking about the resurrection of the dead. In this letter he addressed sexual dysfunction as one of its main emphases and then at the end finds it necessary to reestablish them in a clear understanding of the resurrection of Christ. What is Paul doing in ending his letter with the doctrine of resurrection from the dead? It seems to me that he is addressing the Gnostic idea that Jesus did not have a physical body and come in the flesh. It explains the attitude that the Corinthians had because they had devolved into a spirituality devoid of the message of the cross.

In I Corinthians 15:1 - 7 Paul takes us through the gospel story establishing the numerous eyewitnesses of Jesus being the first man raised from the dead as the basis of our faith and confession. In verse 17 - 19 he says: "if Christ has not been raised, your faith is futile and you

---

[137] Gordon D. Fee, The First Epistle to the Corinthians, p. 253.

are still in your sins. Then those also who have fallen asleep in Christ have perished. If in Christ we have hope in this life only, we are of all people most to be pitied." He basically says why do you even meet together? If Christ did not rise from the dead, then we are all just living a lie and therefore we should just live however we want to live.

Living by the Spirit vs. Embracing Lawlessness

Paul then makes a statement that I've had to ask myself many times on my journey of faith. If the dead are not raised, then why am I struggling against sin? Why am I taking up my cross daily and fighting this good fight of faith? Why don't I just live like the rest of the world who says: "Let us eat and drink, for tomorrow we die." The antichrist gospel of lawlessness is to live without restraint and self-control. The actual motto of Satanism is "do what thou wilt".

Do whatever you want and get the most out of this life. Eat and drink with no restraints because there are no consequences beyond this life. The spirit of antichrist says, "Jesus has paid for all our sins, and we live under grace not the law. We aren't religious, we are spiritual, and we live by the winds of the Spirit. We can fulfill the desires of our hearts because that's what really matters. We deserve the best in this life, and we should not be restricted by some outdated moral code. The Spirit doesn't restrict us. The Spirit gives us freedom to do what we want."

It's why foundations are so important because resurrection from the dead and eternal judgment tell us something completely different. It teaches what Paul taught us wrapping up his first epistle to the Corinthians that we will all appear before the judgement seat of Christ. It's why he says in I Corinthains 15:33 "Do not be deceived: 'Bad company ruins good morals.' Wake up from your drunken stupor, as is right, and do not go on sinning. For some have no knowledge of God. I say this to your shame." The Bible not only warns us over and over concerning sexual immorality, but it also clearly warns us against those who would promote a gospel of lawlessness. We are being deluged daily to worship at the altar of sex and to compromise what the Bible explicitly says to turn away from.

The power of Groupthink is a powerful force! It's the frog in the kettle that happens in the church as scripture is twisted, perverted and sexual immorality takes on an appearance of godliness. What word do you use other than apostasy when large segments of what used to be called the Christian church in America are now preaching a gospel of lawlessness? Oh, it's couched in the terms of inclusion, acceptance and the love of Christ. However, make no mistake Jesus along with all the other apostolic writers would call it sin, idolatry and a departure from the foundation of Christ.

If you do not take up the cross of Christ and put to death the deeds of sexual immorality you will not inherit the kingdom of God. I wish I could tell you there was middle ground. In my personal experience along with the testimony of scripture the only way to live for Christ is to eat of his flesh and drink of the blood of his covenant in total surrender. Jesus said except a seed falls into the ground and dies it remains alone.

He clearly told us in Matthew chapter 16 the same thing. Remember this is just after Peter's confession and Jesus establishing his *ekklēsia* or the body of Christ upon the clear understanding of who he is as the very foundation. He then says: "If anyone would come after me, let him deny himself and take up his cross and follow me. For whoever would save his life will lose it, but whoever loses his life for my sake will find it. For what will it profit a man if he gains the whole world and forfeits his soul?" We try to explain away the command of Christ to complete surrender our lives to him using Paul's message of grace. However, its adulterating Paul's message of grace and taking it out of context.

If you take the time to read all of Paul's teaching in context you will see that he is preaching the message of the cross in all his epistles. Paul in Romans was saying that to abandon God takes you on the descent into the dark abysses of idolatry and lawlessness. It's rejecting the God who created all things through the power of his word. It's rejecting his majesty displayed through his power, its majestic beauty and design clearly seen in creation. It's also rejecting the God who showed us his glory and holiness through the Mosaic law.

The Danger of Exchanging Truth for Lies

Paul in Romans chapter 1 speaks of those who exchange the truth of a God who created all things for a lie that you can find him through searching the futility of your own heart. The result is that you become your own god, doing whatever is right in your own eyes. However, there are those who take it a step further. You have those who are not just content with rejecting any moral standards, but they join with likeminded people to become suppressors of the truth and give approval to those who practice the works of the flesh.

We are not without moral standards. Paul in Romans 6:15 - 18 says: "Are we to sin because we are not under law but under grace? By no means! Do you not know that if you present yourselves to anyone as obedient slaves, you are slaves of the one whom you obey, either of sin, which leads to death, or of obedience, which leads to righteousness? But thanks be to God, that you who were once slaves of sin have become obedient from the heart to the standard of teaching to which you were committed and having been set free from sin, have become slaves of righteousness."

Grace is the free gift of Christ. Grace gives us the ability to live in the power of the Spirit free from the works of the flesh. Romans 8:2 - 4 says: "the law of the Spirit of life has set you free in Christ Jesus from the law of sin and death. For God has done what the law, weakened by the flesh, could not do. By sending his own Son in the likeness of sinful flesh and for sin, he condemned sin in the flesh, in order that the righteous requirement of the law might be fulfilled in us, who walk not according to the flesh but according to the Spirit."

John, Peter and Jude all spoke of the danger of allowing lawless attitudes towards sexual sin to dominate our lives. Jude wrote one of the smallest epistles in the New Testament, but it's packed with a punch striking right at the feet of the idolatry of lawlessness.

- Jude was contending for the faith, and he was contending against those who turned the grace of God into a free for all with no restrictions (Jude 1:4).
- Jude was saying what all the apostolic fathers clearly articulated which is to follow Christ then you must embrace the altar of the cross by denying yourself because there can be no compromise with sexual sin. To deny this truth is to deny that Jesus came in the flesh because you are denying the cross (Jude 1:5-8).
- Jude 1:11 - 13 is speaking about those who proclaim this gospel of lawlessness: "Woe to them! For they walked in **the way of Cain** and abandoned themselves for the sake of gain to **Balaam's error** and perished in **Korah's rebellion**. These are hidden reefs at your love feasts, as they feast with you without fear, shepherds feeding themselves; waterless clouds, swept along by winds; fruitless trees in

late autumn, twice dead, uprooted; wild waves of the sea, casting up the foam of their own shame; wandering stars, for whom the gloom of utter darkness has been reserved forever (emphasis mine)."

The way of Cain is rejecting the blood sacrifice of the cross and doing your own thing. It's being your own god and saying that you know better. Instead of bringing your sexuality to the cross it's embracing the freedom of postmodern sexuality that says, 'did God really say'? It's saying I will do whatever my heart tells me, but the problem is as Proverbs 14:12 says: "There is a way that seems right to a man, but its end is the ways of death."

Balaam was a man with a prophetic gift, but it was adulterated for profit and power. He became a false prophet when he became motivated by greed. Peter talked about those who entice unstable souls and adulterate the word of God promising them freedom while they themselves are slaves of corruption.

It's the false message of grace that says you have the freedom to live however you want to live. It's Gnostic spirituality that says believing in Jesus is enough. It's *gnōsis* that saves you and your personal conduct does not matter. It's a message that says Jesus wants you to be free to express yourself. You don't have to take up your cross that's religion, and we are free from religion.

Peter uses almost the same language in his second epistle and his added commentary brings additional insight. In 2 Peter 2:19 - 21 he says it's a false message that Jesus promises you freedom to get all you can get out of this life. Jesus never said be the best version of you. He never said do what's in your heart. He said repent, turn, surrender and lay down your life. Peter is confronting the false Gnostic teaching that says you can do what you want, if you say you follow Jesus.

Confessing Jesus came in the flesh is not just saying you have the *gnōsis* that Jesus is lord, but it's living a life that demonstrates that Jesus is Lord over your life. [138]Confession of Christ cannot be separated from obedience; true belief issues in righteous living. It's a life submitted to the cross not just a belief like James said the demons believe and tremble (James 2:19). It's a faith that is demonstrated by a changed inward life along with outward conduct because of surrendering to the power and wisdom of the cross.

---

[138] Colin Kruse, The Letters of John (PNTC), p. 146.

The gospel of lawlessness has consequences. Peter says: "whatever overcomes a person, to that he is enslaved. For if, after they have escaped the defilements of the world through the knowledge of our Lord and Savior Jesus Christ, they are again entangled in them and overcome, the last state has become worse for them than the first. For it would have been better for them never to have known the way of righteousness than after knowing it to turn back from the holy commandment delivered to them. What the true proverb says has happened to them: The dog returns to its own vomit, and the sow, after washing herself, returns to wallow in the mire."

No that's not legalism and religion, but it's the clear teaching of the New Testament. Peter was warning us to completely dedicate our lives to the message of the cross because there is no middle ground with the flesh. Greed and sexual immorality are always married together, but they have no place in the kingdom of God. If you give your heart to them then you make yourself an enemy of the cross. Jesus, Paul, John, Peter, Jude and James all said the same thing.

Korah's rebellion is about pride and rejecting Christ authority over your lives upon whom our faith is established. Jude and Peter are not using Korah as an example of those who oppose the apostle set over them, which is a false teaching or opposing any church authority. It's talking about rejecting the way of the cross and making yourself equal to Christ which is rejecting the authority of Christ to rule over our lives.

The Deception of Apostasy: A Warning from Paul

I want to remind you of Paul's words and what he said it would look like in the last days. He said you will see those who are: "lovers of pleasure rather than lovers of God, having the appearance of godliness, but denying its power. Avoid such people." Apostates can talk about God and some even appear to be godly. However, it's a different gospel. It's one made in the image of man where you become your own god enslaved to the wickedness of your heart. It's the gospel of lawlessness that allows you to live in your sin loving this world, but you have made yourself an enemy of the cross.

The wrath of God is a common theme in the New Testament. Did you know that? The New Testament opens with John the Baptist saying in Luke 3:7 - 8 as he spoke to the crowds coming to be baptized: "You brood of vipers! Who warned you to flee from the wrath to come?

Bear fruits in keeping with repentance." John talked about repentance and fruit. He did not say "all you have to do is think the right thoughts". Just follow steps 1, 2 and 3 so that you can prosper. He didn't give us 5 ways to command our angels. He didn't say look inside yourself to find the real you. He said look at your wicked heart, repent and turn away from wickedness.

Paul goes from Romans chapter 1:18 all the way through to Romans 3: 23 to show that the Jew who had the Mosaic law and the Gentile who had the natural creation that: "all have sinned and fall short of the glory of God." Paul leaves no man standing because it's the wickedness of man's heart that is the problem. The creation speaks of God's power and divine nature. The Mosaic law showed us God's moral standard. The book of Romans is taking us back to the Genesis story of man being made in the image of God and created to worship him.

God told man in Genesis chapter 2 to cultivate and keep the garden. The Hebrew word for cultivate is *abad*, and the Hebrew word for keep is *shamar*. These same Hebrew words are used to describe how the priest cared for the tabernacle of Moses. The tabernacle was a precursor to the temple of Solomon.

The priests were to cultivate and keep the tabernacle. In addition, we are told that God walked in the garden during the cool of the day. God also walked in the midst of the temple. The meaning is clear. The garden was a temple for God. Like the temple, the garden was the joining together of God's space and man's space - the intersection of the heavenly realm and the earthly realm.

The Crucial Role of Worship in Shaping Behavior

The human heart is made for worship and there is no such a thing as non-worship. [139]Humans are worshiping creatures. If they cease worshiping the true God, they do not stop worshiping; they substitute something else. The redemptive story from Genesis to Revelation reveals the decisions we all must make about whom we are going to worship. Embedded and hardwired into the heart of man is the desire to worship. The problem is many times instead of acknowledging God and giving him his rightful place in our hearts that we exchange the truth.

Instead of choosing the narrow path of the cruciform life found

[139] N.T. Wright, Paul and the Faithfulness of God, p. 754.

centered in Christ we chose a substitute. Modernity is much more subtle in its idolatry, but whether you realize it or not you are shaped by that which you worship. It's what you give your time, attention and money too. Jesus said the heart of man is like a well. It's our center. It's our core and what the heart is dedicated to is what our lives will display through our conduct. Inner motivation and affections make their impact on outward attitudes and actions.

Paul is unveiling the human heart to us in the book of Romans because the history of humanity whether Jew or Gentile is that we prefer to worship idols because they make fewer moral demands and promise much more freedom. It's worship at the altar of McGospel where you can have it your way. The testimony of scripture, history and our own personal lives should tell us that being our own god is an easy pathway, but it never has a good ending. Sin masquerades as freedom but always results in bondage.

You are promised freedom in the worship of sex, but it's bondage, pain and heartache. At the heart of the Sexual Revolution was the resurgence of Gnostic spirituality which has transformed America's views of sexuality. [140]The Sexual Revolution involved the collapse of sacred order and moral authority. Instead of sticking with the foundations of a Christ centered gospel parts of the church turned to deconstructionism. The deconstructionists found inspiration in reappraising Gnostic spirituality.

Deconstructionist Dilemma: Replacing the Foundations of the Faith with Special Spiritual *Gnōsis*

The deconstructionists have torn down what they saw as an oppressive heterosexual patriarchal system embedded in institutionalized Christian beliefs and practices. However, in their quest to modernize the church they threw out the very foundations upon which the faith is built. Instead of returning to the roots of our faith they replaced the message of the cross. It's been replaced with special spiritual *gnōsis* not bound by restrictions of any moral standards, immediately accessible and connected to the spiritual.

The Gnostic heresy supplants the truth and suppresses morality.

---

[140] Philip Rieff, The Triumph of the Therapeutic, p. 13.

It's because there is no vacuum of worship, only the exchange of worship. Once you *exchange your worship* and *embrace the lie*, you then defend that which you worship because it's now the god by which you find identity. [141]Human beings are created to reflect God, and what they worship they resemble, either for ruin or restoration.

The reaction to the tearing down of moralized Institutionalized Christianity is to invert it with a lawless form of Christianity. However, it's a Catch 22 because you cannot escape the futility, bondage and wrath found in the false worship of idolatry. Paul in Galatians 6:7-8 says: "Do not be deceived: God is not mocked, for whatever one sows, that will he also reap. For the one who sows to his own flesh will from the flesh reap corruption." It's not hard to look at the church and American society to see that the reaping has been costly.

The Wrath of God: A Present and Future Reality

Let's talk more about the wrath of God because it's both a present and future reality. The wrath of God as a present reality is first realized through the spiritual law of sowing and reaping. Just like a farmer is going to reap that which he sows, the scriptures clearly teach that if you sow to the flesh, you will reap corruption. The prosperity teachers make sowing and reaping all about money. The 29 times sowing and reaping is talked about in the New Testament only one has the context of giving money and that is found in II Corinthians chapter 9.

The book of Romans uses the word wrath 11 times. If you reject the loving God that sets boundaries speaking to us through the creation of his natural order and the Mosaic law. If you disregard worshiping him, but instead fill your heart's with idolatry the scriptures are clear that you will reap corruption. Corruption is what happens to our lives when we live them separate from the life of the Spirit. It's what happened to Adam and Eve when they partook of the tree of knowledge of good and evil. Death, corruption and the wrath of God.

The picture is that of a decomposing body where vultures begin to circle. [142]God's wrath is presently revealed in his handing the rebellious over to the consequences of their choices. You may not see the results quickly many times, but sin destroys lives. It destroys the

---

[141] G.K. Beale, We Become What We Worship, p. 16.
[142] Thomas Schreiner, Romans (BECNT), p. 93.

lives of those who practice lawlessness and the lives of others who may become the victims of lawless acts. Have you ever watched a life destroyed by Meth? It's a vivid picture of how fast a life can corrupt, fall apart and be destroyed by a flesh ruled life. It normally leaves a trail of carnage in its pathway, fracturing families and communities.

The gnostic heresy leads to destruction and confusion. Just think about the destructive behavior of transgenderism. To think that you can mutilate the body to release the true inner self as an act of free expression is confusion. It's the ultimate end of destroying the flesh to create a new you and statistics show that it never produces the soundness of mind for which is being sought.

The levels of mental health problems in American society should concern us all. I do think there are varying reasons for this deluge of mental health problems, but it is primarily a spiritual problem. Paul spoke of this in terms of the wrath of God. Yes, call me old fashioned, but I do believe that repentance and turning to the mercy of the cross is a major solution to the mental health problem. As I previously said I am not against Psychiatrist, Psychologist or Counselors, but the root of mental health problems is rooted in the curse of sin. The main part of the solution for the believer is found in the cross.

God's Wrath For Disobeying Civil Authorities

Paul also talked of the wrath of God being administered through the rule of law. I'm going to be addressing this more fully in the next chapter, but Romans chapter 13 Paul said those who uphold the law are: servants "of God, an avenger who carries out God's wrath on the wrongdoer." The government who administers laws for the protection and safety of citizens whether you like them or not the scriptures say they administer God's wrath.

Yes, until Christ rules as king over this earth injustice will be in all societies and we should peacefully support justice. However, if you choose to fight against the government then be prepared to receive the wrath of the government. No matter how righteous you feel your cause may be, the governing authorities could become a tool of God's wrath, and you may pay the price of jail time or death. It's the price you pay for breaking the law so be sure to count the cost.

The Wrath of God and a Coming Day of Judgment

The vast majority of scriptures concerning the wrath of God look forward to the final consummation of the 'day of the Lord'. [143]Paul's references to wrath regularly have a future orientation toward final judgment. History is barreling towards the second coming of Christ to this earth. It will be a day of great glory and great wrath combined when the ruling King of kings returns.

At the cross, the wrath of God was satisfied by the love of God. All of creation stopped to watch the lamb of God that stepped into time to be the propitiation of our sins. [144]Propitiation means the averting of wrath by the offering of a gift. Like a sponge he absorbed the wrath of God on our behalf. The cross is where mercy and judgment kiss together, but you cannot separate the mercy of God from the judgment of God, or you neuter the power of the cross. In our day we want to strip out the consequences for sin.

We would rather not talk about sin, wrath and judgment since all of that is outdated Old Testament stuff. A false picture of a Jesus who tolerates the practicing of sinful lifestyles has been presented. Jesus is the Pattern Son, and we are to follow in the pathway of his dedication to the Father's will. He did not just die for our sins, but he also set an example that we are to follow in our journey of faith.

Ephesians 5:6 says: "Let no one deceive you with empty words, for because of these things the wrath of God comes upon the sons of disobedience." Colossians chapter 3:5 - 6 says: "Put to death therefore what is earthly in you: sexual immorality, impurity, passion, evil desire, and covetousness, which is idolatry. On account of these the wrath of God is coming." [145]The wrath to come clearly refers to the final judgment at Christ's return.

In 1 Thessalonians 1:9 - 10 Paul said to them that: "you turned to God from idols to serve the living and true God and to wait for his Son from heaven, whom he raised from the dead, Jesus who delivers us from the wrath to come." Go open the book of Revelation and you will see

---

[143] Douglas J. Moo, Romans (NICNT), p. 168.
[144] Leon Morris, The Apostolic Preaching of the Cross, p. 144.
[145] Gene L. Green, The Letters to the Thessalonians, p. 95.

that wrath is mentioned 11 times. [146]Revelation intensifies the Old
Testament portrayal of divine wrath in the final judgment.

The Power of Propitiation: Mercy Triumphs Over Judgment in the Gospel

The gospel is that yes, the wrath of God is real. He judges sin
and lawlessness, but in Christ we are covered under the power of the
blood of the cross because mercy triumphs over judgment. Propitiation
is one of those words that is not very well known today, but it lies at the
heart of the gospel. It was central to the Mosaic law and lay at the heart
of the sacrifice system of worship.

Paul uses the word in Romans 3:25 in the context of saying: "all
have sinned and fall short of the glory of God and are justified by his
grace as a gift, through the redemption that is in Christ Jesus, whom God
put forward as a **propitiation by his blood**, to be received by faith
(emphasis mine)." The author of Hebrews uses the word once speaking
of Christ becoming a man in chapter 2 verse 17 saying: "he had to be
made like his brothers in every respect, so that he might become a
merciful and faithful high priest in the service of God, to **make
propitiation for the sins of the people** (emphasis mine)."

John in his first epistle uses the word two times. 1 John 2:1 - 2
he says: "My little children, I am writing these things to you so that you
may not sin. But if anyone does sin, we have an advocate with the
Father, Jesus Christ the righteous. He is the **propitiation for our sins**,
and not for ours only but also for the sins of the whole world (emphasis
mine)." He then uses the word in the context of loving one another.

1 John 4:10 - 12 he says: "In this is love, not that we have loved
God, but that he loved us and sent his Son to be **the propitiation for our
sins**. Beloved, if God so loved us, we also ought to love one another. No
one has ever seen God; if we love one another, God abides in us and his
love is perfected in us (emphasis mine)."

Propitiation is all about blood sacrifice. It is the story of
redemption from the fall where God stepped in covering the man and
woman. It's found in the life of Abel, Noah, Abraham and it was central
to the Mosaic law established on Mt. Sinai. As a matter of fact, the law

---

[146] G.K. Beale, The Book of Revelation, p. 392.

says without the shedding of blood there could be no remission of sins. It all pointed to the cross where mercy triumphs over judgment.

Yes, it's only the propitiation of Christ's blood that can deliver us from the wrath of God. It's why Jesus came, which is to give us freedom as a child of God to live in peace, reconciliation and the freedom of the Spirit. He wants us to be free from sexual dysfunction. Christ has come to help us through our pain and walk with us during our journey of faith. We just have to let him into the door of our hearts. The only unforgivable sin is rejecting the Holy Spirit's conviction bringing you into a place of true repentance falling upon the mercy of the cross.

Embracing the Father's Heart in a Broken Society

John in his epistle spoke in very contrasting terms, but he could easily be called the apostle of love. The two encounters in the New Testament showing us the Father's heart reaching into our sexual dysfunction were recorded in John's gospel. He wrote his gospel showing us that Jesus was God, but in so doing he presented to us the heart of our merciful Father. It's important as we walk through this fallen, broken and dysfunctional society regarding sexual immorality that we embrace the heart of the Father.

John was the only gospel that told us the story of the woman caught in adultery and the woman at the well. In both stories we have a temple, a mistreated woman, societal rejection and systems of injustice. A lot could be said about patriarchal systems, the subjection of women and sexual abuse that is inevitable in such systems.

John gave us these two stories to look at something and examine. I personally think he was showing us the merciful heart of the Father for those whose lives have been affected by systems of injustice and sexual dysfunction. The moral life that the New Testament clearly outlines is about freedom. The Father is trying to protect our lives from the inevitable destruction that sexual dysfunction brings into them.

The woman caught in adultery was not just caught having sex, but she was caught in an unjust system. We are left to assume a lot about this story, so the text gives us a little license to create the back story. It only tells us that the woman was caught in the very act of adultery. It does not say the woman was married.

As a patriarchal society this was most likely a married man and a young single woman. If it was a married woman, then where was the husband and the man committing adultery? According to the Mosaic law the husband should have been present if she was married. The Pharisees were trying to catch Jesus teaching against the Mosaic law. It seems they set this scenario up so it must have been a woman who could easily be manipulated and used for this occasion? She was a victim and probably already a rejected woman living on the outskirts of Jewish society.

The Pharisees bring the woman to the Temple where Jesus is teaching then sit her in the midst of the people. She is publicly shamed and then they misuse the Mosaic law. Leviticus 20:10 says: "If a man commits adultery with the wife of his neighbor, both the adulterer and the adulteress shall surely be put to death." The man, wife and husband of the wife would be present under the law so the judges could look at the evidence first and judge justly. It's not what was happening here. What's happening here is an abusive system unjustly using a woman of lower status and one who is clearly being taken advantage of by powerful men.

Jesus Cuts Right to the Heart:

- He is sitting in front of the Temple with men who worship power and use weak women.
- He's looking at a bunch of snakes who use religion as a weapon to abuse.
- He is looking at a bunch of men who have adulterated the very scriptures they claim to be protecting.
- He is looking at a woman caught and used as a pawn of the power grab of men with wicked hearts.
- He bends down to write in the sand.

A lot of speculation has been made about what he might have written. I heard one commentator speculate that he might have written what was recorded in Daniel 5:25 when the hand wrote on the wall: "Mene, Mene, Tekel, and Parsin." Translated as: "you have been weighed in the balances and found wanting."

- Jesus then looked up at the brood of vipers and said what Paul told us in Romans 3:23 that all have sinned, mess up and fall short.
- Jesus then turned the tables on their self-righteous religious abusive

leaders. He basically said look at yourselves because you all have sexual sin in your hearts.

- Jesus then looked at the woman and said bring forth the fruit of forgiveness and mercy.

We always need to have a heart of justice and restoration. Sexual dysfunctions affect us all and our society has been greatly damaged due to the false worship of sexuality. James in his epistle says it this way: "So speak and so act as those who are to be judged under the law of liberty. For judgment is without mercy to one who has shown no mercy. Mercy triumphs over judgment." Understanding our own weakness and frailty. Fully dependent on the power of the cross must be our merciful attitude in helping those who have been overcome with sexual sin.

John also told us the story of the Samaritan woman at the well. It's not just a story of worship, but it's also a story about sexuality and societal rejection. John shows us the heart of the New Covenant in this story and the redemption Jesus came to bring as God manifested in human flesh. It was Jesus the prophet getting to the root of the issue which realigns everything with the heart of the Father. I do a more detailed explanation of worship in my free online School Of Discipleship found in Lesson 27: The Place Of Worship.

The Samaritan's had exchanged their worship and suppressed the truth. Samaria had a history of idolatry. The Samaritan's did not outright reject the Mosaic law, but it was a syncretized form of Judaism. The Samaritans set up their own temple on Mt. Gerizim and had their own system of worship separate from Jerusalem.

The Transformative Power of Compassion in Worship

What you find in this story is that the woman at the well had been affected by a false system of worship and her own bad choices. The Jews had no association with the Samaritans and believed them to be an unclean accursed people. In the story we have Jesus a male Jew sitting at a well in Samaria at noon asking an outcast woman to give him a drink. I could go into a lot of detail about this story, but I want to focus on Jesus' compassion to this woman.

The woman at the well in Samaia was a low status Samaritan woman, and you couldn't get much lower than that. Jesus went out of his way to encounter this woman, so it wasn't just a happen chance encounter. To get water at midday meant that this woman was shunned by society. What we see in Jesus interaction with this woman is as a prophet who reads her heart. Now as all true prophetic ministry its purpose was to bring healing and restoration. The heart of the Father once again displayed through Jesus' life was to bring healing to those entangled in sexual dysfunction.

The story is not only a story about directing us to true worship from the heart, but how true worship is the pathway to the healing of sexual dysfunction. True worship bypasses geography, ethnicity and gender. Jesus reordered worship to the place of the heart because if he has your heart then he can heal your sexual dysfunction. The New Covenant is all about redemption and restoration. It's not the absence of God's judgement but it is that through the blood of the cross we can be covered with his love.

You cannot compromise with sin and lawlessness, but you can have compassion on the hurting. It's what Paul was saying when he said: "knowing the fear of the Lord, we persuade others." Jude said it this way: "keep yourselves in the love of God, waiting for the mercy of our Lord Jesus Christ that leads to eternal life. And have mercy on those who doubt; save others by snatching them out of the fire; to others show mercy with fear, hating even the garment stained by the flesh."

Our mission as the body of Christ is to be the broken bread and poured out wine showing compassion. It's only because of the propitiation of Christ blood where judgment and mercy kiss together.

The Transformative Power of Christ's Love

Paul in II Corinthians chapter 5 opens talking to us about resurrection from the dead and how we will one day stand before the judgment seat of Christ. We are free through the propitiation of Christ merciful blood from the wrath of God, but we will each stand giving an account of how we treat others. Paul continues saying in 2 Corinthians 5:14 - 15 that: "the love of Christ controls us, because we have concluded this: that one has died for all, therefore all have died; and he died for all, that those who live might no longer live for themselves but for him who for their sake died and was raised."

I pray that this will be your attitude towards a world that has been overtaken with idolatrous views of sexuality. Let us be those who worship in spirit and in truth with hearts full of the love of our Father.

Paul says in verses 17 - 21 that in Christ, we have been born of the Spirit and as new creations we are to display the love of the Father. "The old has passed away; behold, the new has come. All this is from God, who through Christ reconciled us to himself and gave us the ministry of reconciliation; that is, in Christ God was reconciling the world to himself, not counting their trespasses against them, and entrusting to us the message of reconciliation. Therefore, we are ambassadors for Christ, God making his appeal through us. We implore you on behalf of Christ, be reconciled to God. For our sake he made him to be sin who knew no sin, so that in him we might become the righteousness of God."

I can testify that there is hope, healing and restoration in the love of God. He is compassionate, loving and helps us through our struggles. He works in us both the will and the do of his good pleasure. We just have to surrender our lives daily to the cruciform way of living with Christ.

CHAPTER 9

CULTURE, POLITICS & THE KINGDOM OF GOD

Jesus answered, "My kingdom is not of this world. If my kingdom were of this world, my servants would have been fighting, that I might not be delivered over to the Jews. But my kingdom is not from the world."

~ John 18:36 ~

Politics and religion are two topics I was always told not to discuss when I was growing up. In today's America both subjects are polarizing and vitriolic to say the least. It's a very confusing subject and far too many in the pulpit are pushing a political agenda. I want to talk to you about politics and being a citizen of the kingdom of God in an evil world. It's important how we address this subject so that we stay focused on our mission as ambassadors of Christ and are not sidetracked into polarizing political issues.

It was in the spring of 1988, and I had recently come to faith in Christ getting delivered from drugs. AM radio was where you went to get alternative news and Christian teaching. I was tuning in and getting as much Bible teaching as I could. It was a smorgasbord of differing views.

I was 19 and didn't really know what I believed spiritually or politically. One political commentator that caught my ear and my attention was Rush Limbaugh. I was soon hooked, finding myself tuning in for 3 hours a day and five days a week. Yes, I became what they called a 'Ditto head'. Rush was my introduction to the ethos of the political right, and I was soon to be indoctrinated with the philosophical ideas birthed through the Reagan Revolution.

I was born in 1969 and very representative of Generation X. I grew up in a home that was not particularly political nor particularly religious. I grew up in Lancaster, TX, a suburb just south of Dallas TX. I had a mother who embraced the Civil Rights Movement and worked her way into the Management of one of the biggest Tobacco companies in the world. I had a father who was a Teamster truck driver but was not a Democrat nor particularly political. He voted for Ross Perot in the 1992 presidential election because as a truck driver he was witnessing firsthand the rapid decline of the middle class due to outsourcing of American manufacturing.

We were not rich, but comfortably upper Middle Class. Neither of my parents pursued degrees of higher learning, but both graduated high school and were the last generation to go to Jim Crow schools in the city of Dallas before racial integration. I can remember my mother and her friend starting their own Boy Scout pack and getting the poor kids along with Black ones to come join. It was not a welcome jester in the little town.

I grew up being taught by my mother to treat people of color and the poor with compassion. Both of my parents grew up with very little and both came from broken homes, so they were outcasts in the white religious culture of 1950's America.

I didn't understand it as a kid, but I remember spending the night with one of my black friends on the other side of the tracks. Yes, railroad tracks ran on the outskirts of our town and Blacks were not allowed to live on the other side of the tracks up until the late 1980's. I grew up watching the world around me change in a positive way due to the Civil Rights Movement taking root, but it took a long time. Sadly, it took laws put into place to give women and people of color their deserved place in our society.

As I mentioned we were not particularly religious, but my mother did see the importance of faith. As a kid we went to the First Baptist Downtown Dallas and my parents were married by W.A. Criswell. Once we moved to Lancaster we started attending the First Baptist Church there. I don't ever remember my father or brother going to church, but my mother regularly took me.

I have a few lasting memories of that time. I remember my mother bringing poor children to church. I remember her bringing one of her close black friends to the church and maybe the only person of color to ever attend a service up to that point. Needless to say, the deacons of the church did not like my mother, but she really didn't care, and the pastor supported my mother's heart towards the unfortunate.

1988 was the first election I could vote in, and I voted for George Bush Sr who easily won coming out of 8 years of the Reagan presidency. I was 19 years old and didn't know much, but Rush Limbaugh had convinced me that Bush was the better candidate. I soon found myself thrust into a culture war that had been brewing in the country since the Civil Rights Movement of the 1960's.

The Interplay of Faith and Politics in America: A Journey into the Religious Right

America has always combined faith with its politics. It's the bread and butter of the American way of life on both the left and right side of the aisle. I embraced the religious right and their brand of politics. It was presented to us in militaristic terms of a war against the evil Liberal forces that were trying to overtake the United States as a Christian nation. Pat Robertson, the founder of the 700 Club, was probably one of the most influential individuals in creating our current political situation.

Follow me on my journey because I soon found myself thrust right into the middle of the beginning of a movement that we are witnessing come into its fullness today. The 'Kingdom Now Movement' birthed the ideas of our current religious right, but it started as a fringe movement in the Charismatic church of the 1980's.

Let me take you on a little history lesson so you can see where it all came from because if you embrace it you are drinking from a poisonous well. The origins of the current religious right go back to the Presidential election of 1964 at the height of the Civil Rights Movement. John F. Kennedy was just assassinated, and the country was going through one of its greatest changes since the Civil War. The election was between Lyndon B. Johnson and Barry Goldwater.

I don't want to focus on Barry Goldwater. I want to focus on John Rushdoony who though not well known has left a legacy. Rushdoony was the brainchild behind what came to be called 'Christian Reconstructionism' in the 1980's and the Theological framework for what became known as the 'Kingdom Now Movement' transforming the Charismatic church.

Rushdoony cut his teeth as one of the main political organizers galvanizing support behind Barry Goldwater's run for the president against Lyndon B. Johnson. Rushdoony built a grassroots political organization in Southern California through the John Birch Society. Barry Goldwater went down in flames, but one of the most influential think tanks on the religious right, the Chalcedon Foundation, was born and founded in 1965 by Rushdoony as a result.

The Theocratic Vision of Rushdoony for America

John Rushdoony's parents fled the Armenian Genocide of 1915 in what is today Turkey, and he was primarily raised in California. His family converted to Presbyterianism and his father became a pastor of an Armenian Presbyterian church. He received a master's in education from the University of Berkeley and then graduated from the Pacific School of Religion in 1944. In a nutshell, Rushdoony saw his life's mission and calling to develop a framework to implement a Christian government subject to Biblical law in the United States.

John Rushdoony was an effective organizer, but he knew where the true power lay. True power lay in creating the ideas that could transform the institutions of power. Just as the Hippie counterculture movement dreamed of an America that could be free of the power of Institutional Christianity, Rushdoony started dreaming about bringing the American System completely under the control of Institutional Christianity.

The group of men he gathered such as Gary North, Greg L. Bahnsen and others began to publish articles and books in the 1970's espousing their ideas in a very scholarly manner. Rushdoony was a Postmillennialist, but he developed the theology out to its logical end. He simply concluded that if we have been called to rule the nations as the church, now in this age, then we must have a framework for implementing our ideas.

Rushdoony was intellectually honest believing that modern America was being taken over by the false religion of secularism and that the only path to salvation for America was to reconstruct the nation according to Biblical law. As a Calvinist he believed that American had a covenant with God primarily basing it on the Puritans, the Calvinistic sect that founded Plymouth Rock.

He was a man who saw no middle ground because to him it was all out war. He saw the political left as the incarnation of demonic activity. He argued that the Bible must govern every aspect of American life if we are to restore the greatness of America. It was a view that looked back to John Calvin in Geneva and the Puritans who have come to be known as the Pilgrims as attempts at establishing the kingdom of God on earth. Any honest observer can see that both experiments ended very poorly.

The Myth of Establishing God's Kingdom on Earth Prior to Christ Second Coming

The myth that man can establish the kingdom of God on earth using the state as its vehicle lived on in Rushdoony's heart till the day that he passed away. He was never completely embraced by his peers in the Evangelical church because his militant postmillennial dominion theology views carried out to their logical end would look more like 'The Handmaid's Tale' than the kingdom of God on earth.

Rushdoony never gained popularity, but his son in law Gary North who broke away establishing the Institute for Christian Economics in Tyler, TX was embraced by the political right. He was a brilliant Austrian Economist, which is a very anti-establishment Libertarian view of Economics. Ronald Reagan in his 1980 political campaign fully embraced the religious right in his pursuit of the presidency.

It was at the 1980 National Affairs Briefing Conference that was held in Dallas, TX where Ronald Reagan addressed around 15,000 attendees that included more than 2000 pastors. Gary North was one of the guest speakers along with Robert Billings who had worked in Jerry Falwell's Moral Majority Organization.

Pat Robertson and the political organization that he built the Christian Coalition was simply a watered-down form of Christian Reconstructionism. The last 30 years in America I've witnessed the forming of two polar opposite political movements. The Progressive religious left embodied in the Woke Revolution and the Religious right embodied in what has blossomed into the Patriot Movement. 2020 was the year that a religious war that had been brewing for over 30 years spilled out into the streets of America.

Pat Robertson ran a primary against George Bush Sr in the 1988 Republican primary. Pat did not fully embrace the theory of 'Christian Reconstructionism' as espoused by Gary North, but he was advised by him. Pat chose the milder form of Postmillennialism proposed by Francis Schaefer and others who influenced Ronald Reagan helping to form the political right. Pat failed to get the Republican nomination, but he successfully formed the Christian Coalition that swallowed the Moral Majority where the power of the Christian right shifted from Mainstream Evangelicalism to the Charismatic Mega churches that began to explode in the early 1990's.

Postmillennial views pair well with the doctrine of American prosperity and the doctrine of Manifest Destiny which is the belief that it is America's density to govern the nations. According to historian William Earl Weeks, there were three basic tenets behind the concept of Manifest Destiny.

- **Number one**: The assumption of the unique moral virtue of the United States based on its Judeo-Christian legal system.
- **Number two**: The assertion of its mission to redeem the world by the spread of republican government and more generally the 'American way of life'.
- **Number three**: Faith in the nation's divinely ordained destiny to succeed in this mission.

The 'Christian Reconstructionist' take it a step further in their idea that America has a special covenant with God and only if we obey his commands will we succeed as a nation. If not, then we will be judged like the nation of Israel. Yes, it is Replacement Theology on steroids.

The Rise of the 'Kingdom Now Movement'

I found myself in the middle of the start of the 'Kingdom Now Movement' when I was 20 years old. During Pat Robertson's primary campaign, he flew a private jet into the small town of Marshall, TX and did a campaign event with Randy Shankle the leader of what was then called The Church In Marshall.

Randy was part of the 'Kingdom Now Movement' and one of the leading figures on the Trinity Broadcast Network at that time. The best way to describe 'Kingdom Now' Theology was the merging of Rushdoony's Theocratic ideas with Charismatic spiritualism. It was a toxic brew, and I was about to get a good drink from it not really knowing what I had got myself into.

I didn't go to their discipleship school in East Texas until late 1989. I was told the story of how Randy had gone to a city council meeting around the time that Pat Robertson had come to visit. He got up in the meeting and told the city leaders that he was going to take over the city for God. He was extreme in his rhetoric and theology, but he wasn't violent. However, the city leaders were concerned enough that they called the FBI, and they did investigate the church.

Randy had the biggest church in the city, but the growth came from people moving there from all over the nation after hearing him on TV through the Trinity Broadcasting Network. At its height there were 1,000 church members in a town of 20,000. It had a daily discipleship school of 150 attendees and affiliated churches all over the nation. 3 times a year they would rent out the Marshall Convention Center in town. Pastors from all over the nation would attend and they would have guest speakers of the 'Kingdom Now Movement'.

Randy had a meteoric rise and just as big of a crash. His sin was not sexual immorality, but it was arrogance and pride that brought him down. I left in 1991 as his organization dissolved into a mess of 'authoritarian control' and spiritual abuse leaving many shattered lives in its wake. I escaped, but it took me many years to deconstruct and truly understand the experience I went through.

A Journey Of Faith and Discovery: From New York City to the Nations

I soon found my way to New York helping a group of pastors who went home to Long Island, New York to plant a church, but quickly found it was another version of what I had just left. I left after 3 months politely telling them what they were doing was not for me because I could see where it was headed. Yes, I found out later it was just another train wreck because authoritarianism was the foundation.

I was introduced to a group of church planters in Upstate New York in the Catskills Mountains where I moved. I became a youth pastor at the age of 23 in one of their churches and taught in a school of discipleship they had for 3 months every summer on a 100-acre old farm in the Catskills Mountains. It was a great experience and challenged my way of thinking. It moved me away from what I can only describe as an American centered gospel.

The leaders of this group New Life for All Nations were from England, South Africa and Australia. It was a small organization focused on discipleship, world missions and church planting. The vast majority of those involved in this organization were young men and women in our early 20's. One of the main appeals to me is that it was a nonauthoritarian style of ministry that gave us a lot of freedom. It was egalitarian in function viewing men and women as capable ministers of the New Covenant. We had a few churches in New York, but it was primarily focused on international ministry.

It was the first time I had ever looked at the Bible and my faith outside of the context of an American viewpoint. I was asked to go to England to teach in one of their schools of discipleship. Then go to South Africa and spend some time in Zambia with a church in Livingstone just north of the Zimbabwe border. I had no idea how much my views were going to be challenged on this adventure.

I spent 6 months in Zambia. It was both exhilarating and eye opening being one of the poorest African nations. I got to know the people and saw the sincere faith of people who lived sacrificially in the face of daily lack. I left on a train headed to South Africa giving away all the clothes I had with just enough in my backpack to get me to South Africa.

I arrived in Pretoria the capital of South Africa in 1994. It was just after the first elections after the ending of Apartheid. I was around Pentecostals who had come out of the Dutch Reformed Church. The Dutch Reformed Church was practically the White Afrikaner national identity. It used the Bible to support segregation and the Apartheid system.

The South African Apartheid system was very similar to how Southern Christian Democrats supported Jim Crow laws and the cultural power of segregation. Lincoln emancipated the slaves, but particularly in the South the Klu Klux Klan was used to intimidate Blacks from participation in the voting process. No matter what you think of Nelson Mandela or Martin Luther King Jr. it was their vision of a more just world that brought down the injustice of entrenched systematic racism.

I stayed at the home of a University Professor who was Afrikaans and a part of the bilateral negotiations transitioning the government from the all-White National Party to Nelson Mandela's African National Congress. He told me a lot of stories. International sanctions and embargoes brought the white ruling party to the negotiating table. However, he said it was only through prayer and the church helping the leaders see their need for repentance that kept the nation from an actual blood bath.

I went to Johannesburg and preached in one of their largest Townships which looked like a war zone. I grew up in South Dallas, but this was poverty and despair on a different level. I then went and spent time in Port Elizabeth on the coast and from there I traveled along the coast to Cape Town. I spent 3 months in South Africa, and I can only imagine it felt very much like Alabama in 1950. It was a different continent, but you could still feel the injustice of Apartheid in the nation. I then flew to England where we did a school of discipleship.

I arrived back in New York City and spent some time at a church plant we had done in College Point, Queens NY. Once summer arrived, I spent 3 months teaching at our summer school of discipleship in the Catskills Mountains. I met a Canadian girl who had come to school the summer of 1994 and we got married. We moved to Cambridge, Canada just an hour outside of Toronto. We started pastoring a small church and I was about to get another eye-opening experience.

Exploring Canada: A Journey of Learning and Perspective Shift

Canada was a historical learning experience for me. I knew very little about the people or government other than what I had heard from the political right concerning it being a socialist country. In the eyes of the political right, Canada was just cold, irrelevant and evil socialism. However, after spending almost, a year outside of the United States I had begun to have a different view of the world.

I was no longer seeing the world through the lens of what can only be described as the echo chamber of right-wing rhetoric. I began to realize the power of the media to shape my views. The radio and TV were no longer filling my mind with a certain way of framing the way I saw the world. In a Biblical sense the strongholds and thought patterns in my heart were being challenged with a different reality.

Canada is distinctly different from America. It was part of the British Commonwealth and did not become independent from the United Kingdom until 1982. It has more in common with Great Britain, Australia and South Africa. It's also a country that has been heavily influenced by the French because of the almost 8 million Francophone speakers. Montreal is considered the second largest French speaking city in the world next to Paris.

Just a short history lesson to help you understand the Province of Quebec. The city of Montreal is located along the Saint Lawrence River going up to Quebec City which is one of the oldest cities in North America. Quebec City was founded by French Huguenots who were

Protestants being influenced by John Calvin who was a Frenchman. A few attempts were made to create a French Protestant settlement at the mouth of the Saint Lawrence River, but a group of French Huguenots were finally successful in 1608 fleeing religious persecution in France.

The city of Quebec was founded and the main way to fund the new colony was through the fur trade. A successful fur trading enterprise was set up from the City of Montreal going up the Saint Lawrence River to Quebec City then out the mouth of the river back to Europe to sell their fur to the Aristocrats back in Europe. It was so successful that French Catholics came in and took over from the Protestants' endeavors with the authority of the king of France.

The French and the English have a long bloody history which spilled out into North America. England and France were at war in Europe. The English saw the presence of New France to the north of the American colonies as a threat. Europe was embroiled in what has come to be known as the 7-year war being led by England against France along with their allies. In 1759 the English forces combined with soldiers from the American colonies defeated the French in a battle called the Plains of Abraham taking the stronghold of Quebec City. At the end of the 7-year war in Europe France ceded New France to England officially so New France became an English colony.

It was the American Revolutionary war that set into motion the forming of what is today called Canada. Once the British were defeated, they retreated to what was then lower Canada along the Saint Lawrence River. At that time the Catholic Church had established itself as the authority in lower Canada over the French speaking population of around 70,000 people.

A long story short is that the English made a deal with the French Catholic Church and pretty much ceded lower Canada to the French Catholic Church as long as they could control the French population. The British established Ottawa as the capital just two hours north of Montreal and went West establishing Toronto around the Great Lakes.

The French population grew to around 5 million people in Quebec by the 1960's. It was due to the Catholic Church's influence upon the French to have as many children as possible. In addition, it was a very rural population that lived primarily on farms until modernization. It cannot be underestimated the power that the Catholic Church wielded over the people of Quebec.

Up until the Quiet Revolution of the 1960's the Catholic Church ruled the government, banking system, media, labor unions, healthcare, social services and the entire educational system. It was essentially a modern Theocratic state. Today if you go driving through the beautiful Province of Quebec you will see that every town is built around a Catholic Church that is literally the center of the town.

Today people from all over the world come to study the social transformation that happened in French Speaking Quebec literally overnight in what has come to be known as the Quiet Revolution. In the 1960's Quebec over a 10-year period transformed itself from a Theocratic state to a Socialist Democracy very similar to France with very little bloodshed.

One of their historians summed up the period quite poetically as he reflected upon that time. He said the French people of Quebec "threw the Catholic Church into the Saint Lawrence River and went on living life as if it never existed". Quebec today is still one of the least evangelized areas in all North and South America with no more than 1% considering themselves Evangelical.

Following the Spirit's Call: A Journey to Quebec

In 1996 my son was born in Canada, and I was pastoring a small church while I was finishing a Theology degree. As I was praying, I began to feel the leading of the Spirit to go to Quebec. At that time, I was married to my first wife who was raised in Ontario by French parents and went to French schools. We had met some couples from Quebec, and they began to talk to us about coming there.

Arriving in Canada during the summer of 1994 the media was on fire with hysteria about the upcoming vote of Quebec to succeed from Canada and form its own French nation. It would have literally split the country in half, so it was a big deal. I had never heard that level of panic and doom in the media. It was vitriolic to say the least. The only comparison would be the religious right's meltdown with the election of Bill Clinton in 1992 which was quite dramatic.

I would read the English newspapers, and they literally painted the separatist French leaders as Hitler and any newly formed French government as Nazis. You had no internet, talk radio in Canada did not exist and you only had two national newspapers. The referendum for separation happened on June 12, 1995. The proposal to separate from

Canada and setup an independent French nation was rejected by voters, with 50.58% voting "No" and 49.42% voting "Yes"

We moved to Montreal at the beginning of 1997. We did not plant a church in Quebec, but I worked with a few churches teaching what became my workbook, Building Your Spiritual House. I had one church translate the workbook into French which is still being used today. I also had a weekly radio program that was broadcast out of Plattsburgh, NY just one hour south of Montreal.

As I got to know the people of Quebec the picture painted by the English media was totally distorted. It was fiction and a complete aberration of the truth.

The Power of Culture Upon Our Political Views

I told this series of stories because this was my journey of being transformed in my political thinking and how I viewed the Bible regarding how politics should affect us. [147]All of us read Scriptures from within a cultural context that shapes what we see. I saw the enormous power of culture and how it affects us more than any of us really realize. The culture in which we live can greatly affect how we view the world, which can affect how we treat others. It took Paul having a Damascus Road experience and Peter's vision to challenge their hard ingrained cultural bias against Gentiles.

Jesus said that at the end of the age lawlessness would abound causing the hearts of many to grow cold and quenching the love of God from our hearts. [148]Wickedness produces a chilling effect on genuine love. Cultural, ethnic and political bias can cause you to act contrary to the love of Christ. Yes, even believers can be caught up in their power causing them become enemies of the cross of Christ.

Have you ever watched 'Hotel Rwanda'? It is an extreme picture and is a window to see where political rhetoric which demonizes the other side can lead to unthinkable chaos. Totalitarian propaganda works by dehumanizing opponents. Study history and the rise in totalitarian societies. If you look at political opponents as vermin, trash and demons then the only alternative is to destroy them. Dehumanizing

---

[147] Bartholomew and Goheen, The Drama of Scripture, p. 20.
[148] D.A. Carson, Matthew (EBC), p. 507.

language precedes violence. [149]The language of extermination always prepares the ground for wicked behavior against the other.

Go look at the history of our own Civil War and you will see the North and the South using the Bible to justify killing the other side. The Civil Rights Movement was a very religious movement with both sides using the Bible to justify their positions. [150]The Civil War was a theological crisis because the Bible was used to support both sides. Healthy societies, communities, businesses, families and churches must have the ability to communicate. If the church is to be the pillar and foundation of truth, then we must possess the wisdom to communicate in a civil rational way. [151]Truth must be communicated in a way consistent with Christ's love.

Spiritual Warfare: Breaking Strongholds Through The Power of Truth and Love

If you look at Paul when speaking in II Corinthians 10:3-5 he says: "though we walk in the flesh, we are not waging war according to the flesh. For the weapons of our warfare are not of the flesh but have divine power to destroy strongholds. We destroy arguments and every lofty opinion raised against the knowledge of God and take every thought captive to obey Christ." [152]The battleground is ideological; the weapons are truth and proclamation.

A stronghold is a wall in our hearts and minds. In the context of this scripture Paul was talking about false apostles who had taken the Corinthians captive with false ideas. False ideas that had led them away from a simple devotion to love Christ with all their hearts and loving others because Paul opens chapter 11 saying exactly that. The stronghold of political extremism is a powerful weapon especially when hysteria, panic and fear are combined.

What is our primary role as believers? Our primary role is to be an ambassador for Christ. We are sons and daughters who represent the king of heaven. The king we serve is a humble servant who laid his life

---

[149] Alison Des Forges, Leave None to Tell the Story, p. 67.
[150] Mark Noll, The Civil War as a Theological Crisis, p. 8.
[151] Andrew Lincoln, Ephesians (WBC), p. 261.
[152] 2 Corinthians (NICNT), p. 466.

down. He overcame death itself and his motivation was love. We must always stay rooted in love because love casts out fear. Fear confuses, distorts our perception and is the motivational power of the kingdom of darkness.

We are called to follow the way of the cross. In the exact same conversation that Jesus had with Pilate where he was asked, 'What is truth?' Jesus said this statement and it is only found in John's gospel 18:36, "My kingdom is not of this world. If my kingdom were of this world, my servants would have been fighting, that I might not be delivered over to the Jews. But my kingdom is not from the world." We are sojourners in this present evil age and our responsibility is to live by the Spirit of the age to come.

Abiding in the truth of the kingdom of God found in the person of Christ and seeking peace above all else is how you fulfill the mandate of being an ambassador for Christ. Romans chapter 12:17-18 says: "Repay no one evil for evil but give thought to do what is honorable in the sight of all. If possible, so far as it depends on you, live peaceably with all." If you read the whole context, it's teaching us something very similar to what Jesus taught us in the famous Sermon On The Mount.

We are called as believers to live by a higher law than the law of Moses or the law of Caesar. We are called to live by the law of the Spirit of life found in Christ. It's not an option, but it's the nature and fruit that should be displayed through the lives of those who are born of the coming age of peace when our King sets his feet upon the Mt. of Olives.

Paul helps us to understand in Galatians 3:26-28 that ethnic, social, cultural, and hierarchical views are not to separate us. He says that those who have identified with the cross of Christ through baptism being found in him: "are all sons of God, through faith. For as many of you as were baptized into Christ have put on Christ. There is neither Jew nor Greek, there is neither slave nor free, there is no male and female, for you are all one in Christ Jesus."

If we are to be salt and light in this present age, then we must understand our mission is to live by the power of the Holy Spirit which is the only way to walk in the love of the Father. The glory of God only rests upon the nature of the lamb. Jesus is our leader, and he said just as he came to serve our lives are to exemplify his heart of serving. We are not like the nations who live by the power of the beast fighting, killing and destroying.

Our purpose in this age before Jesus returns is to live as harmless lambs lying down our lives and motivated by love. It is living the cruciform life and allowing the Spirit to live his life through us. The kingdom of God is not the meat and drink of this evil age (Romans 14:17). It's not political activism that makes you angry, drunk with the pride of self-righteousness and causing you to display character traits totally contradictory to the cross. The kingdom of God is righteousness, peace and joy in the Holy Spirit. Disciples preserve society by distinctly righteous living.

The Destructive Power of Political Extremism: Fear, Myths, and Hatred

If you become a servant of right-wing extremism or a servant of left-wing political extremism, you become an enemy of the cross. Political extremism is built on myths, distortions of truth and hatred. The greatest power and the most effective motivator in politics is fear. History shows us that if you can mix fear with religion then you can get groups of people to do the unthinkable.

One of the most concerning things for me in America is how both sides of the political aisle mix politics with religion. It is an American thing, and we have a long historical tradition dating back to our founding. I don't agree with a lot of Karl Marx theories, but I do agree with one of his most famous quotes: "Religion is the opiate of the masses."

Right wing religion or left-wing religion are powerful tools in the hands of demagogue's grasping for control and using fear of 'the other' as the motivating factor. It is giving allegiance to systems and making politics the center of our life's struggles.

We are being faced with some of the most extreme political viewpoints on the left and right that I've ever witnessed in America. The question I am asking is a simple one. Are we willing to sacrifice the church's mandate to be a pillar of truth for political gain? Jesus left the church with a clear mission, and we cannot let the idolatry of politics push us into the ditches of left wing or right-wing extremism. I think most Americans have a form of Stockholm syndrome with American politics in our two-party system. A lot of us don't like the Democrats or Republicans but feel like political captives in what has become a blood sport.

Political Discourse in the Era of Echo Chambers

I'm concerned that we live in the echo chambers of the far left and far right. The result is that we are only hearing one extreme point of view being reinforced by a chorus of similar points of view. The internet has opened many avenues of information, but many times people are eating a buffet of ideas that reinforce what they already think.

It's easy to listen to those with whom you agree. The challenge is to be humble enough to listen to someone you disagree with and that is what made America a great nation, which was our diversity of ideas along with a willingness to find the best solution. Political discourse means compromise and that's what living in a civil society means.

Paul talked to us about strongholds. Cultural and political strongholds are some of the most powerful forces regarding the collective human experience. I'm very concerned for the soul of America because we are at a point in our history where the middle ground seems to have been swept away.

John in the book of Revelation talks about the ultimate stronghold in what he calls the image of the beast which demands our complete worship. Revelation 13:16-18 says that the beast: "causes all, both small and great, both rich and poor, both free and slave, to be marked on the right hand or the forehead, so that no one can buy or sell unless he has the mark, that is, the name of the beast or the number of its name. This calls for wisdom: let the one who has understanding calculate the number of the beast, for it is the number of a man, and his number is 666." [153]The mark signifies loyalty expressed in thought and deed.

People have chosen numerous rabbit holes to follow attempting to discover the true meaning of 666. You have those who have swallowed the red pill taking them into the mystical world of personal interpretation concerning these texts trying to determine who this person could be coming up with some wild speculations. The Greek word for mark is *charagma* and it means a stamp, or an imprinted mark stamped on the forehead or right-hand showing ownership. Its primary usage is found in the book of Revelation. Revelation 14:9, 11; 15:2, 16:2, 19:20 and 20:4.

We also see the word used by Paul as quoted in his sermon to the

---

[153] Craig Koester, Revelation, (Anchor Yale), p. 573.

Athenians on Mars Hill in Acts 17:29 as he confronted their idolatrous worship. I think it is safe to say that the mark of the beast on the forehead is symbolic of lives being dedicated to the beast and a mark upon the hand symbolizes putting into practice the agenda of the beast.

John's audience would have understood what the mark was because it was something they saw daily. [154]John's reference to the mark placed upon the back of the hand or the forehead makes perfect sense because in the first century the practice of branding or tattooing slaves with a mark was common practice. It's like cattle ranchers who brand their cattle because it identifies who owns them.

The Romans were a pluralistic society and any land they conquered they would bring conquered slaves back to Rome where they would allow them to continue to worship their gods. John's comments about the mark of the beast should be seen against the backdrop of the imperial cult and the worship of the Roman emperor. The book of [155]Revelation is a sustained critique of the Roman imperial cult.

You could worship any god your heart desired, as long as you bowed to the Roman state and pledge your life to serve it. [156]The beast symbolizes Roman imperial power, and Rome was a beast as are all human governments essentially. The purpose of the *ekklēsia* in this present evil age is to be salt and light while praying to live a peaceful life. It's clearly what the apostolic fathers taught concerning our place in this evil age.

The ultimate god of Rome was the power of the state and anything that got in the way of the beast was annihilated. 6 is the number of man and 666 is the number of men in the fullness of his rebellion against the God of heaven and he becomes nothing more than a ravenous beast devouring. Caesar was merely a symbol of Rome's power, and the cult of Caesar was the closest thing they had to a state religion. It's the picture John paints in the book of Revelation either worship the beast or become food for the beast. [157]Economic exclusion was one pressure faced by those who refused participation.

If a tattoo or computer chip is something forced upon humanity to be a part of the beast system is yet to be seen. The mark is not the

---

[154] Jennifer Glancy, Slavery in Early Christianity, p. 31.
[155] Richard Bauckham, The Theology of the Book of Revelation, p. 35.
[156] Adela Yarbro Collins, Crisis and Catharsis, p. 69.
[157] Craig Koester, Revelation, (Anchor Yale), p. 571.

issue! The issue would be that you have dedicated your life to the beast instead of dedicating your lives to the cross of Christ. If a mark is ever forced upon humanity trust me, you will not have to question what you are doing because you will have to deny Christ or be willing to pay the price of death. The book of Revelation is a book about the conquering Christ, but it's also a book that is clearly about martyrdom.

The scriptures say that Jesus came in the fullness of times. His first coming was at the right time in history and his return will also be. Rome was a mighty power at the time of Christ and provided an avenue for the rapid expansion of the gospel. Revelation does not mention America, and some would argue it's because we are just an extension of Rome. Others argue that we are part of the 10 lost tribes of Israel which is a far-right ideology of white supremacy.

I prefer not to get into endless speculations or outright venomous ideologies, but I think it's safe to look at the comparisons of the ending of Rome to America's current state of affairs. The demise of America has plenty of blame to go around. I think complacency, comfort and decadence is our undoing just like those who ate their last meal on the Titanic as it was sinking. Let's just look at a few keys reasons for Rome's decline comparing it to America's current state of affairs:

- **Endless wars**: I was born in 1969 and I've never known the United States not to be either in open war, supporting a war, talking of war or the CIA infiltrating and overthrowing foreign governments.
- **Domestic Spending on Welfare Programs**: Until 1914, our government spent less than 5% of gross domestic product. Today, it's almost 40%.
- **Debt**: Go ahead google 'Debt Clock'. At present it's 100% of GDP not including unfunded liabilities like Medicare, Social Security, and other domestic spending. At present we will soon be just paying off the interest on our debt. The debt bomb is coming, and it is going to affect us all.
- **Wealth Inequality**: At the end of the Roman Empire the top 1% of its population controlled over 16% of its wealth. In today's America the top 1% control 40% of its wealth.
- **Mass Immigration**: A problem that has been exasperated recently, but not a new problem. I do agree that a nation without a border is chaotic and unsustainable, but any honest observer over the last 40

years can see this has been a bipartisan affair.

- **Internal Conflict**: Government corruption led to internal conflicts where the masses lost trust in the elites who became self-serving. Conspiracy, distrust and mob rule took over society. Law and order which created the Pax Romana or Roman Peace was replaced by internal chaos. America is facing a very similar situation.

I've spent my life watching history happen before my eyes. I do think we are watching the end of the American Empire and as believers in the kingdom of God that cannot be shaken; we must begin to ask ourselves some questions. The main question we must ask is 'who is this Jesus that we serve?' Is he the American god of the left Progressive Woke ideology or is he the American god of the right Patriotic ideology?

Groupthink is a powerful force especially when combined with culture, heritage and religious ideas. Times of societal upheaval or rapid social change tend to generate new political and religious movements. America is going through one of the most rapid paces of change it's ever experienced. If you thought you saw religious cults during the Hippie Movement, well hold on to your hat, because it will pale in comparison to what we are going to witness if America truly unravels. Conspiracy beliefs flourish in times of rapid social change and perceived crisis.

Guarding Against Authoritarianism

The church is supposed to be the pillar and ground of the truth so we cannot get caught up in the hysteria of the moment. American culture is primed to see leaders in the church and government seeking authoritarian power. It's leaders who promise to provide their followers with a sense of having special knowledge and of being members of a vanguard of "chosen ones" who will return the church or society to a lost golden age of virtue and plenty.

Critical thinking skills and being sober minded are always important, but especially in turbulent times. It's why I stress the importance of sound doctrine and foundations. Staying with the basics keeps you grounded when everything is in turmoil. Sound doctrine produces sound living and as believers we should be the most stable people because we are founded on the rock and tethered to the cross.

False ideology is built on myths, partial truth and at times just outright speculation. Conspiracy theories run rampant in times of crisis and false leaders take advantage of the instability. The New Testament does not tell us a lot of things about economics, law and social sciences. It simply does not tell us what type of civil government we should seek. Jesus, Paul nor any other New Testament author argues for any particular form of government. The New Testament simply tells us to submit to the civil authorities. Peter

Arguments have been made for socialism using the Bible and arguments have been made for capitalism using the Bible. Truth be told you can find some arguments for both to some degree, but nothing definitive. However, the reality of this present age is that society needs some form of human government. Laws and a legal system built on justice protecting the innocent are the foundation of any functioning society. Peter in 1 Peter 2:13–17 and Paul in Romans 13:1-3 urges submission within existing structures, not revolution against them.

Man was not created to live in isolation, but in community. As a result of our collective gathering together, we need a system of common rules and enforcement mechanisms to make sure those rules are being followed. It's the only way you have an orderly society, and the community does not dissolve into chaos. Aristotle who lived some 380 years before Christ, said collective life necessitates a constitution or a mechanism of rules, regulations and leadership to enforce those rules for the governing of society.

Approximately 1100 years before Aristotle God brought the children of Abraham out of Egypt, so he could take them to the land promised to Abraham. However, to get to the Promised Land they had to pass through the wilderness of Sinai. Exodus 19 shows us that it was here on Mt. Sinai that Moses was given the law of God to govern the nation of Israel in the Promised Land. Before we go on, I want to do a little detour and take a quick look at comparing the establishment of the American constitution with the Mosaic law.

Comparing Origins: The Mosaic Law vs. The United States Constitution

Unlike the law given to Moses on Mt. Sinai, the United States constitution was written by several different authors and debated among 55 delegates at the Continental Congress. It was then ratified by 39 signers. The U.S. Constitution was debated among men. The law given to Moses came directly from God on Mt. Sinai to one man. There was no debate, it was God's direct communication to Moses, face to face. The U.S. Constitution was debated among the delegates for several months then ratified in 1788 and it has been the law that has ruled the United States since that time.

The U.S. Constitution is for America not for Canada, not for France, not for Brazil or any other nation since it directly relates to the governing of the United States. So, the U.S. Constitution was written to directly govern the United States, in like manner the law given to Moses was a constitution to govern the newly formed nation of Israel.

Unlike the constitution of the United States, the law given to Moses was ratified with a blood covenant, between the children of Israel and God. Exodus 24:7 - 8 says, "Moses took the Book of the Covenant and read it in the hearing of the people. And they said, all that the Lord has spoken we will do and we will be obedient. And Moses took the blood and threw it on the people and said, behold the blood of the covenant that the Lord has made with you in accordance with all these words."

The Mosaic law was given to Israel specifically and exclusively to govern them as a nation. It was a covenant instructing them how to regulate their lives living in a Theocracy, which is a government ruled by God. It regulated how to legislate their legal system, their social way of life and it was instruction on how to worship the God of Abraham, Issac and Jacob. It was Israel's system of common rules and enforcement mechanisms to make sure those rules were being followed.

It was some 2,000 years after Aristotle's time, that America's founders were searching for the best constitution. America was in many ways quite different from Aristotle's Greece. For one thing, the 13 American states were a lot bigger than any of the Greek city-states. Still, the framers at Philadelphia understood Aristotle's political ideas and passed many of them on to us in the document they created called the American Constitution. Contrary to what is taught in many Christian circles, it was the ideas of the Greeks and Romans that had the greatest impact upon the founders' thinking.

It wasn't the Torah that inspired the formulation of our Bill of Rights and the American Constitution. It was the influence of the Enlightenment period affected by a renaissance of Greek and Roman ideas on how to govern societies. [158]The Constitution was more a product of eighteenth-century political science than of Biblical law. [159]The Founders were steeped in the classical tradition…Rome in particular provided models of republican virtue. Among these ideas are the belief in the rule of law, equality, moderation, freedom of speech, freedom of religion, property rights and a government that serves the common interest of all citizens.

As an American I am speaking from an American perspective when it comes to civil authority, because my audience is primarily American. However, as a believer in Christ I'm going to integrate how we should live out our faith under any government. In a day when anarchy seems to be the rule, as members of the royal priesthood we need to understand the role of human governments. It's in Romans chapter 13:1 where we can clearly see that God has ordained human governments as an extension of His rule. We are told to obey the civil authority and if we don't then we can experience God's wrath which is the consequences of disobeying.

The natural tendency we have is to take the easy way out and live anyway we want to live. However, we are not an exception to the rule. There are laws in our cities, laws of our state and laws that come from the federal government. Now as believers in Christ, we are to be ruled by the Spirit of God and our lives are to be governed by him first of all. However, we also live in this world and are subject to the civil laws of the land.

As we look at the Bible as our guide and lens by which we view the world, we have to understand this one truth. The Bible does not tell us everything about world history nor does it tell us everything about how to live life. The Bible is history, but it's telling us the story of God's redemptive history in time. It's God's love story to humanity showing us His redemptive hand through the Hebrew people, his chosen vehicle to redeem a fallen humanity bringing us back to Himself.

The Myth of America as a Christian Nation

Today we are seeing a faction within the Evangelical church gain traction that resembles the Zealots of Jesus day. I will identify them as

---

[158] Gordon S. Wood, The Creation of the American Republic, p. 593.
[159] Carl J. Richard, The Founders and the Classics, p. 3.

the Patriot church and some within that group are Christian nationalist. Spurring the Patriot church and Christian nationalist movement is the idea that America has a special covenant with God.

It's not a new idea but has gained a lot of popularity in recent years. The basic idea is that the founders set up America to be a Christian nation and made a covenant with God. It is a view that sees America almost on the same level as Israel, as both having a covenant with God. The group is becoming more militant in their rhetoric. I go on record as disagreeing with these views. I know good people who hold these views, so I am not going to disparage them, but briefly describe why I disagree:

- **Number one God chose Israel**, separated them from all the peoples of the earth through blood covenant and gave them the words of God. He chose them to be his special possession to bring redemption to the earth.

- **Number two God did not choose America**, that's just a fact. The Puritans did dedicate this land to God when they landed, but that's not a covenant, it's simply not and to make it one is simply a myth. Paul told us not to follow myths and the idea that America has a covenant with God is a myth.

- **Number three America was not set up to be a Christian nation.** It is the agenda of the Christian right to perpetuate this myth that America has a covenant with God. We are compared to Israel and told we need to fight to protect that heritage. The purpose is to use the church for political power and it's not the kingdom of God no matter how religious the terminology is cloaked in.

- **Number four is that the Bill of Rights and Constitution are not based on the Bible**, but Enlightenment ideas along with Greek and Roman influences. I totally agree with the Bill of Rights, freedom of speech, freedom of assembly and the right to petition the government is great. However, freedom of speech is not a Biblical idea.

Go study your Bible. The Bible says we can't say anything we want to say. The Bible tells us to bridle our tongues because it can be a source of evil. How about Bill of right number two which is the right to bear arms. [160]The American right to bear arms emerged from English constitutional history, not from a Biblical mandate. It's not in the Bible. I agree with the right to bear arms regarding self-defense, but I can't find the idea in the Bible. It's an American idea, but let's not call it a Biblical idea.

The founders were not all Christians. You did have Christians, but you also had Deists and Freemasons to name just a few of the pluralistic religious ideas of our founders. It's well documented that George Washington, Benjamin Franklin, and John Hancock were all Freemasons. Now let me be clear that Freemasonry and Deism are incompatible to Christianity. It's like mixing oil and water. It just doesn't mix and if you do mix them, it's called heresy.

I'm not disparaging many of the founders of America. I'm just making the point that I don't see evidence they wanted to set up a Christian nation because many of them were not Christians. Yes, many were religious viewing church attendance as a good way to learn morality, ethics and good citizenship. The founders saw religion as a good mechanism to support a free society, but most of them did not even believe in the Deity of Christ.

The founders wanted freedom of religion. Freedom to practice the faith of your choice without being persecuted by the government. The founders saw the fallacy of a state church like England because they had lived under the tyranny of a king anointed by the church. The founders were very familiar with what happened during the Dark Ages through the Catholic Church. It's clear the founders did not want a government ruled by the church because throughout the history of man ecclesiastical rule always ended in tyranny. The founders wanted the freedom of its people to worship with liberty and free from government influence.

The Progressive Church: A Modern Reflection of the Sadducees

Let's look at the next group in the American church which is what I will call the Progressive church. It aligns itself with left leaning

---

[160] John Witte Jr., Religion and the American Constitutional Experiment, p. 105.

politics and closely resembles the Sadducees party of Jesus day. The Progressive church identifies with such political issues as the environment, social justice issues, LBGTQ rights and pro-abortion to name a few. The Progressives church embraces a Liberal Social Gospel. It's not a new thing. It's been around since our founding, but it solidified itself as part of the American system in the early 1900's.

The American president Woodrow Wilson embraced its teachings and implemented the ideas into the Ivy League Universities and U.S. Governmental institutions. After Wilson's Social Gospel presidency, mainline Protestants and much of American Catholicism got on board to change American culture with the power of religion. It was the Progressive vision of using the Church and religion aligned with the U.S. Government as the principal force for good in American Society. It was where we got such policies as the New Deal under Roosevelt and The Great Society of Johnson's administration.

The Social Gospel, Progressive movement or whatever you want to call it. It resembles the doctrine of the Sadducees who simply used religion for political power. It's the gospel of lawlessness I talked about in Lesson 5: Why the Law of my free online school of discipleship, but today it's dressed up with equity, human rights, social justice, environmentalism and the sexual revolution.

It's empowered with the full force of big tech, big business and the United States government behind it. Today wokeness is their religion and the power of the state is their hammer to chisel out a god made in the image of man. Now the political divide in America is the greatest I've ever seen in my lifetime. It's fracturing American society and the church in so many ways.

Praying For Wisdom to Live Out Our Faith

Jesus said the night before he was crucified in John 18:36, "My kingdom is not of this world. If my kingdom were of this world, my servants would have been fighting." We are rapidly leaving the rails of the last remnants of American constitutional rule and being thrust into the rise of a technocratic state where individual rights are quickly eroding. I wish I was talking about a Sci-Fi movie, but I'm not. We are living through the most transformative time in world history and it's moving so fast it's hard to keep up with what's going on. It's why most people have just checked out because they can no longer handle the disruption of their daily lives, not to mention what's going on in the world.

How to respond to these times calls for wisdom and we need to be daily praying for the wisdom to live as those born of the Spirit. The first amendment in the Bill of Rights says "congress shall make no law respecting an establishment of religion or prohibiting the free exercise thereof or abridging the freedom of speech, or of the press or the right of the people to peaceably assemble and to petition the Government for a redress of grievances". If you lived through the COVID pandemic of 2020 you saw the first amendment pretty much obliterated. To me it was like living in a movie and I was witnessing things happening that would alter our American way of life forever.

It brings us to the answer of when do we disobey civil authority? As Christians we must disobey civil authority when it puts us in a position to disobey God's authority. There are many examples in the Bible of the people of God rejecting civil law in obedience to God. The midwives in Egypt refused to kill the male children. Daniel continued to pray even when he was commanded not too. Daniel modes faithful resistance without rebellion. He and his three friends refused to worship the golden idol in defiance of the king. The apostles continued to preach the gospel in disobedience to the Jewish authorities.

In all these cases they obeyed God instead of the governing authorities and God approved of their actions. [161]If the state commands what God forbids or forbids what God commands, civil disobedience becomes a Christian duty. Just as N.T. Wright says, Romans 13 submission to authority must be read alongside Revelation 13 refusing the mark of the beast. I'm not going to jail for breaking the law, unless it's because meeting together as believers or preaching the gospel is outlawed. I'm not telling you what to do, but I do ask you **to test the spirit** motivating your heart. The Holy Spirit is not violent and full of hatred.

In America we still have the Bill of Rights, but as we witnessed in 2020, we can't take anything for granted. How could these freedoms be restricted? Well, for the first time in my lifetime I am witnessing the mechanisms to restrict freedom of speech and freedom of assembly on a scale I never thought imaginable. I was born in 1969 and got my first computer at the age of 19 which was just MS DOS, so it was a glorified

---

[161] John Stott, The Message of Romans, p. 341.

word processor. I didn't have my first cell phone until the mid 1990's and then came the internet. Today the technological advances going on are happening at breathtaking speed and in the next ten years we are going to see more change than any of us thought imaginable.

America has so many political causes that people spend their time focusing upon. It varies from environmentalism, sex trafficking, social justice, combatting woke ideology in schools, supporting racial issues, anti-corporatism, gun rights, anti-guns, Christian nationalism and the list could go on. A lot of these causes are just and noble. I can find Biblical verses to support some of these issues. I'm not going to tell you what causes you should support and like. I think you must follow your own conscience. I do want to ask you a few questions if you are going to take up a political cause.

1. Are you willing to break the law for any of these causes?
2. Do you think violence is ever justified in supporting one of these causes?

I'm cautioning and encouraging the Jesus movement in America to not get caught up in the extreme political causes on the right or left. I'm going to say it like this. If the cause that you support is making you angry, irritable, hateful and pushing you to attack others then it's not the cause of Christ.

We must have wisdom and discernment in our days, so that we are operating by the Spirit of the age to come which is living by the tree of life. I want to remind you that there were two trees in the garden. The tree of life and the tree of the knowledge of good and evil. The tree of life is found in the wisdom of the cross with the fruit of peace, gentleness, it's open to reason, full of mercy, reconciliation and it's impartial. The tree of the knowledge of good and evil is found in worldly wisdom with the fruit of disorder, jealousy, fighting, murder, hatred, prejudice and refusal to listen to reason. It may be a good cause, but does it take you off mission?

Our mission is not to go to jail for being violent or disruptive even if our American freedoms are being restricted. We are citizens of the kingdom of God first and America citizens second. Remember you are being built up as a spiritual house, to be a holy priesthood, to offer spiritual sacrifices acceptable to God through Jesus Christ. Our mission is to preach, teach and live the ministry of reconciliation by being good stewards of the mystery of Christ.

Some rulers and governments may be wicked, but we must pray for the rulers to change and obey the laws they have made, unless those laws cause us to disobey the word of God. As a holy priesthood we should be model citizens to our neighbors, relatives and working partners living the cruciform life by faith working through love. God has ordained the civil authority to set the laws and enforce them, but it is the Christians' duty to support that process with prayer and godly counsel.

I honestly don't have answers on how to fix our problems as a nation and quite honestly, I don't think anyone does. We are headed for difficult days ahead. It's my desire to navigate the tumultuous times with the wisdom and power of the cross. Will you come with me? I can't promise you it's going to be safe, but I see no way forward, but through the redeeming power of the cross.

We should not retreat to some cave thinking everything will take care of itself instead, we need to be salt, proclaiming the soon return of the King of peace, who will bring his kingdom rule to this earth, establishing justice once and for all.

CHAPTER 10

DISTORTED SPIRITUTALITY

"For false christs and false prophets will arise and perform great signs
and wonders, so as to lead astray, if possible, even the elect."

~ Matthew 24:24 ~

If we believe in the truth found and grounded in Christ, then
there is always a counter truth. Just as John told us in his first epistle that
"it is the last hour, and as you have heard that antichrist is coming, so
now many antichrists have come." Jesus and the apostolic fathers clearly
addressed the subject of false teachers (II Peter 2:1), false prophets
(Matt. 7:15), false apostles (2 Corinthians 11:13–15), and false Christ's
(Matthew 24:4-5).

In Revelation 2:2 Jesus commended the church in Ephesus for
testing "those who call themselves apostles and are not and found them
to be false." He corrected the church in Pergamum for putting up with
false teachers and the church in Thyatira for putting up with false
prophets. Paul ended the book of I Thessalonians chapter 5 just after
talking about the return of Christ to "not quench the Spirit. Do not
despise prophecies, but test everything; hold fast what is good."

Discerning Spiritual Encounters

It was 1988 and I just got delivered from drugs and dramatically
saved. I had just started the Spring semester of my first year of college. I
did not know a lot and was trying to find my footing in society along
with the spiritual world I had awakened too. I went from being a drug
dealer to sharing my faith in Christ literally overnight. People in the
town I grew up in did not know what to do with me and I was trying to
figure out how to live out my newfound faith at the same time.

In college I had to take an elective and Art was an easy 3 credits,
so I took the class. I remember my first day in Art class as the professor
was very openly anti-Christian and told us he was a practicing, Shaman.
He was the real deal and emanated a spiritualism of other worldliness.
He looked the part, and he lived on 20 acres along the Trinity River

where he practiced Shamanism. He was an extremely creative pottery artist. He was a professor at Cedar Valley College which was part of the Dallas Community College system, but he also traveled in New Age Circles selling his pottery.

He told us a story in class one day about something he experienced in the Green Mountains of Vermont at a New Age ceremony. He said they had cut out the trees on the side of a mountain and set up a place to have a spiritual ceremony. He claimed there were hundreds of people involved in a ritualistic ceremony where at the end clouds gathered above them and fire like a bolt of lightning came down in the middle of their ceremony. Now you can say the professor was just making things up, but I tend to believe that he experienced something spiritual and powerful.

Jesus talked about false prophets and false Christ's. I think for most it would be easy to discern that a practicing Shaman is not a follower of Christ, but what happens when it's not so easy to discern? We are living in times where all types of spiritual activity are more commonly accepted, and discernment is needed.

The church seems to be divided among Cessationist who reject almost any type of spiritual activity and then you have those open to almost any type of spiritual activity. I think like politics in our nation most followers of Christ are found somewhere in the middle.

Now Cessationism is a belief that the gifts of the apostle and prophet along with the spiritual gifts mentioned by Paul in I Corinthians chapter 12 have ceased since the formation of what is called the Canon of scripture or the formation of the Bible. You have variations of Cessationism, but it is this idea in a nutshell, and it is vastly a Western idea.

I am a Continuist who believes in the continuing gifts Paul mentions in Ephesians chapter 4, Romans chapter 12 and I Corinthians chapter 12. It was during the time that I was pastoring a church just outside of Toronto Canada that I took college credit hours that I had from my associate's degree and applied it to getting a bachelor's degree in theology. At that time, you did not have internet, so I knew a Pentecostal Bible College that I was able to do correspondence courses, and they accepted my 2 years of college credits, so I started studying while I was pastoring.

I was living in Cambridge, Ontario at the time and they had a Baptist Seminary. It had a good library, and I got to know the Librarian.

She allowed me to use their library and check out books while I was studying. The two years I was there finishing my bachelor's degree in theology I spent my time not just studying from a Pentecostal perspective, but I challenged myself with contradictory viewpoints.

I read a lot of books in those two years, and I am better off today having opened myself up to being challenged. It was from the years 1995 to 1997. It was at this time that what came to be known as the Toronto Blessing, which started at the Airport Vineyard Church just outside of downtown Toronto was happening and I lived just one hour away. I was experiencing the Toronto Blessing which had some extreme spiritual activity happening while examining the Bible to see what I really believed. It was John MacArthur's book Charismatic Chaos that introduced me to really examining that which I had been experiencing in my faith for the last 10 years.

I have a lot of respect for John McArthur and although I disagree with his perspective, I consider him a brother in Christ. I do not consider Cessationism to be heretical, but I do find it to be limiting. I understand the perspective because I do believe it's done out of motivation to stay true to the fundamentals of faith and practice laid out in the New Covenant. I share a common perspective in that regard, and I join all who are willing to defend our common faith in Christ. I've experienced firsthand spiritual extremism among far too many of those who embrace a Continuist view of the spiritual gifts so I can speak from the perspective of an insider.

Jimmi Hendrix, one of the greatest guitarists of all time, had a song called, 'Are Your Experienced?' I don't recommend taking it, but as a teenager I had my share of trips on LSD. A trip into the spiritual world of psychedelics is not something you can explain, but it's something you simply must experience. If you are familiar with the movie the Matrix then you know the main line in the film when Morpheus says "You take the blue pill... the story ends, you wake up in your bed and believe whatever you want to believe. You take the red pill... you stay in Wonderland, and I show you how deep the rabbit hole goes."

2020 was one of those eye-opening experiences for me in so many ways. It was as if 35 years of a spiritual journey brought me face to face with levels of instability and deception I had never experienced. It was like sleeping and then waking up on a roller coaster. Everything was turned upside down, moving around and shaking. I was working for one of the largest transportation companies in the world and we did not stop, but just kept on moving trying to figure out things as we went along.

It took me a while to get my footing because the levels of information warfare were intense. I watched people whom I thought were very rational people acting very irrational. I understood cultish behavior and what I was watching had all the signs of cultish-like tendencies, but it was on a scale that was frightening to me.

The Gnostic Influence of QAnon on American Politics

Let's talk QAnon because whether you realize it or not it has all the elusive traits of Gnosticism and it had a greater effect upon modern America more than has been recognized. [162]Gnostic groups claimed access to hidden, secret traditions unavailable to ordinary believers. In a nutshell QAnon taught that Trump is a Christian ruler, deputized by God to wage war against the liberal infidels destroying a once great and holy nation. QAnon followers — predominantly Donald Trump supporters believed that the real cause of America's crisis is a religious war being waged against legions of Illuminati demons.

QAnon is a smorgasbord of America's greatest conspiracy theories wrapped up into religious garb that only the truly enlightened could discern and understand. You had to have the hidden *gnōsis* to understand the true battle that was being waged for the sole of America. It was American apocalyptic theology at its best and a great number of Evangelical Christian's became its most ardent followers. [163]QAnon exhibits striking structural similarities to Gnostic myth: hidden knowledge, cosmic dualism and secret elites.

[164]Conspiracy belief creates an alternative reality framework. What I witnessed can only be described as delusional. It was a departure from soundness of truth and soundness of mind. People were living in a different reality from what was happening right before their very eyes. Faith is based on truth, but delusion is based on believing a lie. Delusion is based on a false belief about reality and held despite incontrovertible evidence to the contrary.

---

[162] Elaine Pagels, The Gnostic Gospels, p. 18.
[163] David G. Robertson, Conspiracy Theories and the Gnostic Imagination.
[164] Michael Barkun, A Culture of Conspiracy, p. 30.

Our faith is based first and foremost on the truth that God became a man through the Holy Spirit overshadowing a virgin. It is fundamental and core to our faith. If Jesus was not God, separate from the sin of Adam and blameless then he could not free us from our sins. Historical evidence tells us that Jesus lived and that Jesus died. [165]Biblical faith is rooted in historical claims and communal discernment.

Believing that Jesus was raised from dead in a resurrection body is fundamental and core to our faith. Jesus' resurrection from the dead, ascension to the Father, outpouring of the Spirit and return to this earth when we will be resurrected just like him are all fundamental understanding to our faith. It is the soundness of truth that we must be focused upon because the spirit of antichrist is delusional truth taking us away from these core truths to lies and there are many of these lies wrapped in different forms today.

The story of Thomas in John 20:26 - 29 is one of the most famous stories in the New Testament because I think so many of us understand Thomas's dilemma. Jesus just walked through a wall into the room and said to Thomas, "Put your finger here, and see my hands; and put out your hand and place it in my side. Do not disbelieve but believe." Thomas answered him, "My Lord and my God!" Jesus said to him, "Have you believed because you have seen me? Blessed are those who have not seen and yet have believed." We don't get to physically see or touch Jesus in this age, but we do get to experience the reality of his Spirit.

John's gospel was all about the experience. It was all about experiencing the true Christ who stepped into time as a real man and was raised from the dead in a real body that could be touched. Resurrection from the dead is the hope that the prophetic scriptures pointed towards. Our faith is based on the resurrection of Christ who is the first fruits of those who will rise from the dead. Paul, when discussing resurrection from the dead as central to our faith, called it a mystery.

Resurrection from the dead is core to understanding what it means to be a believer in the risen Christ and it also grounds us in our faith. It's not denying the reality of death, sickness nor the troubles we face in this present evil age, but it is the very hope that keeps us moving forward. It is the reality of our faith that though we live in the shadow of death during this present evil age we can partake of the age to come now.

---

[165] Craig Keener, Acts, (BECNT), p. 923.

It is being grounded in the love of God through Christ who is our very justification, redemption and propitiation of our sins.

It's in the gospel of John that Jesus is quoted as saying to Nicodemus one of the leaders of the Pharisees in John 3:7-8 to: "not marvel that I said to you, 'You must be born again.' The wind blows where it wishes, and you hear its sound, but you do not know where it comes from or where it goes. So it is with everyone who is born of the Spirit."

If you look at the context of the conversation that Jesus has with Nicodemus, he is telling him that we enter the world that we see and touch through natural childbirth. It is the world that the unseen God created and who made all things. However, we enter and see the kingdom God through spiritual rebirth. The doorway is through Christ's blood, water and Spirit.

It's what John told us in his first epistle in the context of overcoming this world. 1 John 5:4 - 8 says: "everyone who has been born of God overcomes the world. And this is the victory that has overcome the world—our faith. Who is it that overcomes the world except the one who believes that Jesus is the Son of God? This is he who came by water and blood—Jesus Christ; not by the water only but by the water and the blood. And the Spirit is the one who testifies, because the Spirit is the truth. For there are three that testify: the Spirit and the water and the blood; and these three agree."

We have so complicated the simple yet profound truths in Christ. We have chased after the new thing, but just as the serpent deceived Eve by his cunning so many have been led astray from a sincere and pure devotion to Christ.

Spirituality can be a very elusive reality. What I mean is that it is not something that is tangible which we can touch with our hands and see with our eyes. If you are not tethered to the cross and deeply rooted in the foundations of the faith, then it is very easy to get lost in the spiritual. I know because I've been caught up in movements that in their pursuit for spiritual insight, growth and simply wanting more of the Holy Spirit departed from foundational truth. It's only the message of the cross that grounds us and keeps us out of the delusion of mysticism.

The Great Awakening's: Revival and Spiritual Manifestations in America

The first Great Awakening was led by English missionary leaders in the American colonies such as George Whitfield and Jonathan Edwards. As these men preached, they saw outpourings of the Spirit mainly in the New England states from around the 1730's till about 1750's and there were very well documented occurrences of people getting filled with the Spirit displaying manifestations like the book of Acts. As these men preached, people were experiencing the power of the Spirit, prophesying, crying out in repentance and getting slain or knocked down by the power of the Spirit.

The Second Great Awakening was from the late 1750's to the early 1840's. The main leaders were Charles Finney a Presbyterian minister, then the English missionary brothers John and Charles Wesley. Charles Finney became credited for starting the mass crusade evangelism model that Billy Graham and Oral Roberts popularized in the 1950's.

The John and Charles Wesley brothers were probably the most prolific church planting missionaries in America and their Movement founded what is today known as the Methodist Church. It is well documented that through the outpouring of the Second Great Awakening manifestations of the Spirit like prophesying, crying out in repentance under the power of the Spirit and getting slain or knocked down by the power of the Spirit. You also have documentation of speaking in tongues although it was not popularized during the Second Great Awakening.

That brings us to the 1906 Azusa Street revival in downtown Los Angeles. The Azusa Street revival was not the first movement of the Spirit in America, but it probably brought the greatest divisions which we still see to this day. One of its main leaders was a black man named William J. Seymour. Out of this revival we have several Pentecostal denominations that were started and separated along racial divisions. Restorationists point to Azusa Street as the beginning of what is termed the latter rain move of the Spirit spoken of by the prophet Joel and Peter in the book of Acts.

Charismatic Restorationist teach that the church age is going to end with the latter rain or outpouring of the Holy Spirit at the end of the age. It will be consummated with a great ingathering of souls spiritually fulfilling the Feast of Tabernacles. In looking at history and the text from the prophet Joel, Restorationist see a progressive restoration of the church from the days of Martin Luther to our present time, restoring the church to its apostolic roots.

The defining issue that arose out of the Azusa Street revival was the issue of speaking in tongues because it was the first time since the book of Acts in nearly 2,000 years of church history that tongues were emphasized on a large scale. It is worth noting that Pentecostalism with its various offshoots has been the fastest growing form of Christianity in and outside of America for the last 100 years. Pentecostal and Charismatic movements represent the fastest growing religious movement in the world.

I do feel I can safely say that the Holy Spirit is saturating all nations with the latter rain of the Spirit. Now you can deny that fact, but it's hard not to look at the expansive church planting missionary movements over the last 100 years and not conclude that we are seeing a worldwide outpouring of the Spirit. I can testify to it because I have been a part of that movement.

It was after WWII during the 1950's that America experienced a large revival. Billy Graham was holding large tent revivals at this time. It was the day when evangelists were going all over America in big tents holding meetings. You had a group who put a great emphasis on healing through the laying on of hands.

One of the most well-known Pentecostal figures resulting from this time was Oral Roberts who eventually founded Oral Roberts University in Tulsa Oklahoma. Gordon Lindsey created a magazine called the Voice of Healing, that brought together this movement, and he eventually founded Christ for The Nations Bible School in Dallas, Texas.

The Movement was not just focused on healing and evangelism. The Latter Rain Movement had a focus on laying on of hands, personal prophecy along with the restoration of apostles and prophets. It was also the birthplace of Charismatic Restoration Theology which took these important Biblical truths but over emphasized them and we are still dealing with some of the false doctrines coming out of this movement today.

Jesus talked to us about the root and the fruit when it comes to understanding false prophets (Matt. 7:16). [166]Jesus teaches discernment

---

[166] Craig Bloomberg, Matthew (NAC), p. 130.

based on observable outcomes. Historically, controversaries surrounding Charismatic Restoration Theology include:

- Authoritarian leadership
- Prophetic excesses
- Doctrinal innovation

The Dangers of Distorted Charismatic Restoration Theology in Apostolic and Prophetic Circles

I can speak as an insider because at the age of 20 I was introduced to the Charismatic Restoration movement in which many of the ideas were reintroduced through the 'Kingdom Now Movement'. The problem Restoration Theology runs into is that most who hold to this teaching start to base their teachings on prophetic declarations, angelic visitations, out of body experiences, visions and dreams.

It literally becomes a smorgasbord of spiritual ideas and fertile ground for spiritual deception. It's because personal revelation and private interpretation are the foundation of Restoration Theology. Today so much of what I'm looking at in what is called the apostolic and prophetic circles has its roots in a distorted, twisted and mystical interpretation of scripture that can only be identified as a form of Gnosticism.

We must go back to Alexander Dowie in America to see the origins of this movement in the United States. Just like political movements are many times founded on myths you will find a lot of myths surrounding Alexander Dowie, but with modern investigative reporting a very troubling picture emerges about the man and the movement he created.

It is undeniable that he had every trait of a false prophet. If it looks like a duck, quacks like a duck and swims like a duck then it's safe to say it's a duck. It's safe to say that Alexander Dowie was a dangerous, deceptive and corrupt man. He was by definition a false prophet, and it is important to clearly articulate that fact.

I'm not going to go into all the history that surrounds this man, but just the end of his life says all we need to know. Dowie was one of the first who began to talk about Restoration Theology. He believed in an end-times restoration of spiritual gifts and apostolic offices. In 1899, he claimed to be "God's Messenger", and, in 1901, he claimed to be the spiritual return of the Biblical prophet Elijah.

Dowie founded the city of Zion in Illinois which was his attempt to form the kingdom of God on earth. It was supposedly a Theocracy, but it ended just like all other attempts in history have ended which is some form of totalitarianism. He died a disgrace, a fraud and left a legacy of destroyed lives.

It was William Branham who supposedly caught the mantle of Alexander Dowie. Well, I tend to agree that he caught the same mantle of deception. You can trace the roots of what is called the apostolic and prophetic Restoration Movement back to Branham because he is the fountainhead from which most of it flows.

I look at Restoration Theology because I do think it helps us understand church history and the current spiritual climate in America. I am a Continuist, so I believe that the gifts Paul explained in Ephesians chapter 4, Romans chapter 12 and I Corinthians chapter 12 are for us today.

I depart from Charismatic Restoration Theology due to the subjective theology. The theology becomes dependent on the apostle or prophet teaching who comes up with their own version. It's because personal mystical revelation and private interpretation are the rock bed of mystical neo-Gnosticism. It's the spirituality that Paul specifically warned us about in Colossians chapter 2 which I have previously discussed.

What I am attempting to do is help you understand how neo-Gnostic thought produced two parallel spiritual movements in the 1950's that are very much with us today. It is uniquely an American spirituality that uses the Bible, but so much of its spiritual roots are not found abiding in Christ and soundness of truth. It is the spirit of antichrist, just America's version wrapped in religious terminology.

Gnosticism is a spiritual parasite that mimics and takes on the traits of its host. It's easy to recognize that Gnosticism has transformed Progressive Christianity where it uses Biblical terminology but has departed from the faith that Jesus and apostolic authors gave us. [167]Gnostic teachers presented themselves as offering deeper knowledge of the same scriptures. Historically, Gnostic systems:

---

[167] David Brakke, The Gnostics, p. 8.

- Used Biblical language
- Claimed secret revelation
- Reinterpreted apostolic teaching

Let's look at William Branham because he is a man that many in the Charismatic American church look back to as part of their spiritual roots. If you examine his life and teaching, you will see that he is the father of many Gnostic ideas embraced today. I'm only going to touch the surface of the man and focus on some of his spiritual ideas that are present in today's spiritual landscape. If you want to do a deep dive, I recommend visiting william-branham.org.

I knew about William Branham, but John Collins, who came out of the cult surrounding Branham, has detailed historical documentation. Like Dowie it's easy to call him a false prophet once you see the evidence and the fruit of his teaching. I'm going to take you through a list of a few things that we see in the teachings of Branham and it's clear to see that he was nothing more than a Gnostic mystic. I know many who testify to his tremendous powers and if he did perform miracles then like Dowie, they would be called lying signs and wonders because he was a false prophet.

William Branham was a supporter of White Supremacy and had direct ties to the highest levels of the Klu Klux Klan. It's an historical fact that cannot be denied. [168]One of Branham's central doctrines was the serpent seed doctrine. Branham believed he had a spiritual revelation that Eve had sexual intercourse with the serpent in the garden and through Cain the serpent's seed produced an evil "hybrid" race. He traced that hybrid line to Africans, multiple figures in Jewish history and ultimately the Antichrist.

Aryan race theology was in America during the 1920's before it manifested itself in Hitlers Germany believing in a super race to rule the world. It is a spiritual form of replacement theology. It is found in the lost 10 tribes' theology or also called British Israelism which undergirds the theology of many who adhere to Christian Nationalism today. I'm not painting all who adhere to Christian Nationalist as racist, but if you sleep with dogs, you will get fleas and the core doctrines supporting Christian Nationalism are rooted in racism.

Let me take you through a few things this man taught. If you

---

[168] David Edwin Harrell Jr., All Things Are Possible, p. 169.

understand the root, then when you see these same ideas, they will be easy to spot:

- **Secret Gnōsis as the key to salvation** – He taught that you must possess his inside knowledge which is not available to everyone but comes only through God's chosen vessels. [169]Braham's authority rested on his claim to supernatural revelation.

- **The holy man myth** - A myth surrounds William Branham's birth. He claimed that at his birth there was a sign that he was the prophet. He said that a [170]light came whirling through the window, about the size of a pillow and circled around where he was, shining upon him in his bed. He also [171]claimed he was born on the same day that Alexander Dowie died therefore catching his spiritual mantle. The only problem is that it is one of many verifiable lies that surround his life.

- **Spoken prophecy on par with scriptures** - [172]He taught that when he spoke under the inspiration of the Holy Spirit it was the voice of God. It is the teaching that prophets have the power to create like God with their words and their messages are oracles that must be listened to on equal par with the words of God. To speak against the anointed prophet is to speak against God himself.

- **Elevating apostles and prophets** - [173]He taught that apostles and prophets are going to be restored to the church. He taught that apostles and prophets would be given authority over the church in the last days. He taught that it was through the ministry of apostles and prophets that the church would be given power to rule the nations before Jesus returned.

- **Authoritarianism and spiritual coverings** - He taught that unless you received his revelation then you were part of Babylon the harlot church. [174]You had to come out of the harlot church and submit to the true authority of apostles and prophets who could only spiritually

---

[169] Matthew Avery Sutton, Aimee Semple McPherson and the Resurrection of Christian America, 2007.

[170] William Branham, The Story of My Life (sermon, April 19, 1959).

[171] William Branham, God's Only Provided Place of Worship (1965).

[172] William Branham, The Anointed Ones at the End Times (1965).

[173] William Branham, Ephesians Chapter 4 (1960).

[174] William Branham, The Invisible Union of the Bride of Christ, (19650).

cover you from the deception of the end times. It was only by aligning to the last day apostles and prophets that you could be protected from the demonic activity of the Antichrist.

- **Spiritual Elitism** - He taught that God was [166]raising up a spiritually elite group of Christians who were going to be part of the Bride of Christ, Joel's Army, the Manchild, the 144,000 and Overcomers. Unless you are a part of this move of God then you are going to be deceived by the Antichrist.

- **Mystical interpretation of scripture** - To say that [175]he butchered the scriptures and took them out of context using personal revelation would be an understatement. It is Gnosticism that emphasizes the hidden meaning of text. It's very easy to make the Bible say pretty much anything you want it to say especially when you are getting personal revelation from an angel, vision, dream, out of body experience and the audible voice of God. It's always based on a mystical interpretation of scripture taken out of context usually received from some spiritual experience.

- **Extreme ideas on spiritual warfare** - Branham focused on the spiritual battle going on in the heavenlies and taught that he was given special insight into this spiritual realm. He believed an elite spiritual army made up of warriors for Christ would rise up in the last days casting Satan down, release creation from sin and bring in the kingdom of God before Christ returns to the earth.

- **Angelic visitations** - Branham said he was visited by an angel and commissioned with his healing ministry. He said that he ministered with an angel. His ministry normalized being visited by angels, talking to angels and getting revelation from angels. He introduced a very mystical form of spiritualism that saw angels as a vital part of the lives of the spiritual elite.

- **An incorrect view of Christ** - Branham taught that Christ the Logos was created by God. He taught that Jesus did not become God until he was baptized in water and filled with the Holy Spirit. He taught that Jesus was just a man until that time, but then he became the God-man. The man, the body was not Deity, but Deity was in the body. He taught that before the crucifixion that the Spirit left Jesus in the Garden of Gethsemane where He became just a man once

---

[175] David Edwin Harrell Jr., All Things Are Possible, p. 167.

more and died as a man and not as God.

- **Man can become a little god** - Branham was the originator of the manifest sons of God doctrine that teaches a time is coming in this age when an elite group of believers will literally overcome death, be given immortality and set this creation free triggering the return of Christ. He taught that this had to happen before Christ could return. It was a spiritualized form of postmillennialism and dominion theology.
- **Focus on signs, wonders, visions and spiritual experiences** - Branham focused on signs, wonders, visions, spiritual experience and it was the central focus of his ministry. Sound doctrine and critical thinking were seen as enemies to these spiritual experiences. He considered education, intellectualism and Theology as demonic activities opposing the Spirit.
- **Sexual immorality** - It is documented that several homosexuals were part of Branham's entourage and inner circle. There were a lot of accusations of homosexual behavior concerning William Branham, but no solid evidence. We do know for a fact that Paul Cain, who was a close associate to William Branham and took on his ministry was a confirmed and a practicing homosexual.

The overwhelming evidence clearly defines William Branham as a false prophet and to not look at those facts is to suspend disbelief. The stories written about this man in books like 'God's Generals' by Roberts Liardon are nothing more than William Branham myths and make him into a demigod. Historical facts matter and truth matters. The myths of William Branham as some figure to be looked at as an example of living the Christian life is dangerous.

We cannot overlook facts, and we must use our critical thinking skills, or we wind up in Jim Jones territory. Did you know that Jim Jones was a close associate of William Branham? Jim Jones had his own set of problems, but the only thing Jim Jones seemed to turn away from was the White Supremacy of Brahman. Jim Jones embraced the Civil Rights Movement and integrated his church, but the foundations of his movement were rooted in the message of William Branham.

It's important that we learn from the past because as I look at the current spiritual landscape in America, I'm very concerned about what I see. I'm looking at the fruit of some very bad seeds that were planted in this nation that are leading a lot of people down spiritual paths of deception. We must put a premium on soundness of truth and critical thinking because in a world that is falling apart, foundations are very important.

The Bible talks about strong delusion deceiving people where they suspend critical thinking and start believing lies. I am talking about these things because I've experienced firsthand the effect of false teachings and the power that a false spiritual leader can have when people come under their spell.

The power of a false leader and the Groupthink that can develop around someone should not be taken lightly. However, just because false spiritual leaders lead people astray using scriptures taken out of context doesn't mean we should throw out the Bible. It doesn't mean that we should cut out portions of the Bible just because bad actors twist, adulterate and abuse them to manipulate others.

Recognizing the signs of false teachers, false prophets and false apostles is the responsibility of us all. Paul told us to test all things and in 1 John 4:1 he said: "beloved, do not believe every spirit, but test the spirits to see whether they are from God, for many false prophets have gone out into the world."

The Jesus Movement: A Cultural Revolution in 1960s America

During the 1960's America experienced revolutionary change in so many ways which altered the cultural foundations of America. During the ending of the Latter Rain Movement the Jesus Movement emerged primarily starting on the West coast spreading through the Hippie communities of the 1960's and 1970's documented in the recent movie 'Jesus Revolution'. The movement was very counterculture and like the Hippie Movement of the time, the Jesus Movement challenged traditional Western cultural thought. The Jesus Movement challenged traditional Christianity in the way that Mainline Denominations practiced their faith.

The Jesus Movement had a very dramatic effect on the church in America and I personally think it created some really good ideas on how to contextualize our faith in a society that is changing very rapidly. At the same time, it had a lot of problems mainly due to some extreme ideas and many of those ideas came from segments within the Latter Rain Movement producing some very unsound doctrines and practices. It was putting too much emphasis on unrealistic ideas of communal living and spiritual experience over soundness of truth.

Like the Hippie Movement the Jesus Movement was very mystical in the way that it viewed the world. The most lasting legacies that came out of this movement were the Shepherding Movement, the Deliverance and Healing Movement along with the Spiritual Warfare Movement. We are still dealing with some of the extreme ideas today around these three topics and you can find their roots in some of the extreme factions of the Latter Rain Movement.

Let me say this because I think it is important. The outpouring of the Spirit in the book of Acts was very disruptive, chaotic and it challenged those who experienced it into a different way of thinking. It affected the way they viewed the world because it was the very Spirit of Jesus filling clay jars. I think I'm safe saying that the day of Pentecost had a great amount of emotional exuberance. Putting new wine into hearts is sure to produce a variety of effects, but it's the messy pathway of renewal. One thing to understand is that any genuine outpouring of the Spirit will have some level of disruption.

I was involved with some outpourings of the Spirit in the mid 1990's from the Toronto Blessing to the England and South African outpourings during this same period. Like the First Great Awakening, the Second Great Awakening, the Azusa Street revival and 1950's along with the 1970's renewal movements there were excesses. It's why sound doctrine focused on the word of the cross is so important. We need both the power and wisdom of God to effectively make disciples.

One lasting change that resulted from the moving of the Spirit over the last 50 years has been the transformation of music and worship which has affected almost all evangelical churches. Some of the fastest growing US denominations of the late 20th century, such as Calvary Chapel, Hope Chapel Churches, the Vineyard Churches, trace their roots directly back to the Jesus Movement as do influential worship music such as Jesus Culture and many others.

I would be so bold to say that it has literally transformed most Evangelical church services which are conducted with a contemporary style of worship music and atmosphere. The lifting of hands during worship services and the laying on of hands has become a common practice today.

Jesus did not leave us an instruction book laying out the details of how we are to operate as his body. One could say it's why we have so many different expressions of church life. I'm not of the opinion that is a bad thing. To be a part of Christ's body doesn't mean we all have to look, act and practice our faith the same way. It does mean we have a common identity found in the wisdom and power of the cross. Paul in 1 Corinthians 3:11 said: "no one can lay a foundation other than that which is laid, which is Jesus Christ."

Paul never gave us a detailed instruction book on what the church should look like. He did warn us to take heed as to how we do it. We will all be held accountable as to how we build our personal lives and ministries that affect other people's lives (I Corinthians 3:10-17). We will all stand before the judgment seat of Christ and must give an account (2 Corinthians 5:7). It is an inescapable fact and part of the foundation of our faith. It should be a motivating factor for us to be humble, transparent and let love be the motivation of all that we do.

Religious Movements Gone Wrong: Insights from Podcast Interviews

At the time I was writing this book I was greatly impacted by 3 podcasts. The power of the internet cannot be underestimated today because at no other time in church history have, we been able to learn in real time as today. I watched 3 podcasts chronicling 3 spiritual movements in the modern American Church that have affected probably everyone reading this book and there are lessons we need to learn. Honestly, I was grieved at the levels of dysfunction that I saw in the American Church as I listened to these podcasts, but hopeful at the same time.

Grieved because I know the pain, heartache and trauma that can happen when you experience spiritual abuse and deception. It's a life altering experience to realize that you've spent a lot of time, money and wasted years on things that were simply wrong. It can have a paralyzing effect upon your faith, and I've witnessed many walk away from the faith because they were confused, disgusted and felt like they had been living a lie.

I was hopeful because of the response to renewal, a sincere desire to follow Christ no matter what the cost and a newfound humility in the cross. I was inspired to see people just like me realizing our faith is not about following the holy man or holy woman but following the humble Christ who came in the flesh. I was inspired because I saw this renewal taking place across the body of Christ and not just in one movement.

I am afraid it takes going through great difficulties many times to start asking the right questions and being sober minded enough to look at our own lives. You know my experience is that many times we are deceived because something in us is broken, and we are looking for someone to fix us. What we fail to realize is that those we are looking to are cracked jars of clay too. We overlook clear and obvious flaws because we have become mesmerized by a gift. We make the person into an idol and once we do that, we no longer see each other clearly.

Let's look at these three interviews and the lessons that we can learn. The first one I want to talk to you about is a podcast by Christianity Today called 'The Rise and Fall of Mars Hill'. If you have not listened to this series of podcasts, I would really encourage you to listen. You can find the podcast on Spotify. It is for everyone in the modern American Church, but especially the millions of believers who are in abusive authoritarian churches or have been affected by abusive systems.

I've never listened to a full sermon of Mark Driscoll's or read any of his books, but I was aware of him. As I listened to this podcast, I found out I knew him very well because it was the same story I lived through. It's what happens to so many renewal movements that become fixated on a dynamic spiritual leader. It was just a modern version of the Shepherding Movement. It overemphasized following a set church structure, submission to authority and male dominated leadership.

I agree that we need men to embrace the gospel, but raw male masculinity is an enemy of the cross. It's been my experience that those who focus heavily upon the so-called Jezebel spirit and see women as being the source of so many problems in the church and the world usually have issues in their lives concerning women. I've watched this same movie play out so many times in church and it's why I write what I do. I've been through it, and I hope to help others realize there is hope in the cross.

As I listened to Mike Cosper from Christianity Today narrate this story and interview people I identified with their story because I had lived their story. I heard the tragedy of broken lives. I know a lot of people re-examined their faith, some walked away from the faith for a season and some sadly will walk away from Christ all together. In the end I was left with the hope that I heard in Mike Cosper's message. A hope that we will re-examine our faith and realize the frailty of man. A hope that we can listen, learn and be humble enough to recognize any of these traits in our own lives.

The next interview I listened to was Julie Roy's, who is the founder of the Roy's Report. She is the one that broke the IHOP Kansas City story about Mike Bickle. IHOP KC was considered the MECCA for the Spiritual Warfare Movement and Prophetic Movement, but it was simply an extension of the Charismatic Restoration Movement. I never visited Kansas City, but at the age of 20 I was introduced to these ideas and spent 25 years of my life working with various aspects of this movement. Scriptures teach about spiritual warfare and prophecy, but this movement moved over into the realm of mystical Gnosticism.

It was an overemphasis on the spiritual unseen world that the foundation of IHOP KC was built upon. It was built around a series of prophetic messages that were used by Mike Bickle to build a movement on faulty foundations. In looking at IHOP KC we are left with so many lessons to learn about idolatry, deception, spiritual, sexual and ministerial abuse of power. It's a story that I've watched over and over, but never on this scale impacting so many lives.

I listened to the interview of Julie Roy's on the 'Wake Up and Win Podcast' and I was struck by a few things that she said. Let me go down a little rabbit hole first because you have a major teaching in the body of Christ, and it's been around for a long time called 'touch not God's anointed'. I addressed this earlier, but I want to dig into this subject further because it is used as a weapon by ministers to shield themselves from legitimate questions, concerns and accountability. I was introduced to this teaching 35 years ago so I can spot it quickly when I see it. It changes clothes quite often, but inside the doctrine is always the same wolf hiding.

I spent the last 20 years of my life working in an American Corporate structure. We lived, ate and breathed the chain of command structure. It is the way of the Gentiles according to Jesus. Chain of command and submission to authority is the way of the world and you have different variations of this structure.

Jesus taught us that his organizational structure should be the direct opposite. Jesus said that chain of command authority structure is not the basis of his leadership model but serving. He gave us the example to follow and humility, not exerting power over others is the way of Christ. In the New Testament we are all anointed and given the Holy Spirit. Yes, just like the priests, prophets and kings were anointed in the Old Testament.

The New Testament does not teach a hierarchical model of leadership. Yes, we have leaders, but they are simply mature facilitators whose main function is to help with conflict resolution and keeping us on mission according to Matthew chapter 18. Jesus leaves us little detail on how to build his church so I do conclude that gives us a lot of flexibility and that should be done with a great amount of humility.

The concept that spiritual leaders in the New Testament are like kings, priests and prophets in the Old Testament is simply absent. The idea that they are to be CEO's is purely an American concept. The problem is that far too many extend those roles into leadership models producing an unhealthy reliance on one man. Samuel the prophet warned Israel of this problem that it would lead to idolatry and our failure to heed the same warning has produced a lot of spiritual abuse.

IHOP KC demonstrated all the traits of an abusive spiritual system and the tragedy that happened to so many lives are once again a stain on the church's reputation. In listening to Julie Roy, I was struck by the fact that she found herself in the place of having to report on a situation brought to her. If she did not have enough courage to speak truth to power, then an abusive spiritual system would have continued to harm people's lives.

I once again found myself grieving while at the same time hopeful. Grieving as I knew the numbers of lives that would be affected by this tragic story of what can only be described as deception on a grand scale. I was left with hope as I listened to Julie who is a very humble woman that brought down a spiritual empire by exposing and pulling back the curtain on what can only be described as a house built on lies. I was encouraged by the fact that what might seem like the crumbling of the church can be an opportunity to return to humility, transparency and the accountability found in the cross.

The last interview I want to discuss is one that Charisma Magazine did with Mike Winger. Mike Winger is a Continuist, but he exposes what he sees as misleading and extravagant excesses in the modern-day Charismatic Church which is a big umbrella. He put together a 4-hour video just using Benny Hinn in his own video clips exposing false teaching, false prophecies, manipulative giving practices and deceptive techniques around healing.

I go on the record that I've been in at least 5 Benny Hinn crusades. It's been over 30 years, but I can say that I experienced the genuine power of the Holy Spirit in those meetings. I don't personally know anyone that has ever been healed in one of his meetings so I'm agnostic on that point. I will say that I read his first book 'Good Morning Holy Spirit' and again it's been over 30 years, but it benefited me greatly in understanding the third person of the Trinity and understanding that the Holy Spirit is God. Now as I watched the 4-hour video that Mike Winger put together I was left with no choice but to agree with most of the presentation.

Well, it obviously had a tremendous impact because Benny Hinn was forced to do damage control. I've always had issues with Benny's showmanship, his abuse of scripture and his promotion of false doctrines around the issue of prosperity. The wing of the church Benny represents is hyper Charismatic healing and deliverance ministries. Benny is not alone in what I consider extreme ideas around the man or woman whose ministry is solely focused on healing, deliverance and prosperity. It's been 35 years and I've never seen a sound ministry that solely focuses on these areas.

Benny Hinn went into damage control mode after he was unable to get this 4-hour video taken off YouTube and sought out Charisma Magazine for an interview. He did an interview with Steven Strang, and it was nothing but a puff piece by Steven Strang to prop up his old friend Benny Hinn. The interview that impressed me was by John Matarazzo who is with Charisma Magazine, and he interviewed Mike Winger. I would really encourage you to watch this video of John Matarazzo interview of Mike Winger.

No matter what you think of Benny Hinn it is undeniable that Mike Winger does a great job of speaking to a segment of the church that needs a great deal of help and is leaving a lot of people shipwrecked in their faith. Mike effectively uses the word of God, sound teaching and critical thinking skills to bring correction. He does this in a very constructive way.

The Power of Transparency in Exposing Deceptive Doctrines and Abusive Practices

Now as I watched this interview along with the other two

interviews I was left with hope for the church in America. Hope that with the power of exposure deceptive doctrines, false structures of authority and abusive practices would be exposed. As Supreme Court Justice Louis Brandeis said over a century ago: "Sunlight is said to be the best of disinfectants." Transparency and exposure are either going to produce humility and repentance or digging in the hills with pride leading to further delusion.

In the New Testament we are all anointed with the Holy Spirit, and no one is to be set up on a pedal stool. Celebrity has infected American culture and the church in America, but the internet is showing it to be a double-edged sword. Meteoric rises and meteoric falls are happening quickly and as the old saying goes 'be careful what you wish for, lest it come true!' As I watched these three interviews, I was hopeful that the disinfectant power of truth would lead to a restoration of a more authentic, transparent and humble faith model in the cruciform way.

I'm not writing this as a Heresy Hunter trying to tear others down. Honestly, I prefer not having to talk about these topics, but I've walked down these paths, and I escaped out of the darkness of deception. Now I do feel like I have a responsibility to teach the truth, and I simply want to equip you to discern the body. If I can reach 10 people and help those people to live a more fruitful life for Christ then it's worth my time, investment and sacrifice.

Finding Our Way Forward

Today you have so many differing and contradictory voices coming from all parts of the church. It can make you feel overwhelmed. I know I'm not alone because a lot have just given up altogether. I want to encourage you to keep moving forward and stop looking at all the things that you cannot control. I encourage you to take control of what you can change, which is your own spiritual life. If you are finding yourself confused and damaged due to spiritual abuse, I encourage you to get your heart restored into the soundness of truth.

If the church is built out of living stones, then that means each of our lives is to be a pillar and foundation of truth. Jesus warned us about false prophets for a reason because it would be a reality, and we need to have discernment.

I understand firsthand the power of deception and the power of getting caught up in spiritual movements. I don't have all the answers, but I've done a lot of deconstructing over the years. I'm going to walk you through some things that I've learned. What I am going to walk you through will help put you on a path to restoration. I am going to walk you through 3 simple ways that I've discovered to recover from spiritually abusive situations.

We overcome spiritual deception by rediscovering Christ and getting back to basics. Spiritual deception happens because we have been pointed away from Christ to something else. It really is that simple, but it happens so subtly.

As a kid I always loved to hike and explore where no one had gone. I was always the scout who found the path for others to follow. In a forest it can be easy to get turned around and not sure exactly which way you are going. One thing I learned was that as soon as I was not sure where I was going, I went back to where I had lost my way. Don't just keep going because it gets harder and harder to find your way.

If I am not sure where I am going, I use 1 John 5:4 - 9 as my compass. It says: "everyone who has been born of God overcomes the world. And this is the victory that has overcome the world—our faith. Who is it that overcomes the world except the one who believes that Jesus is the Son of God? This is he who came by water and blood— Jesus Christ; not by the water only but by the water and the blood. And the Spirit is the one who testifies, because the Spirit is the truth. For there are three that testify: the Spirit and the water and the blood; and these three agree. If we receive the testimony of men, the testimony of God is greater, for this is the testimony of God that he has borne concerning his Son."

The blood, water and Spirit is my compass. You may say Darren, that's too simple. Yes, and I never leave that threefold cord because it is the key to overcoming the spirit of antichrist. We are not overcoming the world through secret *gnōsis*. We are not overcoming this world through the 7 Mountain Mandate. We are not overcoming this world because the wealth of the wicked is being given to us. We don't overcome this world by casting out demons or healing the sick. We are not overcoming this world by doing greater works than Jesus. We are not the saviors of the world!

Number 1: The Power of the Blood in Overcoming the World

The blood of the cross is one of the main keys to overcoming the world according to the Bible. Taking up our cross and discipleship is not following some man or movement. It's not submission to a church! It's submission to Christ the redeemer of your soul and him alone. He is the foundation and only him!

Let me go down a rabbit hole and ask you a question. What if you get put in jail for preaching the gospel? Is your apostle going to be there to hold your hand? Is your faith in your pastor? When you die are you taking your prophet with you to stand before the judgment seat of Christ? All of that seems kind of silly when I say it out loud, but I would encourage you to ask yourself those things. We have elevated the holy man or holy woman to a very unhealthy place in the church.

The blood of the Lamb is our sole foundation. If it is not yours then you are going to be deceived and you need to examine your faith. Revelation 12:11 says we overcome the Antichrist: 'by the blood of the Lamb,' by the word of our testimony and loving not our lives even unto death. It's our testimony and our personal faith. It's not what someone else says. It's us answering Christ when says: "Who do you say that I am?"

Number 2: The Transformative Power of Water -Embracing Our Identity in Christ

The water speaks of two things: our baptismal identification with Christ and daily renewing our minds to the word of God. We are children of God dependent on the Father. We are vine's connected to the Branch. We are sheep dependent on our Shepherd. We need to daily spend time in prayer and reflection upon his word because we are dependent on him.

We cannot expect to not be deceived if we do not spend time reflecting upon the truth of the word of God. The Foundation Publications School of Discipleship is a result of me seeking truth for myself. I have a teaching gift, so I put my personal study into a form for others to learn. I don't know everything, but the course I put together is my personal study and pursuit of truth based on the Bible. It is my journey to assimilate scripture in my daily life which has helped me become established in Christ. I made this a free resource because I desire others to understand the word of God even if you don't have the resources to pay.

Number 3: The Crucial Role of the Holy Spirit in Our Covenant with Christ

Let's look at the third cord of our covenant with Christ which is the Holy Spirit. Now the Bible does not tell us everything about how to live life. Does the Bible tell us where to live? Where to work? Who to marry or not to marry? The Bible does not tell us a lot of things about the decisions that we have to make daily. The million-dollar question is how do we make these important daily decisions? I'm going to call this subjective truth, and this is where the Holy Spirit plays a role in our daily lives.

Jesus ascended to the right hand of the Father and sent the Holy Spirit to be with us here as the third person of the Trinity until he physically returns at his second coming. John 14:18 Jesus said: "I will not leave you as orphans; I will come to you." In verse 26 he said: "the Helper, the Holy Spirit, whom the Father will send in my name, he will teach you all things and bring to your remembrance all that I have said to you." In John 16:13 Jesus said when: "the Spirit of truth comes, he will guide you into all the truth, for he will not speak on his own authority, but whatever he hears he will speak, and he will declare to you the things that are to come."

The primary role of the Holy Spirit is to lead us into the objective truth found in Christ. He keeps us centered on the redemptive work of the cross and our common foundation. The Holy Spirit also has a role in declaring to you things to come which is subjective truth. John in his first epistle says that we have all been anointed and given the Holy Spirit.

In 1 John 2:26 - 27 it says: "I write these things to you about those who are trying to deceive you. But the anointing that you received from him abides in you, and you have no need that anyone should teach you. But as his anointing teaches you about everything, and is true, and is no lie—just as it has taught you, abide in him." Just as the prophet, priest and king were all anointed in the Old Testament as New Testament believers we are all prophetic because we all have the Spirit of truth. We are all priests because we all have been given direct access to the Spirit. We are all kings because we have all been given the power of the Spirit.

The author of Hebrews in 8:10 - 11 says it this way: "I will put my laws into their minds and write them on their hearts and I will be their God and they shall be my people. And they shall not teach, each one his neighbor and each one his brother, saying, 'Know the Lord,' for they shall all know me, from the least of them to the greatest." It's not saying that we don't need teachers who help us to understand the word of God. It is saying that the Holy Spirit makes the redemptive work of the cross a reality in our hearts.

The Holy Spirit is with us to support, comfort and lead us in our daily lives. What I want to help you understand is that you can know the guidance of the Spirit in your day-to-day life. It's been my experience that we complicate things. Simplicity is the key and in the cross is the very wisdom of God. The wisdom of the Spirit guides us in the way of peace. We have an anointing in us, and the Spirit will give us a green light and a red light. Peace is a green light.

If you don't have peace, then begin to ask questions. James 3:17 says: "the wisdom from above is first pure, then peaceable, gentle, open to reason, full of mercy and good fruits, impartial and sincere." It says here that we are also to be open to reason. The Bible is not opposed to critical thinking skills, and it is part of being discerning.

Discerning of spirits is a manifestation of the Spirit, but discernment is also using your critical thinking skills and assessing a situation. It's okay to judge because we are told to judge, but we are not to be judgmental. You make judgments all day long and if you don't then you are just being naive which leaves you open to deception. If you are not feeling good about a decision then be cautious, investigate and don't move forward until you have understanding.

It's important that you learn how to make daily decisions based on wisdom. I'm not against godly counsel, but it should not be what you turn to first. You have an anointing of the Holy Spirit and the wisdom to critically assess situations. You need to learn to make godly decisions on your own.

Discerning Spiritual Experiences: The Role of Visions, Dreams, and Prophetic Words

I'm not against visions or dreams, but remember you have the Holy Spirit and those are not normal everyday experiences. I'm not against prophetic words, but they are not normal everyday experiences, but the exception. You don't need personal prophetic word's to direct your life. Angelic visitations are not normal Christian living and if anyone is telling you they are then they are very dangerous people.

It's important to always recognize manipulation. Anyone who has been through a spiritually abusive situation then you know that spiritual wolves are masters at manipulation. Spiritual wolves want you to be dependent on them because it's how they survive. It's why they build systems to manipulate you, isolate you and then take advantage of you. One of the hardest things to come to terms with if you have been in an abusive system is to realize you have been deceived and are being taken advantage of. It really is a form of Stockholm syndrome.

Stockholm Syndrome is a psychological phenomenon where hostages identify with, become emotionally attached to and sometimes even fall in love with their captors. They often defend, protect and develop strong emotional connections with their abusers. The first step to getting out of a spiritually abusive situation is acknowledging that you are in one and that you made some wrong decisions. It's coming to terms with the truth and acknowledging all the signs. It is painful, humbling and, depending on the programming, scary because it's people you have come to trust. It's people you've been very vulnerable too and dependent on spiritually.

Let's look at a few tale-tale signs. False prophets, false teachers and false apostles all have one thing in common they twist the truth using it to their advantage. I've said this before, but it's worth repeating which is wolves run in packs so it's normally a group of likeminded people. Let what Jesus and the apostolic writers said be your guide.

Jesus said a false prophet, false teacher or false apostle will have a heart that is ravenous. The Greek word ravenous is used 5 times in the New Testament and is normally translated swindler. A swindler is someone who takes from you and uses deceptive techniques to take advantage of you. It's the opposite of serving with sacrificial love but using others to benefit themselves and their organizations.

Jesus specifically said you will know them by their fruit (Matt. 7:15-16). The fruit is not signs, wonders, miracles or even church growth. Healing, deliverance and moving in spiritual manifestations of the Spirit are things that we should desire, but remember Jesus said people could do those things and still be workers of lawlessness (Matt. 7:23). I want you to sincerely think about that because he said people could do those things and not even know him. Its why Paul put I Corinthains chapter 13 in the middle of I Corinthians 12 and 14 where he was speaking about the manifestation of the Spirit. Love which is the very personification of Christ is the main thing, period.

The fruit is love, joy, peace, kindness, goodness, faithfulness, gentleness, self-control; against such things there is no law. If you belong to Christ, then you will display the fruit that flows from the Spirit. The Spirit points to Christ and if you are operating by the Holy Spirit then your message will focus on the redemptive work of the cross. If the message is something else that should cause critical thinking skills to jump into high gear. The message and conduct will display the true heart of the Father. Love doesn't do wrong to others. Love is not controlling, domineering and abusive.

I'm a Continuist, but I reject the extremism I see in so much of what is called the Prophetic Movement. Visions, dreams, angelic visitations, out of body experiences, trips to heaven and prophecy are not the signs of a prophet. A false prophet could have all those things happening in their lives and many of them do, but they are operating by a different spirit other than the Spirit of Christ.

A New Testament prophet's focus is to be the word of the cross which is the gospel just like all the other gifts mentioned in Ephesians chapter 4:11. Yes, a prophet will operate in the manifestation of prophecy, the word of knowledge and word of wisdom, but the centrality of their message is Christ and him crucified.

The role of the Holy Spirit is to point to Christ and when the Holy Spirit is involved Christ will be exalted. A person with a prophetic gift is not infallible and it's why we are encouraged to test all things. Jesus and the apostles defined being false as something inwardly corrupt which leads to deception taking you away from the foundation of Christ. Humility is a sign of true prophetic ministry centered in the cross. Pride refuses to be tested and corrected if it is warranted through the testing of prophetic revelation (I Corinthians 14:29; I Thessalonians 5:19-22).

Deception in Prophetic Circles

The level of deception that I am witnessing in far too many Prophetic circles is breathtaking and troubling. I know many of these people and it goes to the very top. The deluge of mystical activity and false spirituality happening in certain sectors of the church is widely accepted while rarely being tested.

I could turn on spiritual programs right now that millions of Christian's listens to and it's outright fantasy land. It's a mystical spiritual world that they call prophetic, but it flows with a spirit of error. Yes, they use the Bible, but it's allegorized and most of the time taken out of context. No one is held accountable for the numerous false prophecies, wild speculation and false teaching because again it goes to the very top.

A lot of the fruit is rotten because the root is grounded in Gnostic ideas of spiritually. It's hitting so many trip wires of a false spiritualism which leads away from Christ the head and if not adequately addressed will just evolve into another Jesus. I'm afraid just like the Deity cult of William Branham is still around today, those who don't disengage from these same ideas will wind up in the same location of deception. The trends are not in the favor of the Prophetic Movement's future as a viable part of Biblical Christianity if a return to sound doctrine does not happen.

The reason these spiritual experiences are put at the forefront is simply to manipulate people. It's conmen and women for Jesus because they have been deceived. It really is that simple. As I said before, if it quacks like a duck and walks like a duck then it's simply a duck. Remember as John said, "the anointing that you received from him abides in you, and you have no need that anyone should teach you. But as his anointing teaches you about everything and is true and is no lie." I've learned to trust that anointing and I encourage you to do the same. Jesus told us to beware of false prophets and I concur that all that glitters is not gold.

Recognizing False Apostles

Let's not leave out false apostles because it's an issue that we must address. Yes, as a Continuist I believe apostles are for today. No, they do not have authority to write scripture or establish new doctrines.

No, they do not have authority over churches and leaders. Yes, they will plant and extend the church into new territories and work with leaders, but as humble servants not as authoritarians.

Apostles do not have some kind of mystical power to pull down territorial spirits. No, the church is not built on the vision of the apostle but on Christ and the foundation that's been securely laid down by the original apostles detailed in the New Testament. The faith has been established (Eph. 2:20; 3:4-6) both scriptures are past tense. Just because someone says it's true or even if a group of people says it's true does not make it true.

Apostolic ministry is foundational, but not hierarchical. I think it would be more appropriate to liken them to feet than heads since they are more about support and partnership than domination. If we use Paul as an example, he saw himself as a servant and a steward. He was a spiritual father who had to correct at times, but it was done with a fatherly heart of love and restoration. I fully cover spiritual gifts in my book Empowered: Discover Your Gifts, Develop Your Gifts and Do Your Part.

I've been around false apostles and yes, I concur they are dangerous. False apostles should be avoided because they love power, thrive on manipulating people and are masters at taking advantage of others. It's their bread and butter because Paul called them deceitful workers. The number one sign of a false apostle is control and domination. False apostles are power hungry and divisive, but master's at deception. Money is a byproduct, but what they truly thrive on is power over others. False apostles emphasize structure and normally their particular type of structure to capture unsuspecting prey. It's always presented as the newest and shiniest car on the block to draw unsuspecting victims.

Yes, they will tout the unity of the church, but it's unity under their spiritual covering because it's only by aligning with them that you can be spiritually safe. Fear is used to manipulate, control and dominate, which is the sign of ravenous wolves. Paul in 2 Corinthians 11:20 talked about such false apostles who take: "you into bondage...devoureth you...taketh you captive" and exalt themselves. I've seen it resort to verbal and physical threats which Paul also addressed in this text.

Healing from Spiritual Abuse: Finding Grounding in Christ

If you have been in a spiritually abusive situation then it's hard to trust others and I've been there. It takes time to heal. In my personal experience getting grounded in Christ is one of the main paths to healing. Back to basics and renewing your personal devotion to Christ is the main key to finding soundness of mind. I live my daily spiritual life in the basic foundational truths of the faith. Maturing in Christ is simply growing into a greater understanding of what he's done for us. The depths and the riches of the word of the cross is a well of spiritual life that never runs dry.

It's also important to connect with others because isolation is not healthy. I found the toxicity of spiritual abuse and spiritual deception is very similar to coming out of a hard-core drug life. It can send you into a spiral of despair and hopelessness. Getting connected to others who are grounded in sound truth is very important. Look for healthy leadership that is loving, supporting and looking for nothing in return.

Leaders have a role, but leaders are simply mature facilitators, and their main role is conflict resolution along with keeping the church on mission. I Timothy chapter 3 gives us a list of character qualifications for leaders. Leaders are not supposed to be quick tempered, violent or domineering, but should be gentle when helping others. Paul laid out a clear list of character qualifications for leadership that should not be laid aside. Look for spiritual leaders who display these character traits. In the next lesson we will dig into the word of the cross and the focus that we need to keep for living a healthy spiritual life grounded in Christ our foundation.

CHAPTER 11

THE MYSTERY OF CHRIST &
THE MISSION OF THE *EKKLĒSIA*

"This is how one should regard us, as servants of Christ and
stewards of the mysteries of God. Moreover, it is required of stewards
that they be found faithful."

~ I Corinthians 4:1-2 ~

In the Bible, stewardship is another way of talking about how
you live your life. In the New Testament, the word steward is rooted in a
Greek word meaning the manager of a household. A steward planned,
managed the work, the finances, the strategy and the records of the
master. The important thing for stewards was faithfulness and efficient
management of the master's resources. A steward never owned the
property or resources, he simply managed them for his master and was
required to manage those resources faithfully.

The Mystery of Christ: Paul's Apostolic Mission

The focus of Paul's apostolic mission was to be a steward of the
mysteries of God. It's important we get the mystery of Christ correct
because like Paul we are also called to be faithful stewards over this
mystery. If we don't get this foundation correct, then the whole house is
built on a faulty foundation.

Paul out of all the other apostolic writers was given special
insight into the mystery of Christ. Paul wrote two thirds of the New
Testament. Paul was a master teacher and called himself a wise master
builder of the community of the faithful. Paul was able to take large sums
of information, digest it and break it down to simple understanding. He
was a learned Jew in the Torah along with being fluent in Greek, so he
understood Roman culture too because he was born a Roman citizen.
His comprehension and understanding of Christ's purpose compared to
none other. He tirelessly labored in the grace of God giving us an
example of being a faithful steward. Let's look at what Paul had to say

about this mystery.

[176]The word translated mystery doesn't mean mystery as we think of something mysterious, mystical, strange or weird. It means something previously unrevealed. A secret and something kept hidden until the appointed time by God. Paul used the term to describe the gospel that had been revealed to him. The mystery refers to God's saving plan now revealed in Jesus Christ.

The book of Romans was a theological masterpiece that Paul wrote. He ends this book saying, "now to him who is able to strengthen you according to my gospel and the preaching of Jesus Christ according to the *revelation of the mystery* that was kept secret for long ages but has now been disclosed (emphasis mine)." Did you hear that? It says the mystery has been disclosed and made known.

The mystery is not hidden anymore. It's not something we can't understand. I want you to get that, so I am going to say it again because this was written almost 2,000 years ago and Paul said the mystery of Christ has now been disclosed. The mystery is the gospel. [177]The mystery refers to God's saving plan now revealed in Jesus Christ. It's not some hidden *gnōsis* that someone reveals to you.

The Simplicity and Power of Christ's Message

Now Paul, although he was a very well-educated man was able to make his message so simple that the uneducated could understand it. It's so simple that we stumble over it. He said we preach that Christ was crucified. The Jews are offended, and the Gentiles say it's all nonsense. "But to those called by God to salvation, both Jews and Gentiles Christ is the power of God and the wisdom of God (I Corinthians 1:24)." The simplicity of Christ is a stumbling stone and at the same time the foundation that the whole household of faith is built upon. [178]For Paul, 'mystery' refers to God's salvific plan, once hidden but now revealed in Christ.

Paul told the Colossians in 1:25-26 of his epistle that he became a minister according to the stewardship from God that was given to him "to make the word of God fully known, the mystery hidden for ages and

---

[176] Douglas J. Moo, The Epistle to the Romans, p. 936.

[177] Thomas Schreiner, Romans (BECNT), p. 809.

[178] Gordon D. Fee, The First Epistle to the Corinthians, (NICNT), p. 105.

generations, but now revealed to his saints". Did you hear that? Paul said it again, which is that *the mystery* is no longer a secret.

Paul goes on to say to them in verse 27 that "God chose to make known how great among the Gentiles are the riches of the glory of ***this mystery, which is Christ in you, the hope of glory*** (emphasis mine)." Again, listen to what he said. He wants the mystery to be made known and no longer hidden. Paul then said, Him we proclaim. Who is him? Christ in you, verse 28 says "warning everyone and teaching everyone with all wisdom, that we may present everyone mature in Christ". [179]The 'mystery' is not an esoteric doctrine for a spiritual elite but the open secret of God's redemptive purpose.

The mystery is that God became man. It's the incarnation when Christ took the humble position of a slave and was born as a human being. When he appeared in human form, he humbled himself in obedience to God and died a criminal's death on a cross. The prophetic writings from Genesis to Malachi have woven throughout them the redemptive story. One author has called it the scarlet thread that ties the scriptures together from Genesis to Revelation.

The mystery is that through Christ's death, burial, resurrection and ascension to the right hand of the Father He has dealt with sin once and for all through the cross. Subsequently through the outpouring of His Spirit, the God who created all things by the power of his word, has now chosen to fill those who identify with his blood, water and Spirit (I John 5:6-8).

The Body of Christ in the Book of Ephesians

It's not just a cliche, we are literally the body of Christ. Jesus enacted a new Exodus, created a new law-making love the central guiding rule, implemented a new sacrificial system through his body and blood, then created a new temple, the body of Christ along with a new priesthood including all its members. The resurrected Messiah is the head of a new humanity made up of both Jews and Gentiles. Paul teaches this same message to the church in Ephesus. Ephesians is the sister letter of Colossians and both letters would have been read among all the believers in that region.

---

[179] F.F. Bruce, The Epistles to the Colossians, to Phelemon, and to the Ephesians, (NICNT), p. 75.

Paul in Ephesians 3:2-10 says I assume that you have "heard of the stewardship of God's grace that was given to me for you how *the mystery* was made known to me by revelation, as I have written briefly. When you read this you can perceive my insight into *the mystery of Christ*, which was not made known to the sons of men in other generations as it has now been revealed to his holy apostles and prophets by the Spirit (emphasis mine)." [180]The mystery was not that Gentiles would be saved, but that Jews and Gentiles would be united equally in one body.

The mystery is that the Gentiles are fellow heirs. Fellow heirs with whom? Fellow heirs with the natural sons of Abraham the children of Israel. Gentiles whom the Jews consider dogs have been brought into the family of God through Christ. Jew and Gentile have been reconciled through the cross and made members of the same body and partakers of the promise in Christ Jesus through the gospel.

Paul said of this gospel I was made a minister according to the gift of God's grace, which was given me by the working of his power. Paul was a faithful steward of this mystery, which is simply the good news of what Christ accomplished.

The Controversy Surrounding Apostles and Prophets in Modern Times

Let me address an important and relevant topic which is the place of apostles and prophets. If you are a Cessationist then it's easy because you can disregard portions of scripture writing them off as completely in the past. No apostles and prophets for today so that's not a topic discussed and if anyone does it's pretty much written off as heretical.

If you are a Continuist then it's important to adequately address this topic because it raises serious questions that are foundational as to how we practice our faith. Paul is the only one who addresses this subject, and it's mainly done in the book of Ephesians. Ephesians 2:19-21 which says: "you are fellow citizens with the saints and members of the household of God, built on the foundation of the apostles and prophets, Christ Jesus himself being the cornerstone, in whom the whole

---

[180] Harold Hoehner, Ephesians, (Baker 2002), p. 429.

structure, being joined together, grows into a holy temple in the Lord." The metaphor suggests a once-for-all foundation.

You also have Ephesians chapter 3:4-6 telling us that all believers are made one in Christ no matter the ethnicity, gender or social status and that was revealed to the apostles and prophets by the Spirit. It echoes what Paul said in Galatians 3:26-29: "in Christ Jesus you are all sons of God, through faith. For as many of you as were baptized into Christ have put on Christ. There is neither Jew nor Greek, there is neither slave nor free, there is no male and female, for you are all one in Christ Jesus. And if you are Christ's, then you are Abraham's offspring, heirs according to promise."

I 100% agree with Cessationist that if you read Ephesians chapter 2 and 3 when talking of apostles and prophets it's past tense. Not concluding that can lead to some serious errors in how we practice our faith. Scripture is overwhelmingly clear that the foundation is Christ, and it's built upon a clear understanding of him (Matthew 7:24; Matthew 16:18; I Corinthains 3:11; I Peter 2:8)

The apostles along with New Testament prophets are the ones who interpreted and helped us to understand what the Law, Psalms and Prophets said concerning God becoming man. It's already been done and it's a clear understanding of the gospel. Our job as stewards of the grace of God is to share the gospel and "to contend for the faith that was once for all delivered to the saints" as Jude 1:3 put it.

The unique and permanent place of the original apostles is confirmed in Revelation 21:14 when the vision of the new heaven and the new earth describe the presence of "twelve foundations ... the twelve names of the twelve apostles of the Lamb." This means that the initial establishment of the apostolic foundation will have an eternal significance in God's *ekklēsia*. This will not be changed, updated, or renewed. Charismatic Restoration Theology and its adherents go off the tracks when they start teaching a restoration to something that has already happened.

To teach that we are coming into some new apostolic age where we are going to have apostles and prophets on par, or some say even with greater revelation and power than the ones who established the *ekklēsia* then that lays the groundwork for all kinds of deception. It's not just a wrong interpretation of scripture, but it's dangerous and I've seen it result in some very troubling practices.

The potential for spiritual abuse goes off the charts when you start teaching that apostles and prophets have some kind of special authority today over the church. As the old saying goes, power corrupts, but absolute power corrupts absolutely. Spiritual wolves masquerading as apostles and prophets is a problem in certain sectors of the church and extreme views of Charismatic Restoration Theology have opened the door. [181]Authoritarian leaders who claim special revelation often create environments where dissent is equated with rebellion against God and [182]when spiritual authority is divorced from accountability, abuse becomes almost inevitable.

Yes, as a Continuous I believe in current day apostles and prophets, but today they are just one of the five gifts that Paul later tells us about in Ephesians 4:11. [183]These are gifted persons given to the church for its growth, not hierarchical rulers. [184]The emphasis is on equipping the saints, not on establishing a new ruling class because [185]spiritual abuse thrives where leaders claim divine authority that cannot be questioned.

[186]New Testament churches were led by a plurality of elders, not by a single authoritative figure (I Tim 3:1-7; I Pet. 5:1-2). I firmly hold to the need for teams of spiritual leaders and apostles along with prophets should be team members with teachers, evangelists and shepherds. The APEST gifts are not offices or some sort of authoritative structure, but simply servants to help extend and build the *ekklēsia*. (I fully cover spiritual gifts in my book Empowered: Discover Your Gifts, Develop Your Gifts and Do Your Part).

The Centrality of Christ in Paul's Teachings

Paul never gives a hierarchical structure for these gifts, nor does he ever say apostles are spiritual coverings. He never says these five gifts have any type of authority over others. He simply says in verses 12 thru 13 that they are given to: "equip the saints for the work of ministry, for building up the body of Christ, until we all attain to the unity of the

---

[181] Ronald Enroth, Churches That Abuse, p. 41.
[182] Diane Langber, Redeeming Power, p. 29.
[183] Harold Hoehner, Ephesians, (Baker 2002), p. 544.
[184] Clinton E. Arnold, Ephesians, (ZECNT), p. 256.
[185] Wade Mullen, Something's Not Right, p. 77.
[186] Alexander Strauch, Biblical Eldership, p. 45.

faith and of the knowledge of the Son of God, to mature manhood, to the measure of the stature of the fullness of Christ." Clearly the gospel of Christ is the centrality of all that Paul taught and us being grounded in that understanding was his primary focus.

Paul spoke of the gospel as a mystery because it was hidden from the eyes of the vast majority of those who walked in Jesus day. Remember the conversation Jesus had with Peter in the first instance that this new entity called the church (*ekklēsia* in Greek) was mentioned.

"Now when Jesus came into the district of Caesarea Philippi, he asked his disciples, "Who do people say that the Son of Man is?" And they said, "Some say John the Baptist, others say Elijah, and others Jeremiah or one of the prophets." He said to them, "But who do you say that I am?" Simon Peter replied, "You are the Christ, the Son of the living God." And Jesus answered him, "Blessed are you, Simon Bar-Jonah! For flesh and blood has not revealed this to you, but my Father who is in heaven" – Matt. 16:13-17

It's hard for us to imagine the magnitude of this revelation because we have the Old and New Testament which gives us 20-20 hindsight and a viewpoint that is much clearer. You had varying ideas in Israel about what the coming Messiah was going to look like, his message and his purpose. [187]The word translated "messiah" (*machiach*) is fairly common in the Old Testament. It occurs over three dozen times. It simply means "anointed". And there is no Old Testament verse that has a dying and rising *machiach*. If you're thinking Isaiah 53 is the exception, it isn't. The word *machiach* does not appear in that passage. That doesn't mean Isaiah 53 isn't part of the messianic profile – it means that the content of Isaiah 53 is just one piece of a much larger whole.

[179]By God's design, the Scripture presents the messiah in terms of a mosaic profile that can only be discerned after the pieces are assembled. Jesus during his earthly ministry spoke in parables and mysteries. The pieces were kept separate to obscure the big picture. Just after Peter recognized Christ as the Messiah, he fails to understand Jesus

---

[187] Michael Heiser, The Unseen Realm: Recovering the Supernatural Worldview, p. 241-243.

announcement of going to die in Jerusalem. [179]He couldn't read it in his Bible because there was no single verse for the idea. Rather, the concept of a dying and rising messiah must be pieced together from a scattering of disparate fragments in the Old Testament that, each taken alone, don't seem to have anything like a messiah in mind. None of the garments reveal the final assemblage.

It was not until after Christ resurrection with the help of the risen Christ and his Spirit that they could have their minds opened to see a suffering messiah. [179]Jesus had to enable the disciples to understand what the Old Testament was simultaneously hiding and revealing. God's plan to redeem humanity, reclaim the nations, and revive Eden depended on the incarnation of the second Yahweh figure and his subsequent death and resurrection.

The story of the cross is the Biblical-theological catalysts to God's plan for regaining all that was lost due to Adam's sin. It was the secret and hidden wisdom of God that was concealed so the powers of darkness would be misled as Paul explains in I Corinthians 2:6-8. If the plan of God for the Messiah's mission had been clear, the powers of darkness would never have killed Jesus – they would have known that his death and resurrection were the key to reclaiming mankind's redemption and the nations forever. Paul called this 'they mystery', and Peter said even the angels didn't know nor understand the plan (I Peter 1:12).

The hidden mosaic in the Old Testament scriptures of the redemptive story of the cross was only truly revealed once the Spirit was poured out. It was the apostles and prophets during these formative years before we had the New Testament scripture who clarified the purpose of the Messiah. As Paul clearly tells us in Ephesians 3:4-6 that "you can perceive my insight into the mystery of Christ, which was not made known to the sons of men in other generations as it has now been revealed to his holy apostles and prophets by the Spirit. This mystery is that the Gentiles are fellow heirs, members of the same body, and partakers of the promise in Christ Jesus through the gospel."

If you become firmly grounded in the message of Christ then Paul says in Ephesians 4:14-16 that you will: "no longer be children, tossed to and fro by the waves and carried about by every wind of doctrine, by human cunning, by craftiness in deceitful schemes. Rather, speaking the truth in love, we are to grow up in every way into him who is the head, into Christ, from whom the whole body, joined and held together by every joint with which it is equipped, when each part is working properly, makes the body grow so that it builds itself up in love."

It's a simple pattern and can be accomplished in varying ways. It doesn't take the superstar. It just takes those who are willing to lay down their lives at the cross where the power and wisdom of God are given to build his *ekklēsia*. Every member of the body has gifts that they have been given for the furtherance of the mission. It's about each member discovering, developing and putting into practice their gifts for the furtherance of fulfilling the ultimate mandate of being the body of Christ.

Paul in I Corinthians chapter 3 then lets us know those with the leadership gifts of Ephesians 4:11 are simply servants. Jesus laid down the pattern for those who would lead his body, and it was the night before he was crucified at that last Passover. Serving others should be the primary quality of leadership. The character qualifications Paul laid out in I Timothy chapter 3 are clear and precise.

Understanding the Flexibility of the Body of Christ

Jesus nor did the apostolic fathers give us clear instruction on how to plant, govern and make disciples. We can look at the book of Acts and piece together ideas from varying scriptures or look at church history. It's just not that clear and it's why we have so many ways that it's done.

It's not a particular pattern that matters because that can depend on the context. The structure or how you do things can and should be flexible. The character traits of spiritual leadership cannot be flexible because it's the integrity of the mission. It's why Paul gave clear character qualifications in I Timothy 3. Leadership is like the rudder on a ship. It's a small, but important part and if the rudder is broken the ship drifts. I personally see leadership teams as the healthiest pattern. A team that is truly accountable one to another. Paul and Peter used the plural term elders when describing spiritual leadership.

Paul demonstrated servant leadership because it's what Jesus taught. In 1 Corinthians 3:5 - 8 he says: "What then is Apollos? What is Paul? Servants through whom you believed, as the Lord assigned to each. I planted, Apollos watered, but God gave the growth. So neither he who plants nor he who waters is anything, but only God who gives the growth. He who plants and he who waters are one and each will receive his wages according to his labor."

Paul seems to emphasize a teamwork mindset when it comes to forming the *ekklēsia* (I Peter 5:1-2; Acts. 20:28). Paul and Peter both show that leadership is best demonstrated through a plurality of leaders demonstrating the humility of the cross in submitting one to another. Partnership, fellowship, serving and encouraging every member to do their part was an emphasis in all of Paul's letters.

One Foundation and One Source of the Spirit

Paul then says in verse 11: "For no one can lay a foundation other than that which is laid, which is Jesus Christ." The word of the cross is the redemptive story of Christ. Christ is our all in all and for us to fulfill the mandate we must keep him as our all in all. We must defend the faith that was once and for all delivered to us. It's only this foundation that will stand the test of time.

It's not a difficult message and it's something each one of us are called to do which is to be a steward over the mystery. So many are stumbling around in the dark looking for some hidden key of *gnōsis* while they are tripping over the very cornerstone. The secret key is Christ and us crucified with him. It is the very wisdom and power of God to live this life of faith. It's a deep well of living water that never runs dry.

Just as Jesus told the Samaritan woman at the well that: "whoever drinks of the water that I will give him will never be thirsty again. The water that I will give him will become in him a spring of water welling up to eternal life (John 4:13-15)."

I want to help you understand that your source is Christ. I want to help you understand that your foundation is Christ. I want to help you understand that your head is Christ. I want to help you understand that Christ is your all in all. If you don't get this foundation correct, then you are going to be led into deception. You will fall for false apostles and false prophets who lead you away from this foundation to come under their superstructure of a false covering. You will be taken captive by false teachers who take you "captive by philosophy and empty deceit and not according to Christ."

The Mandate of Our Faith: The Centrality of Christ

Let me just take you through what Paul called 'the mystery', the 'day of salvation', the 'word of the cross' and the 'gospel of your salvation'. Peter called it the 'prophetic word'. Jude said it is our 'common salvation' and simply called it 'the faith'. John simply called it 'the message'. The centrality of our faith is based in Christ and as believers in the risen Christ we must be established in him.

Our mandate is Matthew 28:18-20: "All authority in heaven and on earth has been given to me. Go therefore and make disciples of all nations, baptizing them in the name of the Father and of the Son and of the Holy Spirit, teaching them to observe all that I have commanded you. And behold, I am with you always, to the end of the age."

Our mission is to make disciples of Christ not of ourselves. We are pointing others to the one who has the words of eternal life. We are pointing them to the one man in the whole history of mankind who has ever been born of a virgin or ever will be. [188]The virgin birth is doctrinally important because it shows that salvation ultimately must come from the Lord.

The virgin birth is central and core to our faith. Yes, it's mysterious, but it's non-negotiable. God becoming man separate from the bloodline of the curse of sin is core to understanding the gospel. It's why the gospels open telling us about the conception of Jesus by the Holy Spirit and his natural lineage all at the same time. [189]The genealogy places Jesus squarely within Israel's story and the story of the whole human race. [190]Without the virgin birth, the Biblical presentation of Christ's sinlessness is imperiled.

The prophetic scriptures are wrapped in the redemptive story going back to the origins of man. To undermine the reality of God coming to us in human flesh through the lineage of Adam is to undermine the very foundation of our faith. [191]The genealogies are theological affirmations of Jesus' place in the history of God's promise.

---

[188] Wayne Grudem, Systematic Theology, p. 532.
[189] N. T. Wright, Matthew for Everyone, p. 5.
[190] Robert L. Reymond, A New Systematic Theology of the Christian Faith, p. 617.
[191] Richard Bauckham, Jesus and the Eyewitnesses, p. 92.

It's part of the mystery that's been revealed. Our roots don't just go back to Adam, but to Abraham, Isaac, David and the lineage of Christ up to Mary the mother of Christ.

Jesus lived as a man just like you and me. He had all the bodily functions of a man except he was still God and therefore sinless. He appeared like any other child playing and growing. We get a glimpse into who he was at the age of 12 as recorded in the gospel of Luke when he stayed behind in Jerusalem and did not join the family caravan back home after the feast of Passover. It says it took them three days to find him. [192]Luke emphasizes both Jesus' normal development and his unique sonship.

Jesus was in the temple "sitting among the teachers, listening to them and asking them questions." His reply to his parents was: "Why were you looking for me? Did you not know that I must be in my Father's house?" Jesus could read so that would mean he was educated, and Jewish custom would also mean he did carpentry work since Joseph his father was a carpenter. [193]Jesus' trade identifies him as an artisan within first-century Jewish society.

At the age of 30 when priests were eligible to enter service, he was baptized in the Jordan River by his cousin John the Baptist. [184]Luke's not of Jesus' age may evoke priestly service imagery. It was so the prophecy concerning Elijah the prophet being sent to prepare the way for the one called Immanuel which means God with us could be fulfilled. Matthew 3:16 - 17 says: "when Jesus was baptized, immediately he went up from the water, and behold, the heavens were opened to him, and he saw the Spirit of God descending like a dove and coming to rest on him; and behold, a voice from heaven said, "This is my beloved Son, with whom I am well pleased."

We see God in human flesh go under the water then come up and God the Spirit anoint him for his ministry while God the Father speaks from an open heaven. The mystery of the Trinity is seen in open view. [194]The baptism scene is one of the clearest narrative manifestations of the Trinity. [195]The incarnation is the supreme mystery of the Christian faith. Jesus spent 40 days in the wilderness just like the children of Israel spent

---

[192] Darrell Bock, Luke 1:1-9:50, (BECNT), p. 266, 298.

[193] Craig Keener, The Gospel of Mark, p. 208.

[194] Craig Bloomberg, Matthew, (NAC), p. 81.

[195] J.I. Packer, Knowing God, p. 53.

40 years in the wilderness, yet Jesus was without sin. He passed the test. He fulfilled prophecy after prophecy through his ministry. He came for one purpose, which was to fulfill the will of the Father.

Jesus was a prototype or a model of the perfect man. Paul called him the Last Adam. [196]Paul presents Christ as the representative head of a new humanity. Jesus' virginal conception breaks the pattern of natural birth that has been the norm since Adam and places Jesus as the holy head of a new humanity. His obedience in the face of temptation is a first step in reversing the results of the curse that came because of Adam's disobedience. Christ is the obedient last Adam who fulfills humanity's original calling.

Peter in the book of Acts describes the ministry of Jesus like this in chapter 10:37-38: "beginning from Galilee after the baptism that John proclaimed: how God anointed Jesus of Nazareth with the Holy Spirit and with power. He went about doing good and healing all who were oppressed by the devil, for God was with him."

Jesus was God, but he was also a man who needed the anointing of the Holy Spirit. He did not demonstrate power to heal the sick and cast out demons until the Holy Spirit empowered him, yet he was God. Jesus demonstrated the need to rely on the Holy Spirit throughout his ministry. We can never be Jesus because he is set apart on his own as a first fruit or prototype since he alone is God. However, he is our example, and we are his disciples called to follow in his footsteps. We need to be filled and empowered with the same Spirit so that we can complete the will of God for our lives.

Jesus sole purpose was to do the will of the Father. Scriptures are overwhelmingly clear that the central purpose of Jesus becoming man was to be the sacrificial sinless and spotless Lamb of God. The author of Hebrews in 10:4-7 says it this way: "it is impossible for the blood of bulls and goats to take away sins. Consequently, when Christ came into the world, he said, "Sacrifices and offerings you have not desired, but a body have you prepared for me; in burnt offerings and sin offerings you have taken no pleasure. Then I said, 'Behold, I have come to do your will, O God, as it is written of me in the scroll of the book.'"

---

[196] Thomas Schreiner, Romans (BECNT), p. 286.

The Crucifixion of Jesus: A Divine Act of Love

Jesus on the cross in Luke 23:43 said to one of the criminals being crucified beside him and who came to believe in him on the cross that: "Truly, I say to you, today you will be with me in paradise." Verses 44 thru 46 describe the curtain of the Temple housing the ark of the covenant being torn from top to bottom. It was the event that turned the page from the old administration of the Mosaic law and opened the new administration of the law of the Spirit of life found in the Last Adam.

Luke recorded the event saying: "It was now about the sixth hour, and there was darkness over the whole land until the ninth hour, while the sun's light failed. And the curtain of the temple was torn in two. Then Jesus, calling out with a loud voice, said, "Father, into your hands I commit my spirit!" And having said this he breathed his last." [197]The darkness signifies divine judgment, and the tearing of the veil symbolizes new access to God.

God's wrath for the sin of the world was poured out on Jesus and it was satisfied at the crucifixion of the Lamb of God. As John said in his I John 4:10 that: "In this is love, not that we have loved God but that he loved us and sent his Son to be the propitiation for our sins." He also says in I John 2:2 that: "He is the propitiation for our sins, and not for ours only but also for the sins of the whole world." [198]God in love provides the sacrifice that satisfies his own righteous wrath.

The background for propitiation is seen in the Old Testament covenant ceremonies and in the sacrificial system. The bloodshed in those rites represented what sin deserved and merely pointed to the cross. The apostolic authors help us to understand that we are no longer under the Mosaic law. [199]Propitiation indicates that God's righteous anger against sin has been satisfied by Christ's sacrifice.

If you do a thorough study of Hebrews, Romans and Galatians you will see the Mosaic law was completed when the curtain veil was torn from top to bottom. The administration of the Mosaic law was completed through Jesus' flesh and he alone is a new and living way. We all have direct access to the Father through the one mediator Jesus and

---

[197] Darrell Bock, Luke 9:51-24:53, (BECNT), p. 1856.
[198] D.A. Carson, The Difficult Doctrine of the Love of God, p. 63.
[199] Thomas Schreiner, 1, 2 Peter, Jude (NAC), p. 95.

that's the central core of the good news he came to give us. We are no longer under the law, but we are under grace and the administration of the Spirit. [200]The Levitical sacrifices were anticipatory and provisional, pointing forward to Christ.

Reconciliation in Christ: A New Identity

Paul talks about our identity in Christ calling us new creations with very similar language that Jesus used with Nicodemus. He then says in II Corinthians 5:18 - 19 that: "Christ reconciled us to himself and gave us the ministry of reconciliation; that is, in Christ God was reconciling the world to himself, not counting their trespasses against them, and entrusting to us the message of reconciliation." Paul ends this chapter saying in verse 21 that: "For our sake he made him to be sin who knew no sin, so that in him we might become the righteousness of God."

Paul, Peter and John employed imagery of the Temple and its sacrifice system throughout their writings. [201]The temple theme is one of the most pervasive unifying threads of Scripture. It's because they were helping us to understand that Jesus was the fulfillment of all the Law, Psalms and Prophets wrote. The apostles were not coming up with something new but were merely interpreting the Old Testament in the light of God being manifested in human flesh.

Paul was not saying that Jesus literally became sin or that he became a sinner. It means that just like under the Mosaic law the lamb was a substitute. The sin of the people was transferred to the lamb and in the same way Jesus is our final sin offering, but he was not a sinner, but the sin of the world was laid upon him. [202]Christ did not become sinful but was made a sin offering, bearing sin's penalty as substitute. As Peter said in I Peter 2:24: "He himself bore our sins in his body on the tree, that we might die to sin and live to righteousness. By his wounds you have been healed."

Jesus' body was in the tomb, but his inner man went into the depths of the earth for 3 days and 3 nights. He said to the Pharisees who came wanting a sign in Matthew 12:39-40 that: "no sign will be given to" you "except the sign of the prophet Jonah. For just as Jonah was three

---

[200] F.F. Bruce, The Epistle to the Hebrews, p. 206.

[201] G.K. Beale, The Temple and the Church's Mission, p. 17.

[202] Thomas Schreineer, Paul, Apostle of God's Glory in Christ, p. 203.

days and three nights in the belly of the great fish, so will the Son of Man be three days and three nights in the heart of the earth." [203]The 'heart of the earth' refers to Jesus' death and burial, not necessarily to a detailed geography of the underworld. If you look at Luke 16:19-30 it seems the parable reflects common Jewish imagery of the intermediate state where the righteous and the wicked were held with a gulf separating them.

The New Order of Worship: Christ, Our All in All

The resurrection and ascension of Christ established a new order of worship no longer administered on the Mosaic law, but the blood and body of Christ. Christ is now our all in all and our lives are to be found in Him. Hebrews 7:26-27 says we: "have such a high priest, holy, innocent, unstained, separated from sinners, and exalted above the heavens. He has no need, like those high priests, to offer sacrifices daily, first for his own sins and then for those of the people, since he did this once for all when he offered up himself." The finality of Christ's self-offering marks the end of the repeated sacrifices of the Mosaic Levitical sacrificial order.
Hebrews 8:6 says: "Christ has obtained a ministry that is as much more excellent than the old as the covenant he mediates is better, since it is enacted on better promises." The New Covenant is not a revision of the old but it's fulfillment and replacement. [204]The superiority of Christ's priesthood is inseparable from the superiority of the New Covenant he mediates. [205]Believers are no longer under the Mosaic covenant as a governing authority but under the Spirit.
It's important to remember that when the temple veil was torn from top to bottom a new way to approach God was opened and we are now under the new law of the Spirit of life found in Christ. Hebrews 10:19 - 22 says we: "have confidence to enter the holy places by the blood of Jesus, by the new and living way that he opened for us through the curtain, that is, through his flesh, and since we have a great priest over the house of God, let us draw near with a true heart in full assurance of faith, with our hearts sprinkled clean from an evil conscience and our bodies washed with pure water." We have a New Covenant based on the

[203] R.T. France, The Gospel of Matthew, (NICNT) p. 489.
[204] Peter O'Brien, Hebrews, (Pillar), p. 287.
[205] Thomas Schreiner, Romans (BECNT), p. 402.

death, burial, resurrection, ascension and outpouring of the Spirit of our king/priest Jesus.

On the day of Pentecost as he promised Jesus the resurrected king/priest poured from his throne the oil of the Spirit upon his newly formed body in the earth. [206]Christ's heavenly session marks him as the true temple high priest and Davidic king. The head of the church sits at the right hand of the Father, but he is connected to his body through the blood, water and Spirit which I call the threefold cord of covenant.

Our lives are to be built on Christ who is not just the head, but the very foundation of this new temple. Peter says it this way in 1 Peter 2:4 - 5 that Jesus is: "a living stone rejected by men but in the sight of God chosen and precious, you yourselves like living stones are being built up as a spiritual house, to be a holy priesthood, to offer spiritual sacrifices acceptable to God through Jesus Christ."

Apostolic Doctrine: Foundation of Faith & Practice

Ecclesiology is important because that is how we administer the New Covenant. The believers in the book of Acts began to establish a common core set of beliefs based on the birth, life, death, resurrection, ascension, outpouring of the Spirit and return of Christ. We can look at the gospels, book of Acts and epistles where the apostolic authors helped us to interpret the Law, Psalms and Prophets.

I think I can safely call this apostolic doctrine that is clearly established, and believers should have a common agreement upon. It is what I based the first section of the Foundation Publications School of Discipleship upon. Hebrews 6:1 - 2 which talks about: "a foundation of repentance from dead works and of faith toward God, and the doctrine of baptisms, the laying on of hands, the resurrection of the dead, and eternal judgment."

The question I am sometimes asked is, if there is only one church of the Lord Jesus then why so many denominations and Christian groups? I'll give you an analogy. It's like going into a neighborhood where they're building new homes. If all they had in the neighborhood was the foundation of the homes, you could not really tell one apart from the other. The foundations are all made from concrete. It's not until the

---

[206] G.K. Beale, A New Testament Biblical Theology, p. 615.

house is built that you see the distinction between each one. The foundation is made of the same substance, but the structure of the house is distinct. [207]Christ is not one foundation among others; he is the exclusive foundation of the church.

Our foundation is the common bond that unites the church together no matter what part of the body we identify with. That bond is the basic teachings of our faith in Christ centered around the blood and broken body of the risen Christ. Every local church, denomination or network of churches will have their own distinct house or type of ministry, but there is only one foundation. Paul in I Corinthians 3:11 says that: "no one can lay a foundation other than that which is laid, which is Jesus Christ."

In Acts 2:42 we see that the early church converts, continued steadfastly in the apostle's doctrine, and in fellowship and breaking of bread and prayers. In the New Geneva Study Bible, it says that the basic teachings of Hebrew 6:1-2 can all be found in the books of Acts which are the ABC's of Christian doctrine. [208]These are foundational teachings already well established in the community.

It's like when we go to school. In kindergarten we all learn the same basics or foundation, but by the time we are in college we have our own distinct focus of study. In Acts 2:42 we can see that it is the measure of common teaching between believers which will determine the measure of our fellowship with one another, resulting in our ability to fulfill the purpose of God.

I am under no illusion that we are all going to agree on everything, but my mission is to help believers return to focusing on the foundation of Jesus Christ where Ephesians 4:13 says the unity of the faith is established. I am convinced that if we focus on the centrality of Christ that we will no longer be children, tossed here and there and carried around by every different teaching.

Yes, there are some non-negotiable areas we need to have agreement on. Here are a few examples of what we must agree on as foundational truths:

- Jesus being born of the virgin birth and God manifested in human flesh.

---

[207] Anthony Thiselton, The First Epistle to the Corinthians, p. 312.
[208] Peter O'Brien, The Letter to the Hebrews, p. 210.

- Salvation being by grace through faith because of Christ's death, burial and resurrection.
- The body of Christ being founded on what Christ did for us through the cross and that we are joined to His throne of grace through one Spirit.
- Our common fellowship around the body and blood of Christ.
- The mission of the body of Christ which is to proclaim this message until He returns in a resurrection body. At Christ second coming, we shall be changed, given resurrected bodies and forever be with Him.

The foundation of the church is not some apostles' personal revelation or prophet's spiritual experience, but Christ. A good policy to follow is in essentials unity, in non-essentials liberty in all things love. Another wise little word is to major on majors and minor on minors. If we want to fulfill the mission, then we must stay focused on the main thing. Its why sound doctrine is so important.

The *Ekklēsia*: Embracing Unity and Flexibility

Ecclesiology is about how we build on top of that foundation and it's where we should give one another the liberty to discover. Yes, our hearts are the ultimate place where the Spirit dwells, but we are each individual stones that are built together to be the corporate dwelling of the Spirit. The *ekklēsia* is not a building, but a people filled with the Spirit of the risen Christ. The *ekklēsia* is not to be a rigid organization but filled with the life-giving power of the Holy Spirit flowing from the throne of grace.

How we view being the body of Christ and live out our faith is of practical importance. In saying that Jesus nor did the apostolic writers give us clear specific guidelines on how to practically carry out the mission of making disciples. I do think there are some basic guidelines that we can follow, but ultimately, we are all going to be held accountable as to how we live out our faith in Christ.

Paul in the context of bringing our attention to the foundation of the word of the cross which is the revelation of Christ in I Corinthians 3:12-15 says: "Now if anyone builds on the foundation with gold, silver, precious stones, wood, hay, straw— each one's work will become manifest, for the Day will disclose it, because it will be revealed by fire, and the fire will test what sort of work each one has done. If the work that anyone has built on the foundation survives, he will receive a reward. If anyone's work is burned up, he will suffer loss, though he himself will be saved, but only as through fire."

The Nature of Heresy: Works of the Flesh

Heresy is not just having a simple difference of opinion on how we practice our faith. Paul defined heresy as a work of the flesh in Galatians chapter 5. I break down these works of the flesh into 3 categories. **Hedonism** which are "sexual immorality, impurity, sensuality, drunkenness, orgies, idolatry and sorcery". **Emotionalism** which is "enmity, strife, envy, jealousy, and fits of anger." **Legalism** is rivalries, dissensions and divisions. The word divisions can be translated as factions or heresies in other translations, but all these religious sins are called works of the flesh.

The term heresy and heretic are thrown around so freely today it becomes like the boy who cried wolf. Obviously if you've gotten this far in this book then you know I do think there is legitimate heresy that we need to identify, address and stay away from however Jesus also warned us to beware of the leaven of the Pharisees (Luke 12:1). Jesus defined the leaven of the Pharisees as religious hypocrisy.

Heresy is someone who divisively expresses their opinions creating factions. We think today of heresies in terms of wrong ideas and teachings. It is, but the word carries an emphasis on wrongfully dividing over opinions. [209]The word suggests the formation of sectarian groups that destroy the unity of the body. Heresies can be thought of as hardened dissensions. There is all the difference in the world between believing that we are right and believing that everyone is wrong. It is an arrogant attitude which believes the way we think is the only way to think and not giving room for any differing opinion.

It's not standing on clear laid out principles or clearly stated doctrinal positions, but it's taking obscure positions and making them non-negotiable. It's the attitude that says: it's my way or the highway and it creates a faction. Paul was dealing with this exact attitude when writing to the church in Galatia which had started listening to the

---

[209] F.F. Bruce, Galatians (NIGTC), p. 249.

heretical legalism that certain men started preaching.

We have the same legalists today who want to turn believers away from the focus on the cross of Christ to outward ordinances and rigid viewpoints. It's simply heresy that creates factions because selfish ambitious people want to take you captive and control you. The leaven of the Pharisees is being divisive over positions that are not clearly articulated in scripture. A lot of our ecclesiology is subjective, and we should give room for diversity. As someone who has lived and ministered in different countries, ecclesiology needs to be flexible depending on the context. [210]Paul distinguishes between essential gospel truths and secondary matters.

The Essential Practices of Jesus' *Ekklēsia*

Jesus did not leave us a manual on exactly what his *ekklēsia* should look like and I'm not going to make one up for you to follow. We have been given a lot of freedom regarding outward styles and ecclesiastical formats. The Spirit of Christ works through any format that truly identifies with the water, blood and Spirit. He's given us great flexibility to be ourselves and I'm not going to get hung up on outward appearances nor box anyone into doing things my way. However, I do see four main practices that are necessary if we want to call ourselves Jesus *ekklēsia*. The *ekklēsia* is more than a social club; it's the body of Christ which is fulfilling the mission of Christ by implementing and maintaining these four main practices.

- **Number one** is teaching the pure doctrine of the word which includes discipleship and equipping believers to do the work of the ministry.
- **Number two** is the practice of water baptism which is a public demonstration and a sign or witness that you are a member of the body of Christ.
- **Number three** is the partaking of the body and blood of Christ on a regular basis among the community of the faithful which is essentially fellowship and prayer.
- **Number four** is having some type of leadership structure which is about accountability and formation of Christlike qualities.

---

[210] Douglas J. Moo, Romans, (NICNT), p. 835.

Leadership is for the unity, safety, protection and guidance of the community so that the mission of the gospel is fulfilled. It's simple and it's what the apostle's did in establishing the *ekklēsia* wherever they went. Acts 2:42 says the disciples devoted themselves to the apostles' teaching and to fellowship, to the breaking of bread and the prayers.

In the book of Acts we see 3 things happening which are prayer, proclamation and then formation. It takes implementing all three to fulfill the command of Christ to make disciples. Paul laid out this pattern for building the community of the faithful through his apostolic ministry and it's in the book of Ephesians that he lays out a framework for accomplishing this mission. It's the mystery of the church living between the two Mountain tops of the 'day of the Lord'.

Let's look at a few things Paul says in I Corinthians chapter 1. First, I choose an ecclesiology that is inclusive because the gospel is inclusive. What do I mean? Well in context Paul was telling us not to get caught up focusing on or just elevating Apollos because he is an eloquent speaker.

I do think when we elevate leaders to celebrity status and develop a professional clergy class it has a detrimental effect upon the church. It doesn't mean we don't have good speakers, but if all you have is good services with great speakers that doesn't make a lot of room for the body to be participants. It's important to build systems that encourage everyone to identify, develop and use their gifts.

One Body With A Diversity of Gifts

Leadership has a responsibility to be humble, transparent and not build walls to insulate themselves. Charismatic leaders are fine as long as humility, transparency and mutual submission to one another in a team are all present. Leadership in the *ekklēsia* has two primary purposes which is keeping us on the mission of making disciples and conflict management. It's a small yet very important role. I liken leadership to the rudder on a ship that keeps us on track. Mature leadership finds ways to make room for others always developing new leaders and encouraging everyone to use their gifts.

To be inclusive also means to not divide over race, political identity, gender and social status. Paul in Galatians 3:26 - 28 says: "in Christ Jesus you are all sons of God, through faith. For as many of you as were baptized into Christ have put on Christ. There is neither Jew nor

Greek, there is neither slave nor free, there is no male and female, for you are all one in Christ Jesus." In one text Paul leveled the playing field.

Remember what Paul said 1 Corinthians 1:26-29 to: "consider your calling, brothers: not many of you were wise according to worldly standards, not many were powerful, not many were of noble birth. But God chose what is foolish in the world to shame the wise; God chose what is weak in the world to shame the strong; God chose what is low and despised in the world, even things that are not, to bring to nothing things that are, so that no human being might boast in the presence of God." Our purpose is not to rule nations in this age, but to demonstrate through our lives the love of the Father. A love that lays down its life to serve others because we live by the life-giving power of the blood, water and Holy Spirit.

Inclusive also means that Jesus commissioned his body to be the vehicle to reach this world. Every member has been given gifts to function in their particular way as a part of the body. A gift needs to be identified, opened, developed and used. You find 3 sets of gifts mentioned in the New Testament and as a Continuist I say they are all available for today.

Paul said that after Christ's resurrection he ascended to the right hand of the Father. He ascended to rule in power from the throne of grace, but he also gave gifts to his body for the furtherance of his ministry in the earth. Ephesians 4:11-12 says: "he gave the apostles, the prophets, the evangelists, the shepherds and teachers, to equip the saints for the work of ministry, for building up the body of Christ."

Paul told us in Romans chapter 12 to not be arrogant, but to be humble, realizing our uniqueness due to the gifts of grace in our lives. In verse 5 thru 8 Paul says that we are: "one body in Christ, and individually members one of another. Having gifts that differ according to the grace given to us, let us use them: if prophecy, in proportion to our faith; if service, in our serving; the one who teaches, in his teaching; the one who exhorts, in his exhortation; the one who contributes, in generosity; the one who leads, with zeal; the one who does acts of mercy, with cheerfulness."

Paul in I Corinthians chapter 14 told us to desire to be used by the Holy Spirit. In 1 Corinthians 12:7 - 11 he told us that: "to each is given the manifestation of the Spirit for the common good. For to one is given through the Spirit the utterance of wisdom, and to another the utterance of knowledge according to the same Spirit, to another faith by the same Spirit, to another gifts of healing by the one Spirit, to another the working of miracles, to another prophecy, to another the ability to distinguish between spirits, to another various kinds of tongues, to another the interpretation of tongues. All these are empowered by one and the same Spirit, who apportions to each one individually as he wills."

In the book of Acts, we see 3 things happening which are prayer, proclamation and then formation. It takes implementing all three to fulfill the command of Christ to make disciples and that's what being apostolic means. It means we have been sent into this world with the power for the Holy Spirit to be good stewards of the mystery. We have been sent as ambassadors for Christ because God is making his appeal through us his body and each of us have a part to play.

One of leadership's main roles is to make sure the body is included, equipped, developed and sent. It takes each part of the body using their spiritual gifts to fulfill the mission. It's simply called discipleship, but I'm afraid the church in America has gotten so caught up in putting on a show to attract people that we've many times forgotten the mission.

The Interconnection of Resurrection, Eternal Judgement, and The Mission of the *Ekklēsia*

In this age we are mortal subject to weaknesses. It's why we live the cruciform life because we've learned by experience that we tend to mess things up when left to our own devices. It's what Paul was saying here in II Corinthians chapter 5 that our weaknesses should always lead us to the cross reminding us that the surpassing power belongs to God and not to us. He was showing us that we are not going to be without problems, difficulties and persecution, but it's part of the life of faith. It's to be expected during our journey in this present age.

Resurrection from the dead and eternal judgement are inextricably tied together. What you see Paul do here in II Corinthians chapter 5 and I Corinthians chapter 3 is tie those ideas together as part of our ecclesiology. It is lived out through the knowledge of the cross as part of our continued practice meeting together in fellowship partaking of the body and blood of Christ. Let me show you because it's all about our common foundations and our continued commitment to fulfill the Great

Commission.

Paul in II Corinthians 5:1 - 9 affirms a future resurrection of our mortal bodies with the Spirit being our guarantee. He then ties this new resurrection body to a coming judgment and motivation for completing the will of God. In verse 10 he says: "we must all appear before the judgment seat of Christ, so that each one may receive what is due for what he has done in the body, whether good or evil." Paul taught us to live in the presence of the future. We are all headed towards a day when we will have to give an account of our obedience to faithfully use that which God has given us. None of us will escape that day.

Let's look at 1 Corinthians 3:12 - 17: "Now if anyone builds on the foundation with gold, silver, precious stones, wood, hay, straw— each one's work will become manifest, for the Day will disclose it, because it will be revealed by fire, and the fire will test what sort of work each one has done. If the work that anyone has built on the foundation survives, he will receive a reward. If anyone's work is burned up, he will suffer loss, though he himself will be saved, but only as through fire. Do you not know that you are God's temple and that God's Spirit dwells in you? If anyone destroys God's temple, God will destroy him. For God's temple is holy, and you are that temple."

In context Paul just laid out the message of the cross in chapter 1 showing us how it takes a team to fulfill the Great Commission, and every member has a part to play in building the ekklēsia. In chapter 2 Paul clearly shows us the role of the Holy Spirit saying that out of the cross comes the very power and wisdom of God. In verse 4 he says that the message of the cross must be proclaimed with the "demonstration of the Spirit and of power." In 1 verses 10 thru 13 he says: "God has revealed," the word of the cross, "to us through the Spirit." In context Paul is saying that it is the Spirit who explains the mystery of the cross to us because the depths and riches of God are found in Christ.

Paul opens chapter 3 reminding us once again that it takes a team to fulfill the mission. We each have our place in fulfilling the mission, but we each need to take heed as to how we build because we each will be held accountable before God. None can escape judgment, and it's supposed to be a daily motivation to examine our lives in the light of the purpose of God for our lives.

The whole foundation is laid between the two Mountains of the day of the Lord. Yes, we have been judged for our sins at the first coming of Christ and appropriated the blood of forgiveness through receiving the message of the cross. However, a future judgment awaits us at the consummation of the day of the Lord when Christ returns to this earth where we will be judged for our works. How we live out this life of faith in this body is of utmost importance.

The very foundation of our faith is laid out in the terms of a covenant. Paul in 1 Corinthians 11:23 - 26 says: "For I received from the Lord what I also delivered to you, that the Lord Jesus on the night when he was betrayed took bread, and when he had given thanks, he broke it, and said, "This is my body, which is for you. Do this in remembrance of me." In the same way also he took the cup, after supper, saying, "This cup is the new covenant in my blood. Do this, as often as you drink it, in remembrance of me." For as often as you eat this bread and drink the cup, you proclaim the Lord's death until he comes."

In proclaiming the Lord's death until he comes is living in the light of the future where we each will be held accountable for how we live out our life of faith. It should be the motivating factor that keeps us moving forward to finish the race that we have been given. It should be the source of our daily discipline as we yield to the power and wisdom of the cross.

The ecclesiology of the cross is all about loving God with all our hearts, soul and strength. It's also about loving others and laying down our lives to serve others. Each of us has been given gifts that need to be identified, opened, developed and used. As stewards of the manifold grace of God we must be faithful to pursue our purpose and fulfill the will of God for our lives.

Paul's motivation to labor in the grace of God was not a salvation based on works, but an ecclesiology rooted in the cross. Paul makes this statement in 1 Corinthians 15:10 that: "by the grace of God I am what I am, and his grace toward me was not in vain. On the contrary, I worked harder than any of them, though it was not I, but the grace of God that is with me." The context of this statement is sandwiched in the middle of one of our pillar texts concerning resurrection from the dead.

Grace is more than the gift of salvation, but it's also the motivating power to live a godly life and a life of service. You can't separate grace from the cross and sacrifice because it all flows from the blood, water and Spirit. The end of the age is about returning to foundations and fulfilling the mission that started the age of the grace of God. Each of us are called to be a part of his body and are called to be vessels shining with the glory of the risen Christ until he sets his feet upon the Mt. of Olives.

The very foundation of our faith as Peter so eloquently articulated in his first epistle chapter 2 verse 1 is laid upon the fact that Christ is the foundation, but we are each living stones being built together to be a habitation of the Spirit. We "are being built up as a spiritual house, to be a holy priesthood, to offer spiritual sacrifices acceptable to God through Jesus Christ."

The question we each need to ask ourselves as we walk on this journey of faith is what are we doing to fulfill our part? Our motivation is not to be accepted because that is found in the blood of the cross, but to be found faithful because that is to daily live our lives in the light of the cross shining a path to our blessed hope of his return.

CHAPTER 12

ISRAEL, THE *EKKLĒSIA* AND THE END OF THE AGE

"Men of Galilee, why do you stand looking into heaven? This Jesus, who was taken up from you into heaven, will come in the same way as you saw him go into heaven.".

~ Acts 1:11~

It was the year 1969 when America landed on the moon, started pulling troops out of Vietnam, the Woodstock Festival happened, and the Charles Manson Cult murders took place. We stepped into the modern age, but as we did it was like a door to an ancient age was opened.

I do think, like Rome, America has had a unique place in the history of mankind. If you look at the rise of America power since WWII it's hard to imagine a world without American dominance. I do think the height of our empire was the 1980's and the Reagan Revolution shaped the world we live in today in so many ways. However, like all empires they eventually come to an end.

Decline of Empires: Lessons from the British Empire

Just think of the British empire before WWI. No one ever thought the sun would sit on the British empire and today it's just back to being an island nation. Yes, England is still around, but it's a shell of its former greatness. As the British historian Arnold Toynbee is quoted saying, "Civilizations die from suicide, not by murder." He said they start to decay when they lose their moral fiber, and the cultural elite turn parasitic to exploit the masses. Hubris, arrogance and self-confidence lead to indulgent destruction. It's the picture of the Titanic hitting the iceberg, yet the party continued because no one dreamed it could sink.

In chapter 9 I showed you what I consider some real parallels to the decline of the Roman Empire and to the decline of the American Empire. American power, peace, prosperity, stability and being the sole superpower of the world were the result of the Reagan years. I have a lot of opinions on what has contributed to the decline of America. Living outside of the United States as a missionary and then spending 20 years in some of the most powerful global organizations has given me a certain perspective.

I appreciate having the opportunity to live in America, but that does not make me blind to the reality that like any human government it's just another beast. Human governments in the Bible are always described as beasts and history shows us that some are tamer than others, but in the end a beast is there to feed on others.

A Framework For Interpreting The Book of Revelation

I want to help you understand at least a framework for looking at the book of Revelation because it's important. A lot of people approach the book of Revelation like it's a book that was added to the Bible. It's not looked at as a part of the redemptive story found in Christ. Doing that starts off completely wrong and ends in a tremendous amount of speculation at best.

What you will find in the Revelation that John wrote. Is that over half of the references stem from Daniel, Ezekiel, Psalms, and Isaiah. Daniel provided the largest number in proportion to length and Ezekiel stands out as the most influential. [211]John alludes to the Old Testament hundreds of times and more than any other New Testament books.

I think it would be easy to say that no book of the Bible has garnered more speculation, produced more fanatical movements and has left more people just baffled as to its message. I'm under no illusion that I am going to set the record straight. The book of Revelation is not the unveiling of some New World Order conspiracy theory. It tells us in the opening sentence what it is: "The revelation of Jesus Christ." [203]The Apocalypse is not a book about end-time speculations but about the unveiling of Jesus Christ and his redemptive purposes.

John is the author of the book of Revelation. It is the same author who wrote the gospel of John and the three epistles of John. He was an original apostle of the Lamb, but John was also a prophet. A prophet is one who leads us to Christ. The main role of a prophet is to ground us in covenant and establish us in the mystery of Christ.

Hermeneutics refers to how we interpret the Bible. In looking at the book of Revelation five main methods have developed regarding how

---

[211] G.K. Beale, Revelation, (NIGTC), p. 50, 78.

we are to interpret it. What I want to do is briefly describe these five views and if you are one who likes to study, I will give you a couple of resources espousing each of these views.

The Preterist Interpretation of the Revelation

The first method of interpretation I want to look at is the preterist method. In this interpretive approach to the book of Revelation, it is taught that the symbols and content relate only to events and happenings at the time when the book was written. It is taught that the beast of chapter 13, for example, is related to Rome or some say specifically identified Nero Caesar during the first century. The 'city of Rome' and the Imperial priesthood are seen as the Babylonian whore of Revelation chapters 14, 17 and 18.

An alternative view is that the Babylonian whore is to be identified with Jerusalem and the Jewish system of worship. However, both views see no future prophetic content in the book of Revelation whatsoever, except for the return of Christ to the earth.

Preterist tend to take the postmillennial view of the 1,000-year reign of Christ. The view sees the millennial reign of Christ in Revelation chapter 20 as not a literal 1,000 years but a symbol of completeness. It is an undetermined amount of time during this age, when Christ is going to rule the nations through the church. It is a belief that the enemies of Christ will be put under the feet of the church ruling the nations during this age. It is a view that the body of believers conquers the whole world for the gospel, and the entire world acknowledges Christ. Then, at the end of the millennial reign of Christ, He will physically return to set up a new heaven and new earth.

It is a popular view among Reformed thinkers today and such men as Charles Finney and Jonathan Blanchard who was the founder of Wheaton College. During the 1980's and 1990's in America, many Charismatic ministers began to embrace parts of this theology, which became known as the "Kingdom Now Movement".

Preterist Authors: J. Marcellus Kik, "An Eschatology of Victory" David Chilton, "The Days of Vengeance"

The Idealist Interpretation Of Revelation

The second method of interpretation is known as the idealist or symbolic method. The church father, Augustine, held this view, and it was the predominant view until the Protestant Reformation. In this understanding, the contents of the book of Revelation are not seen to relate to any historical events at all, but only to symbolize the ongoing struggle between good and evil during the church age until Christ returns. In general, the idealist view is marked by a refusal to identify any of the images with specific future events, whether in the history of the church or regarding the end of all things.

The primary benefit of this view is that it renders the book of Revelation quite understandable at a basic level. It is simply a book that was written to encourage suffering saints in the knowledge that God will someday conquer all evil and make things right. Idealists are amillennial in their view of Revelation 20 concerning the millennial reign of Christ. Amillennial means "no literal Millennium. Some people would rather call this view present-millennialism."

Amillennialism holds that while Christ's reign during the millennium is spiritual in nature, at the end of the church age, Christ will return in final judgment and establish the new heavens and new earth. Amillennialism has been the predominant view of believers during the history of the church among Catholics, Lutherans, Reformed, and many of the original Baptists. This view has predominantly been popular among covenant theologians.

Idealist Authors: Oswald Allis, "Prophecy and the Church" Leon Morris, "The Revelation of Saint John"

The Historicist Interpretation Of Revelation

The third method I want to look at is the historicist method of interpretation. Most of the Protestant reformers interpreted the Revelation in this way. In this understanding of the book, the events describe actual events from the beginning of the church until the time of the interpreter.

The Protestant Reformers could say that the Catholic pope was the Antichrist, and the Catholic Church was Babylon. In this view,

Revelation was interpreted in the light of the history of Western Europe through the various popes, the Protestant Reformation, the French Revolution, and individual leaders such as Charlemagne or Napoleon. In unison, just about all of the Protestant Reformers such as Luther, Calvin and Zwingli took this position.

It's not a popular method used today. Historicists vary in their interpretive approach and none of them agree as to how history and scripture correlate. It does make the book relevant to every generation of believers. Today those taking the historicist view have varying interpretations of the millennial reign of Christ.

Historicist Authors: William Hendiksen, "More than Conquerors" Steve Wohlberg, "End Time Delusions"

The Dispensational Futurist Interpretation Of Revelation

The fourth method of dealing with Revelation is the dispensational futurist view or known as 'Dispensational Theology'. Dispensationalism divides the Bible into seven time periods, it is claimed that God's saving activity is organized differently in each. One of the teachings of Dispensationalism is that the present age will end with a terrible seven-year manifestation of the wrath of God upon the whole earth. However, the true church will not partake of this tribulation, for immediately prior to it, Christ will have secretly come and taken the saints away to heaven. This coming, it is taught, may occur at any moment. The teaching is that Christ first comes for the church then comes back to the world after the seven-year tribulation period.

'The Left Behind' fiction series co-authored by Tim LaHaye and Jerry B. Jenkins is based on this interpretation. The series popularized this method in Modern America. The method relies heavily upon the distinction between Israel and the church, and the distinctive plan God has for both.

The view teaches that Revelation Chapter 4 is the rapture of the church, which is a secret event, and the rest of the book is exclusively dealing with national Israel. God's people in Revelation are Israel, restored to Jerusalem with a rebuilt temple where the Antichrist sets up his image for the world to worship. The church does not return to the earth until Revelation 19 at Christ's return to the earth.

Dispensationalist and moderate futurists agree on the

premillennial position on Revelation 20. It is believed that Jesus Christ will literally return to the Mt. of Olives and reign on the earth for one thousand years. All moderate futurists do not take the position that it necessarily has to be literally one thousand years, but an indefinite period of time. It will be the physical reign of Christ on this earth from the nation of Israel along with the resurrected saints from all ages.

Dispensational Authors: Clarence Larkin, "The Book of Revelation". John Walvrood, "The Revelation of Jesus Christ"

The Historic Premillennial Moderate Futurist Interpretation Of Revelation

The fifth method is referred to as a moderate futurist or the historic premillennial view. George Ladd has popularized this view, and it is a departure from the Dispensational view. Moderate futurism finds no reason to cut the cord between Israel and the church. The primary purpose of the Revelation is to describe the consummation of this present age, which includes the church, Israel and the nations.

The view sees the rapture of the church and the return of Christ as one event at the consummation of the age. At the same time the view incorporates the preterist interpretation, which is simply a foreshadowing of the final consummation.

The moderate futurist sees aspects of the idealist view by seeing many aspects of the Revelation as symbolically reflecting the ongoing struggle between the kingdom of God and the enemies of Christ. In addition, it sees the historical judgment of Jerusalem by the Roman armies like the preterist, but merely as a foreshadowing of the final appearance of the Antichrist kingdom at the end of the age. To the moderate futurist Rome was a type or historical figure of the final Antichrist and his short attempt to rule that is yet to appear in the future.

The historic premillennial position believes that the kingdom is presently at work in the earth through the church, but also not yet fully manifested; they believe that the kingdom is in the midst of the world as a witness during this age. It sees the church as 'salt and light' in a wicked world, while at the end of this transitional age, Jesus will return which includes a catching away of the living saints and the resurrection of the saints who have died (I Thess. 4:16-17).

We will meet Him in the air, after a brief complex series of events, which will culminate in the return of Jesus with His saints to set up a one-thousand-year rule on earth with Christ as 'King of kings'. During the millennial reign of Christ both Israel and the nations will embrace Jesus Christ as King and Savior, since Israel will be the capital of the nations in that age.

Moderate Futurist Authors: George Ladd, "A Commentary on the Revelation of John" Dan Juster and Keith Intrader, "Israel, The Church and The Last Days".

Theological Views on Eschatology: Embracing Diversity and Humility

I personally see valid points in all the views, but I do have a hermeneutical method that I prefer and that is the historic premillennial co position which is also called the moderate futurist view, but I pull in aspects of amillennialism. I cut my teeth on the debate between the Dispensationalist futurist view arguing and fighting with the Preterist views in the early 1990's. The debate is still ongoing and will more than likely continue until Christ returns. I'm of the opinion that like ecclesiology we need to give people liberty on how they view the Revelation. I'm not so arrogant to think I have it all figured out and I would recommend avoiding those who think they do.

I'm a defender of faith and I think we all need to be because foundations matter regarding eternity. If the foundations of Christ are abandoned in our lives, then the result is apostasy. We have seen and are going to see a great falling away from the fundamentals of the faith at the end of the age with the result of people no longer walking with Christ.

The Revelation opens with Jesus giving a personal message to 7 actual churches in the region of what is today modern Turkey. We see in these messages that many had already begun to compromise the fundamentals of their faith. John as a prophet spoke words of correction, encouragement, edification and consoled them in their trials. We see in Revelation chapters 2 thru 3 a series of messages helping each church to stay focused on its main mission of the Great Commission and the testimony of Jesus Christ.

Prophecy: Layers of Meaning and Fulfillment

I opened this book up giving you the analogy of an onion and how to view prophecy. To the ancient Jewish mind, prophecy was a pattern which keeps repeating, a prophecy having multiple fulfillments with each fulfillment, each cycle, teaching something about the ultimate fulfillment. It's the concept that history repeats itself. [212]Biblical prophecy is often typological, where earlier events serve as patterns that are escalated in later fulfillments. If you have ever cut open an onion, then you'll see there are layers. Prophecy is like that in how God fulfills them which is progressive escalating patterns.

John in his first epistle said in 2:18 that: "it is the last hour, and as you have heard that antichrist is coming, so now many antichrists have come." [213]The appearance of many antichrists is evidence that the final hour has begun. John as a prophet looks through what I call double vision with his prophetic perspective because [214]prophets frequently saw the future as a series of mountain peaks without perceiving the valleys between them.

A prophet sees the present, the immediate future and the ultimate fulfillment of their prophecy's, but it's many times blended. It's what Paul meant when he said that we see "through a glass darkly". Our present knowledge of divine realities is partial and indirect. At best before the return of Christ even those with prophetic gifts have an obscure or imperfect vision of prophecy.

The Multidimensional Nature of Biblical Prophecy

Biblical prophecy is multi-dimensional and just as the Old Testament prophets blended the near along with the future together painting what seemed to be one picture in like manner, so did John. [215]The visions of Revelation are not strictly chronological but recapitulate the same period from different angles. It is the understanding that the 'day of the Lord' opened with Christ first coming,

---

[212] G.K. Beale, A New Testament Biblical Theology, p. 17.

[213] Colin Kruse, The Letters of John, p. 102.

[214] Walter Kaiser, Toward an Old Testament Theology, p. 137.

[215] G.K. Beale, Revelation, (NIGTC), p. 124.

but time is barreling towards the final consummation of the coming 'Day' when Christ returns. It's one continuous play with varying scenes and interludes along the way. We await with anticipation the final curtain dropping event when Christ returns to set his feet upon the Mt. of Olives.

It is the tension of the ever-present God who steps into our time and space pulling back the curtain so we can see enough to understand. Yes, Rome of John's day embodied antichrist tendencies however the portrait of the Antichrist spoken of in Revelation chapter 13 is far larger than historical Rome.

I do look at Rome as a historical forerunner of the final Antichrist and the final beast system. Jesus as a prophet spoke in Matthew chapter 24 on the Mt. of Olives of the coming antichrist and the beast system of Rome that destroyed the Temple in 70 AD. However, it was just a forerunner to the Antichrist at the end of the age. So, Jesus and John saw the beast in Rome manifested in the present, yet still to come in the future.

As George Ladd has commented: "we conclude the correct method of interpreting the Revelation is a blending of the preterists and the futurist methods. The beast is both Rome and the eschatological Antichrist-and, we might add, any demonic power which the church must face in her entire history."

The Final Consummation of the 'Day of the Lord'

The entire Bible is prophetic. It declares God's redemptive story through the Lamb of God slain before the foundations of the world, Jesus Christ the Alpha and Omega. We are barreling towards the final consummation of the 'day of the Lord' which is the wrapping up of the redemptive story in time. Jesus taught us to pray that his kingdom would come on earth as it is in heaven. We are merely getting a taste of his glory this side of his return. Paul called Christ's second coming the 'Blessed Hope' and told us to fix our hope on that coming day.

In Titus 2: 12 – 13 he told us: "the grace of God has appeared, bringing salvation for all people, training us to renounce ungodliness and worldly passions, and to live self-controlled, upright, and godly lives in the present age, *waiting for our blessed hope*, the appearing of the glory of our great God and Savior Jesus Christ, who gave himself for us to redeem us from all lawlessness and to purify for himself a people for his own possession who are zealous for good works (emphasis mine)."

In an evil age that is cruel and unjust we are longing for the day when justice will reign on the earth. Christ kingdom rule brings peace to our hearts now in this present darkness motivating us to fulfill the purpose of God for our lives. However, a day is coming when Christ will rule this earth from the city of Jerusalem bringing peace to all of mankind. It is going to be a day when creation is judged by fire being freed from the curse of sin and death. The same fire will destroy and dismantle the principalities and rulers of this present evil age. It is the day when we are clothed with immortality being given new bodies and death is swallowed up with resurrection life.

The Interconnection of Resurrection, Eternal Judgment, and the Mystery of Israel

Resurrection from the dead and eternal judgment are inextricably tied to the mystery of Israel. The Hebrew prophets prophesied of a coming resurrection of the righteous and the redemption of Israel. To me it is impossible to read Romans chapters 9 thru 11 and conclude that God is done with the lineage, land and prophetic purpose of the children of Abraham. It is the glaring blind spot of replacement theology. It was the foundation of Martin Luther's reprehensible antisemitic views that paved the way for Hitlers final solution.

Jesus tied his second coming to the Mt. of Olives and the apostolic writers clearly tied Jesus' second coming to resurrection from the dead and eternal judgment. Jesus before he ascended reiterated to his disciples that they needed to focus on the mission. In Acts1:6 - 7 they ask Jesus: "Lord, will you at this time restore the kingdom to Israel?" He said to them, "It is not for you to know times or seasons that the Father has fixed by his own authority, but you will receive power when the Holy Spirit has come upon you, and you will be my witnesses." It's the entire gospel story. It started wrapped up in a child, but the final act will be consummated with a ruling king subduing the nations with a rod of iron. Luke the author of the book of Acts intentionally connects the location of the ascension with Zechariah 14.

Jesus will return as the ruling king upon a literal throne on this earth as the son of David. The prophet's words will be fulfilled not just in an allegorical way, but literally. The unjust corrupt systems of this present evil age will be dismantled. The kingdoms of this world will come under the full sway and control of the heavenly king-priest who will set upon his throne in the city of the King, Jerusalem (Revelation 11:15). [216]The coming of Christ brings both resurrection glory for the believer and judgment for the wicked.

God becoming man wrapped in human flesh as the last Adam was to redeem us from the curse and re-establish the kingdom of God upon the earth. It's why the gospel is about the birth, life, death, resurrection, ascension, outpouring of the Spirit and second coming of Christ to rule. You can't separate Christ first coming in the flesh as a man to his second coming as the ruling king-priest.

If you believe the Hebrew prophets, then Jesus is going to rule the nations as a man from the city of Jerusalem. John in Revelation 20:6 ties resurrection from the dead to us believers being "priests of God and of Christ" who "will reign with him for a thousand years." Exactly how that is going to be fulfilled is yet to be determined, but [217]the Old Testament promises of Davidic rule require a future earthly reign.

Resurrection from the dead and eternal judgment are tied to the promise of ruling with Christ in the fullness of his kingdom upon this earth. Paul in 2 Timothy 2:10 - 12 says: "I endure everything for the sake of the elect, that they also may obtain the salvation that is in Christ Jesus with eternal glory. The saying is trustworthy, for: If we have died with him, we will also live with him; if we endure, we will also reign with him; if we deny him, he also will deny us." The book of Revelation is a textbook about endurance, perseverance, patience and faithfulness during an onslaught of difficulties, but it's also about reward.

The Full Circle of Faith, Works, and Judgment

In the Bible judgment is tied to faithful service and reward. We are not saved by our works, but we will be judged according to our faithful service to God. Justification by faith does not negate works, but James said it should fuel our desire to love God and lovingly serve others. Paul in the context of talking about resurrection from the dead says in 2 Corinthians 5:10 that: "we must all appear before the judgment seat of Christ, so that each one may receive what is due for what he has

---

[216] G.K. Beale, 1-2 Thessalonians, (IPNTC), p. 208.
[217] Craig Blaising, Progressive Dispensationalism, p. 281.

done in the body, whether good or evil."

Jesus tied reward in the age to come to faithful service. Go read Jesus' parables because they are all about hard work, faithfulness, endurance, mercy and treating others justly, but also about being rewarded. How we live this life of faith matters and the fear of the Lord is living our lives in the light of a future judgment when we will stand before God. We will all give an account of how we lived our lives in this body. Paul likened it to a race that we each must run, and he told us to stay focused on the reward of our obedience (I Corinthians 9:24-24).

It's the full circle of faith. The author of Hebrews said it like this: "let us run with endurance the race that is set before us (Hebrews 12:1)." To run with endurance and to receive our reward we need to daily live the cruciform life of faith. To faithfully fulfill the will of God is to be the focus of our lives as those who believe in the God who became flesh. It is us no longer living life for ourselves, but us daily eating the flesh and drinking in the blood of the New Covenant allowing Christ to live his life through us.

The Prophetic Fulfillment of Israel

The roots of our ancient faith go into the deep soil of the Abrahamic covenant. As followers of Christ, we are tied to the fulfillment of the resurrected Christ consummating the final redemption of Israel. [218]The promises to Abraham form the backbone of Paul's understanding of salvation history. If you cut the cord of the prophetic fulfillment of Israel's salvation at Christ's second coming, then you sever yourself from redemptive history.

In the book of Romans Paul dedicates three chapters discussing the place of Israel. To exclude the lineage, land and prophetic purpose of the children of Abraham is to sever yourself from the roots from which our Messiah sprang. In Romans 9:4 - 5 he says that to Israel: "belong the adoption, the glory, the covenants, the giving of the law, the worship, and the promises. To them belong the patriarchs, and from their race, according to the flesh, is the Christ, who is God over all, blessed forever. Amen." [219]The church's identity is inseparable from Israel's ongoing covenantal existence.

---

[218] Thomas Schreiner, Galatians, (ZECNT), p. 206.
[219] Mark Kinzer, Postmissionary Messianic Judaism, p. 211.

The mystery that Paul unveiled in the book of Romans, Galatians and Ephesians are that God through Jesus is the seed of Abraham, son of David and God manifested in human flesh. He was sent to redeem not just Israel, but all who will believe from the nations of the earth. Paul opens Romans 1:1 - 4 saying he was: "called to be an apostle, set apart for the gospel of God, which he promised beforehand through his prophets in the holy Scriptures, concerning his Son, who was descended from David according to the flesh and was declared to be the Son of God in power according to the Spirit of holiness by his resurrection from the dead, Jesus Christ our Lord." [220]Paul frames the gospel as the fulfillment of Israel's royal-Davidic hopes.

Paul then closes the book of Romans his masterpiece of redemption saying in 16:25 - 27: "Now to him who is able to strengthen you according to my gospel and the preaching of Jesus Christ, according to the revelation of the mystery that was kept secret for long ages, but has now been disclosed and through the prophetic writings has been made known to all nations, according to the command of the eternal God, to bring about the obedience of faith— to the only wise God be glory forevermore through Jesus Christ! Amen."

The mystery revealed is that redemption for all of humanity came through the Hebrew nation of Israel. The double vision that I talked to you about in chapter 2 is 'the mystery'. Christ's first coming opened the 'day of the Lord' in Jerusalem with the outpouring of the Holy Spirit and his second coming will consummate the 'day of the Lord' in Jerusalem. [221]The mystery is the inclusion of the Gentiles as equal members of God's people.

Jesus confirmed to his disciples before his ascension that the kingdom is going to be restored to Israel upon his return (Acts 1:6-7) and Paul confirms that in the book of Romans. [222]Jesus does not deny the restoration of Israel; he postpones discussion of its timing. Just as surely as the prophets were vindicated in Christ death, burial, resurrection, ascension and outpouring of the Holy Spirit they will be vindicated at the last trumpet. The prophetic writings of a glorified Jewish Messiah ruling from the throne of David upon this earth will be fulfilled.

---

[220] Richard Hays, Echoes, p. 34.
[221] Frank Thielman, Ephesians (BECNT), p. 210.
[222] Darrell Bock, Acts, (BECNT), p. 69.

The Significance of the Cross in Hebrew Roots

Once you untether the cross from its Hebrew roots then you are left with a Christ that is no longer tied to humanity. Jesus came in the flesh and that means he was born a Jew, died king of the Jews and rose from the dead in Jerusalem as the lion of the tribe of Judah. Paul addresses this very subject in Romans 11:1-2 when he: "ask, then, has God rejected his people? By no means! For I myself am an Israelite, a descendant of Abraham, a member of the tribe of Benjamin. God has not rejected his people whom he foreknew." The earliest Christian proclamation did not detach Jesus from his Jewishness.

Paul in addressing the Jews rejection of the cross in his days says in Romans 11:11-12: "did they stumble in order that they might fall? By no means! Rather, through their trespass salvation has come to the Gentiles, so as to make Israel jealous. Now if their trespass means riches for the world, and if their failure means riches for the Gentiles, how much more will their full inclusion mean!" Paul's denial is categorical: God has not rejected Israel.

To reject the regathering of the Jewish nation into their homeland after 2,000 years and to think that God is done with the descendants of Abraham is the height of arrogance! Paul made a point and went out of his way by putting these three chapters in Romans. The book of Roman's is Paul's last epistle, and he makes a point to explain the place of Israel in the redemptive story.

In Ephesians 2:11-16 Paul tells us to: "remember that at one time you Gentiles in the flesh, called "the uncircumcision" by what is called the circumcision, which is made in the flesh by hands—remember that you were at that time separated from Christ, alienated from the commonwealth of Israel and strangers to the covenants of promise, having no hope and without God in the world.

But now in Christ Jesus you who once were far off have been brought near by the blood of Christ. For he himself is our peace, who has made us both one and has broken down in his flesh the dividing wall of hostility by abolishing the law of commandments expressed in ordinances, that he might create in himself one new man in place of the two, so making peace, and might reconcile us both to God in one body through the cross."

Yes, I can say unequivocally that we are no longer under the Mosaic law. It was fulfilled in Christ, but that in no way implies that

God is done with the lineage, land and prophetic purpose of the children of Abraham. Paul tethers the *ekklēsia* as being grafted into a very Jewish olive tree in Romans 11:17-19. Using this olive tree analogy, Paul reminded Gentiles that "it is not you who supports the root, but the root supports you". [223]Paul does not erase Israel; he declares that Gentiles are incorporated into Israel's covenant blessings. We are no longer tied to the Mosaic law, but we are tied to the Messiah who is the fulfillment of the Abrahamic covenant and going to rule this earth as the Davidic king through the city of the king: Jerusalem.

Paul called this a mystery, and I personally think it is one that we are not going to fully understand until we see what the Hebrew prophet's declared coming to pass. Just think about Christ first coming and how those prophecies were fulfilled. It wasn't until after they happened that the apostles could point back to and say, "this was that which the prophets declared" (Acts 2:16). What Paul is telling us here in Romans is that we need to walk in humility. We don't want to find ourselves like the Pharisees who arrogantly thought they had it all figured out, but were on the wrong side of the prophets.

Just read the text where Paul in Romans 11:18-26 warns us Gentiles to:

"not be arrogant toward the branches. If you are, remember it is not you who support the root, but the root that supports you. Then you will say, "Branches were broken off so that I might be grafted in." That is true. They were broken off because of their unbelief, but you stand fast through faith. So do not become proud, but fear. For if God did not spare the natural branches, neither will he spare you.

Note then the kindness and the severity of God: severity toward those who have fallen, but God's kindness to you, provided you continue in his kindness. Otherwise, you too will be cut off. And even they, if they do not continue in their unbelief, will be grafted in, for God has the power to graft them in again.

For if you were cut from what is by nature a wild olive tree, and grafted, contrary to nature, into a cultivated olive tree, how much more will these, the natural branches, be grafted back into their own olive tree. Lest you be wise in your own sight, I do

---

[223] N.T. Wright, Paul and the Faithfulness of God, p. 1233.

not want you to be unaware of this mystery, brothers: a partial hardening has come upon Israel, until the fullness of the Gentiles has come in. And in this way all Israel will be saved."

The Prophetic Fulfillment in the Return of Christ

The return of Christ is tied to the deliverance of the lineage, land and prophetic purpose of the children of Abraham. The consummation of the 'day of the Lord' is the summing up of the redemptive story in time and the book of Revelation is the capstone of that story. The harvest is the end of the age. As surely as the first coming of Christ fulfilled prophetic promises. You can be assured that the God who took upon himself human flesh being baptized in the lowest place on earth will set his feet upon the Mt. of Olives. He will return to this earth fulfilling the prophetic promises of justice filling the earth through his government of peace.

To reject the fulfillment of Jesus' rule upon this earth through the lineage and land of Israel is to reject the prophets upon which our ancient faith has been established. It's to reject the words of Christ himself who said before his ascension that he would restore the kingdom to Israel. The Old Testament expectation of Messiah's reign in Zion is not spiritualized but fulfilled in history. Paul called this a mystery, and as I've previously said it is tied to resurrection from the dead which will happen when Jesus literally returns.

Denying that Jesus came in the flesh is what John called antichrist. Denying that Jesus is going to literally return to the Mt. of Olives in his resurrected state as the last Adam is also antichrist. Jesus is not going to just rule from his heavenly throne, but in his second coming he is going to rule the nations with the iron rod of his judgment, justice and peace will flow like a river through the nations of the earth. [224]Revelation brings to climax the prophetic hopes of the Old Testament.

Remember as G.H. Lang so accurately said there were two aspects and periods of the kingdom of God, as foretold by the prophets and was the necessity of the case: an inward and an outward kingdom. The inward kingdom is spiritual in the hearts of men. The outward kingdom will affect human affairs, when Christ judges and rules over the

---

[224] Richard Bauckham, The Theology of the Book of Revelation, p. 6.

305

nations. [225]The kingdom is both a present spiritual reality and a future apocalyptic manifestation.

Now the defining event of redemptive history is what the prophets called the 'day of the Lord'. It's the icing on the cake of all the prophets foretold. It's the Jewish view of redemptive history with the arrival of the Messiah inaugurating the 'day of the Lord', splitting time between this age and the age to come. It's the primary message that ties together the Old Testament prophets and the New Testament apostles. It's the cohesive message of God's redemptive history spoken through the Hebrew prophets and understood through the apostles.

The prophets of old and the apostles both taught inheriting the kingdom of God, the restoration of Israel, a resurrection of the dead, a judgment of the nations and the glory of God filling the earth, along with a final restoration of the heavens and the earth. The prophets saw the 'day of the Lord' as a future event. The apostles taught that 'the day' had already started, because of the Messiah suffering and entering glory, ascending to the right hand of the Father.

Peter started his first epistle saying, "concerning this salvation, the prophets who prophesied about the grace that was to be yours, searched and inquired carefully, inquiring what person or time the Spirit of Christ in them was indicating the sufferings of Christ and the subsequent glories". Christ entered the glory of God, but the promise of his return to this earth as the ruling Messianic king is part of the redemptive story that we need to stay focused upon. [226]The final state includes both the resurrection of the body and the renewal of the earth.

The return of the Messianic king is the hope upon which our faith is founded. It is embedded within the foundation of our fellowship meal when Paul told us in 1 Corinthians 11:23-26 that: "I received from the Lord what I also delivered to you, that the Lord Jesus on the night when he was betrayed took bread, and when he had given thanks, he broke it, and said, "This is my body, which is for you. Do this in remembrance of me." In the same way also he took the cup, after supper, saying, "This cup is the new covenant in my blood. Do this, as often as you drink it, in remembrance of me." *For as often as you eat this bread and drink the cup, you proclaim the Lord's death until he comes* (emphasis mine)."

---

[225] George E. Ladd, The Presence of the Future, p. 221.
[226] Anthony Hoekema, The Bible and the Future, p. 274.

Christ coming in the flesh as the Messiah is the foundation upon which we live out our faith working through love. It is a faith grounded in the prophetic scriptures of the Hebrew prophets and understood by the apostles. A faith where all of Adam's seed both Jew and Gentile, are joined together to form a new humanity in one common bond of the blood of the cross.

The only hope for world peace can be found in the Last Adam and he is the only one who can bring justice to the nations of the earth. It's only the lion of the tribe of Judah who overcame death and Hades that can free us from the curse of sin. He is the only one who conquer the last enemy of bodily corruption when all knees will bow, and every tongue confesses that he is Lord as he returns to this earth resurrecting the righteous.

What I am going to do as I finish this book up is paint a picture with a broad brush. Just as the prophecies concerning the first coming of Christ did not come into focus until he was walking upon this earth. I personally don't think it is going to be any different regarding his second coming.

We are sojourners walking through this present evil age and as Paul so accurately said in 1 Corinthians 13:9 -10 that: "we know in part...but when the perfect comes, the partial will pass away." Our focus in this age is about walking by faith, hope and love longing for the full redemption that will come at the return of the perfect Lamb of God.

Comparative Analysis: The Conditions Surrounding The First & Second Coming of Christ

If the conditions of the last days before Christ return are similar to those in the days of Christ, then let's compare. You have Israel, the church and the known world connected by the Roman Empire and dominated by their beastly rule in the first century. Let's look at our world today. Israel is restored and the Jewish people are once again established in the land promised to Abraham. The *ekklēsia* has become a large worldwide net and has been established to some degree in all the nations of the earth.

The question to be asked is where is an entity comparable to Rome's dominance that fits the descriptions of Revelation? The speculation and theories that surround 'mystery Babylon', the 'beast' along with his number '666' which seems to be an enforcement mechanism to dominate are numerous to say the least. I'm not going to add to the speculation. [227]The beast represents the oppressive power of the Roman Empire, though it also transcends Rome as a symbol of recurring godless empire. [228]Attempts to identify Babylon with a specific modern nation consistently miss the symbolic nature of the text. [229]The solution to 666 is less important than it's symbolic portrayal of incomplete, counterfeit divinity.

The context of the Revelation is a further understanding of Jesus' prophecy in Matthew 24 and Daniel's prophecies about the last days, so it is geographically focused on Israel along with the surrounding Middle East Region. [230]The final form of the beast empire will emerge from the Mediterranean world. Therefore, we can conclude that it's not a book focused on America.

Mystery Babylon, the beast system and Antichrist will arise in the Middle East Region. It does not mean that their reach and dominance will be confined to that region, especially considering modern technology. However, it's not something we should live in fear about, focused upon and spend time endlessly speculating about because we will have wisdom to know what we need to know as 'The Day' approaches. [231]Revelation is not a codebook for anxious predictions but a call to faithful endurance.

The Book of Revelation: The Fulfillment of Prophecy in Light of the 'Day of the Lord'

The book of Revelation is the capstone to the redemptive story and the consummation of the 'day of the Lord'. It can be a perplexing book filled with symbols and apocalyptic language that is not easy to understand. The focus of the book is centered on understanding the fulfillment of the prophecies given through the Hebrew prophets to the

[227] G.K. Beale, Revelation, (NIGTC), p. 680.
[228] Craig Koester, Revelation, p. 675.
[229] Richard Bauckham, The Climax of Prophecy, p. 387.
[230] John Walvoord, The Revelation of Jesus Christ, p. 199.
[231] Eugene Peterson, Reversed Thunder, p. 15.

lineage, land and prophetic purpose of the children of Abraham. [232]The Apocalypse is the consummation of Old Testament prophecy. It is the goal toward which the prophetic movement of the Old Testament pointed. The 'day of the Lord' tradition of the Old Testament is expanded and brought to completion in Revelation.

It is about the full establishment of the kingdom of God along with the reaping of the righteous wheat into his kingdom. Now this includes the *ekklēsia* in all nations and people groups where the gospel has been planted. As a wild olive shoot, Gentiles have been grafted in and now share in the nourishing root of the olive tree of Israel's covenant promises established through Christ.

The book of Revelation is also an unveiling of the reaping of God's judgment upon the evil demonic powers and the tares which have yielded to their power oppressing the people of the covenant throughout the earth. [233]The harvest imagery represents the consummation of God's purposes in salvation and judgment.

The mystery of the *ekklēsia* is tied to the mystery of Israel and both are tied to the return of the Messianic king Jesus. The king-priest Jesus has been ruling from heaven waiting for the fullness of times to bring his rule upon this earth at his return. The Revelation is primarily about showing us this transitional period in the earth as God judges the nations for their rebellion.

The seven seals in Revelation 5-6, seven trumpets in Revelation 8-10 and seven bowls in Revelation 16 make up the bulk of the framework of the book with various interludes. The interludes of Revelation are found in chapter 7 with the 144,00 being sealed. Revelation 11 talking about the Two Witnesses. Revelation 12 describing the Woman and the Dragon. Revelation 13 describing the Beast. Revelation 17 – 18 describing the Mystery Babylon and the Beast. Prior to Revelation 20 which speaks of the millennial year reign of Christ, we have Revelation 19 showing Christ returning as the conquering king.

I concur with George Ladd that Revelation chapter 6 shows "the opening of the first six seals which picture the forces that will be operative throughout history by which the redemptive and judicial purposes of God will progress." G.K. Beale says something similar, "the

---

[232] G.K. Beale, Revelation, (NIGTC), p. 77.

[233] G.R. Beasley-Murray, Revelation, (NCB), p. 219.

seals portray judgments operative throughout the church age.

The first seal releases the **white horse** and represents the progress of the Christian faith until the fullness of the Gentiles is reaped from all the nations of the earth. The second seal, the **red horse** represents war and rumors of war. The third seal, the **black horse,** represents famine, scarcity and inflationary prices. The fourth seal, the **pale horse** represents pestilence, disease and pandemics.

The four horsemen run through the whole of church history and increase in intensity like birth pains up until the return of Christ. [234]The imagery of birth pains suggests escalating crisis prior to the end. Then the next two seals bring us to the very threshold of the last of the last days, the final round of birth pains found in Matthew 24:8 and what Jesus called the great tribulation in Matthew 24:21.

The Time of the Great Tribulation is Connected to Christ's Return

The prophet Jeremiah called this time 'Jacob's trouble' in Jeremiah 30:7 of his prophecy and the prophet Daniel 12:1 also referred to this period calling it the last days of his seventieth week prophecy. Jesus, directly alluded to Daniel and uses almost the exact same language in Matthew 24:21 when saying such tribulation "as has not been from the beginning of the world until now, no, and never will be" immediately preceding His own return. It will not be a long period of time as Revelation and Daniel both reference 1,260 days which is a period of 3 ½ years. [235]Revelation and the Olivet Discourse both depend upon Daniel's vision of the end.

The tribulation will happen simultaneously with the rise of what Jesus called the 'abomination of desolation', John calls the Antichrist and Paul calls the 'man of lawlessness' in II Thessalonians 2: 4 who is destroyed at Christ return. Christ language, Paul's language and John's language in the book of Revelation all draw from the book of Daniel. All of them speak of the fullness of the kingdom of God coming in power on the clouds as the 'Son of Man' comes to destroy the 'little horn'. He is also identified as the last "beast" and the 'day of the Lord'

---

[234] R.T. France, The Gospel of Matthew, (NICNT), p. 903.
[235] George E. Ladd, Revelation, p. 131.

is consummated with Christ rule upon the earth after his defeat.

As the sixth seal is opened in Revelation 6:12-17 John begins to use language that Jesus used in Matthew chapter 24 when Jesus said, "the sun will be darkened, and the moon will not give its light, and the stars will fall from heaven, and the powers of the heavens will be shaken" describing the consummation of the ages.

Peter uses the same apocalyptic language quoting the prophet Joel in Acts 2:19-21 saying, "I will show wonders in the heavens above and signs on the earth below, blood, and fire, and vapor of smoke; the sun shall be turned to darkness and the moon to blood, before the day of the Lord comes, the great and magnificent day." [236]Peter in Acts interprets the Joel prophecy as inaugurated at Pentecost, though not exhausted. Peter in his second epistle uses similar language in II Peter 3:10 "the day of the Lord will come like a thief, and then the heavens will pass away with a roar, and the heavenly bodies will be burned up and dissolved, and the earth and the works that are done on it will be exposed."

Christ's Return and False Teachings

[237]The early church lived with an expectation of the return of Christ. It's why Paul had to correct the understanding of the church in Thessalonica and the false teachers who were teaching that Jesus had already returned. The antichrist spirit teaches that Jesus did not come in the flesh, and it also teaches that Jesus is not going to physically return as the ruling king of Kings over the nations of the earth.

Paul in II Thessalonians 2:1-3 says, "Now concerning the coming of our Lord Jesus Christ and our being gathered together to him, we ask you, brothers, not to be quickly shaken in mind or alarmed, either by a spirit or a spoken word, or a letter seeming to be from us, to the effect that the day of the Lord has come. Let no one deceive you in any way." Paul had previously talked to the Thessalonians' about the consummation of the 'day of the Lord' and connected that final period to the return of Christ.

Paul had previously written to them telling them in I Thessalonians 4:14 -16 that: "God will bring with him those who have

---

[236] Craig Keener, Acts (BECNT), p. 939.
[237] George E. Ladd, The Blessed Hope, p. 19.

fallen asleep. For this we declare to you by a word from the Lord, that we who are alive, who are left until the coming of the Lord, will not precede those who have fallen asleep. For the Lord himself will descend from heaven with a cry of command, with the voice of an archangel, and with the sound of the trumpet of God." Some in Thessalonica were claiming that the 'day of the Lord' had already arrived.

The Hebrew prophets looked to a day when God would step into his creation to redeem, restore and bring peace upon the earth through a ruling king like David making Israel as the head of all nations. The Hebrew prophets were vindicated and shown to be servants of God in Christ first coming. Our faith is built on those prophetic promises found in Christ and it will be no different concerning the return of the king of Kings.

Peter, who's first message declared the opening of the 'day of the Lord' closed his second epistle speaking about the consummation of the 'day of the Lord'. In II Peter 3:2 - 13 he says, "you should remember the predictions of the holy prophets and the commandment of the Lord and Savior through your apostles, knowing this first of all, that scoffers will come in the last days with scoffing, following their own sinful desires.

They will say, "Where is the promise of his coming? For ever since the fathers fell asleep, all things are continuing as they were from the beginning of creation." For they deliberately overlook this fact, that the heavens existed long ago, and the earth was formed out of water and through water by the word of God, and that by means of these the world that then existed was deluged with water and perished. But *by the same word the heavens and earth that now exist are stored up for fire, being kept until the day of judgment and destruction of the ungodly.*

But do not overlook this one fact, beloved, that with the Lord one day is as a thousand years, and a thousand years as one day. The Lord is not slow to fulfill his promise as some count slowness, but is patient toward you, not wishing that any should perish, but that all should reach repentance. But the day of the Lord will come like a thief, and then the heavens will pass away with a roar, and the heavenly bodies will be burned up and dissolved, and the earth and the works that are done on it will be exposed.

Since all these things are thus to be dissolved, what sort of people ought you to be in lives of holiness and godliness, *waiting for and hastening the coming of the day of God, because of which the*

*heavens will be set on fire and dissolved, and the heavenly bodies will
melt as they burn!* But according to his promise we are waiting for new
heavens and a new earth in which righteousness dwells." (Emphasis
mine)

Christ's Return the Catalyst to the Coming Transformation

A transformation of this present evil age is coming and it's the
hope of the church, Israel along with all of creation. You may scoff at a
coming day of fiery judgment, but the Hebrew prophets and apostolic
fathers point us towards this transformative event where all of history is
barreling. [238]Paul speaks of a cosmic redemption in which the created
order itself will be freed from corruption (Romans 8:19-23).

It's what the book of Revelation is all about which is the
summing up of all things in Christ. [239]Revelation portrays the
consummation of God's kingdom and the restoration of creation. It's
about the one new man made up of both Jew and Gentile who is going to
rule with him as a kingdom of priest upon a renewed earth free from the
curse of Adam's failure. [240]The new earth will not be an entirely
different creation, but this present creation renewed.

Just as God judged and cleansed our current earth through the
flood of water in the same way he is going to judge and cleanse our
current earth through fire. II Peter 3:7 says, "the heavens and earth that
now exist are stored up for fire." Vs 12 says "the heavens will be set on
fire and dissolved, and the heavenly bodies will melt as they burn." Fire
is going to separate the righteous from the wicked. [231]Revelation
climaxes with the destruction of Satan and his forces. The principalities
and rulers of darkness that rule in this present evil age will be deposed
and their authority to deceive the nations will be destroyed as the
heavens are set on fire at the return of the king of Kings to this earth
subduing his enemies.

The *sixth seal of Revelation brings us to the beginning of the
end.* The previous seals represent forces that will be taking place during
this age much in the same way as a woman during her pregnancy. As we
approach the end of the age the birth pains and contractions of a new age

---

[238] Douglas J. Moo, The Epistle to the Romans (NICNT), p. 516.
[239] G.K. Beale, The Book of Revelation (NIGTC), p. 1040, 1036.
[240] Anthony Hoekma, The Bible and the Future, p. 274.

will continue to grow increasingly closer together then *the **seventh seal** opens up the consummation of the 'day of the Lord'*. The seventh seal contains the seven trumpets.

Revelation 8:1 says, "the Lamb opened the seventh seal." Then in verse 6 it goes right into talking about the *seven trumpets. The seven trumpets are John describing the story in greater detail as the approaching 'day of the Lord' descends upon the earth.* The consummation of the 'day of the Lord' is not one single event, but a complex series of events. George Ladd says, "it includes the outpouring of God's wrath upon a rebellious civilization, the judgement of the Antichrist, and the destruction of his hosts, as well as the resurrection of the dead and the establishment of God's kingdom."

It's not my intent to give you a commentary on Revelation, but to give you a perspective centered in Christ. I'm convinced that there are things in the Revelation of Jesus Christ that we are not going to fully understand with great clarity until they are taking place. However, I can confidently say that the word of the cross is the only remedy for the sins of the world both Jew and Gentile.

Revelation's Parallels to the Passover Story

The book of Revelation shows us the final consummation of the 'day of the Lord'. Christ redemptive work is the interpretive key to the whole book. Just as God separated the righteous from the wicked through obedience to the Passover lamb in the Exodus story bringing the children of Israel out of Egypt. [241]The trumpet and bowl judgments are patterned after the Egyptian plagues. So, you see in the book of Revelation many similarities to the judgments released upon this world and the deliverance of those who fully surrender to the Lamb of God.

Jesus as the lamb of God is mentioned 28 times in the book of Revelation greatly surpassing any other book in the Bible. The Lamb is the underlying theme of the book of Revelation. I want to end this book by sharing with you 7 themes which have helped me in not only understanding the book of Revelation, but they also have given me inspiration to continue in the faith during difficult times. The 7 themes that I am going to cover are interrelated and are all central themes from

---

[241] G.K. Beale, The Book of Revelation (NIGTC), p. 52.

Genesis to Revelation because the 7 themes are found in the word of the cross because [242]the dominant Christological image in Revelation is the Lamb. The Lamb imagery is the theological center of the book.

The Central Theme of Worship in the Bible

The **first theme is that of worship** and I would say is the main theme with the other themes woven into it. The whole creation - the stars, planets, earth, animals and all creation along with the angelic hosts were built for worship. The creation even in its corruption resulting from the curse still displays the glory of God longing for its glorious restoration. Worship is the central theme of the Bible starting in the book of Genesis embedded in the creation story. Man as the central figure of God's created order was fashioned to worship with his heart being formed as a habitation of God and was to be his image bearer.

God told man in Genesis chapter 2 to cultivate and keep the garden. The Hebrew word for cultivate is *abad,* and the Hebrew word for keep is *shamar*. These same Hebrew words are used to describe how the priest cared for the Temple. The priests were to cultivate and keep the tabernacle. In addition, we are told that God walked in the garden during the cool of the day. God also walked in the midst of the temple. The meaning is clear. The garden was a temple for God. Like the temple, the garden was the joining together of God's space and man's space - the intersection of the heavenly realm and the earthly realm which is what you see transpiring in the book of Revelation.

Adam was a priest who walked with God, bore his image, was clothed in his glory and demonstrated servant leadership in the garden. Adam was also a king created to rule, which means man was to be God's representative in the earth and through man God was to exercise his rule and authority in the earth.

The book of Revelation opens up with this same theme in chapter 1:5-6 when it says that our Creator, "has freed us from our sins by his blood and made us a kingdom, priests to his God and Father, to him be glory and dominion forever and ever." The first Adam failed, but in the midst of his failure God made a covenant promise that through the seed of the woman a deliverer would conquer and crush the serpent's

---

[242] Richard Bauckham, The Theology of the Book of Revelation, p. 74.

head.

The Interconnection of Worship and Covenant

It brings us to our **second theme of covenant** which was introduced at this same time when God clothed Adam and his wife with garments of skin. Worship and covenant are intricately woven together throughout the testimony of scriptures forming the battle between covenant keepers and those who oppose the Lamb slain before the foundations of the world. In microcosm it is seen in the innocent blood sacrifice offered by Abel through faith pointing towards the cross which enraged Cain who approached God through the works of his hands.

The rage produced in Cain's heart resulted from the worship produced through the works of his hands which was false and rejected. It caused him to react in a murderous way. He became an enemy to the cross and an enemy to those who identified with the blood of the Lamb. In Jude 11 Cain is used as an example of one who is an enemy of the covenant people of God. He is seen as an apostate who did not share in the faith of God's people, but rather opposed them. The central theme of those who follow the way of Cain is seeking to be justified separate from the cross. Repentance from dead works is the first step in approaching God. It's realizing our complete insufficiency separate from the grace of God.

Cain represents the first picture of the attempt to be justified through self-effort. It is rejecting the pathway of the cross demonstrated through blood sacrifice. The fruit was lawlessness and legalism being seen in the hate filled murder of Abel. Worship in the way of Cain is not submitted to God in a humble and contrite heart. The way of Cain does not seek the covenant keeping God through surrender to the blood of the cross. It is the worship of Baal that opposes Israel. It is self-centered thinking that if you can just pull the right strings, go through the right rituals and tap into the spiritual world then you can have what you desire apart from obedience to the covenant.

John 3:10-15 describes Cain as being of the 'evil one' who hates those who love God with all their hearts in covenant worship and display that love by laying down their lives. Jesus used the same language when speaking to the Pharisees whom he called sons of the devil. The two main enemies opposing the cross; legalism and lawlessness are personified in Cain, the Tower of Babel, Egyptian worship, Canaanite worship, Babylonian worship and it finds its ultimate final fulfillment in the worship of the beast described in Revelation. Revelation presents a stark alternative: allegiance to the beast or allegiance to the Lamb.

Behind the scenes of history lie spiritual powers of darkness opposing the covenant people of the cross and the book of Revelation pulls the veil back so we can clearly see. John says that we are either going to bow in surrender to the beast and his system or we are going to surrender to the Lamb. [243]Revelation unveils the spiritual dimension behind earthly persecution.

Everyone is a worshipper of something or someone because there is no vacuum of non-worship. In the great conflict described in the book of Revelation there is no middle ground. The consummation of the 'day of the Lord' will be the ultimate valley of decision and who you worship will be brought into the light. You will not be tricked into taking the number of the beast or worshipping him. Taking the number of the beast will be an active decision you make surrendering to the beast. It's rejection the blood covenant found in the cross.

The mark of the beasts represents conscious loyalty to the beast. One is either a worshiper of God and the Lamb, or of the beast. One is either part of the new humanity which forms 'a kingdom of priest' dedicated to the blood of the Lamb or is part of a fully apostate demonized humanity thoroughly given over to the illicit worship of the spirit of the Antichrist.

Embracing Sacrifice and Victory in the Midst of Tribulation

Worshipping the image of the beast brings us to the **third theme of tribulation**. The pressures of the last days are going to cause you to bow in obedient service to the Lamb or harden your heart in obstination against the Creator raising your fist in defiance. Paul had just been stoned, dragged out of the city of Lystra and left for dead when he said in Acts 14:22 after: "strengthening the souls of the disciples, encouraging them to continue in the faith, and saying that through many tribulations we must enter the kingdom of God."

Tribulation means pressure, but it's also about suffering. You can't separate suffering and sacrifice from the gospel. The message of

---

[243] G.K. Beale, The Book of Revelation (NIGTC), p. 675.

the cross is one of sacrifice and the surrendering of one's life to the kingdom. Revelation 12:10 - 11 says: "the salvation and the power and the kingdom of our God and the authority of his Christ have come, for the accuser of our brothers has been thrown down, who accuses them day and night before our God. And they have conquered him by the blood of the Lamb and by the word of their testimony, for they loved not their lives even unto death." Revelation calls believers to cruciform witness.

The believer is saved and protected from the wrath of God, but we suffer persecution in this age. [244]The saints conquer not by force but by faithful witness, even to death. The message of the cross is first about our identification with his death and martyrdom is not our defeat but testifies to the resurrection life found in Christ. Stephen the first martyr of the church looked death in the face with no fear and it demonstrated the victory of the eternal life found in Christ.

We don't conquer this world through our political or economic power. We don't conquer this world through our own ingenuity, self-determination and self-righteous superiority, but by the humility of the cross. George Ladd comments saying: "The great tribulation will be a concentration of the same satanic hostility which the church has experienced throughout her entire existence when Satan, in one final convulsive effort, tries to turn the hearts of God's people away from their Lord."

The children of Israel were freed from the power of Pharaoh because they were willing to surrender to the blood of the Lamb and follow the pathway of the cross. [245]Revelation draws heavily on the Exodus narrative as a paradigm of deliverance and judgment. The parallels of the bowls of wrath poured out upon those who submit to the beast and the judgment of Egypt are striking.

I take a post-tribulation view of the second coming of Christ which means the church made up of both Jew and Gentile will go through the 'great tribulation'. I do see parallels in how God protected the children of Israel through the blood of the Passover lamb in Egypt while at the same time he poured out his wrath on Pharaoh and all those who submitted to him. In like manner the wrath of God will be poured out upon the beast, his system and all who submit to the beast openly worshiping him.

---

[244] Ibid, p. 661.
[245] Craig Koester, Revelation (AYB), p. 645.

Satan is seen to energize the whole world system that is opposed to God with its worship. Human sin as Paul described in Romans chapter 1 and the book of Revelation brings out into the open is fundamentally a refusal to glorify the Creator of heaven and earth. The ultimate refusal to acknowledge God is the rejection of the covenant keeping Creator Jesus Christ who became a man and defeated the serpent through the cross. Revelation 14:10 says those who worship the beast, and his image are given to drink the wine of God's wrath in exchange for the wine of the sexual immorality trafficked by the harlot system of mystery Babylon.

[246]Babylon represents the seductive economic and cultural power of empire. Revelation 17 and 18 show us that the beast simply uses the harlot system of Babylon to seduce the nations through the seduction of luxury, sensuality and abominable practices. It's the ultimate personification of the works of the flesh which lead to corruption and are in opposition to the kingdom of God. Mystery Babylon is simply a tool to prepare those who reject the cross for the short reign of the beast.

The final judgment upon Mystery Babylon gives rise to the beast, Antichrist or as Paul calls him the 'man of lawlessness'. Paul in II Thessalonians 2:9 - 12 says: "The coming of the lawless one is by the activity of Satan with all power and false signs and wonders, and with all wicked deception for those who are perishing, because they refused to love the truth and so be saved. Therefore God sends them a strong delusion, so that they may believe what is false, in order that all may be condemned who did not believe the truth but had pleasure in unrighteousness." [247]God's sending of delusion is judicial – confirming prior rejection of truth.

Embracing Justice and Salvation

It brings us to the **fourth theme of justice**. Paul in his first epistle to the Thessalonians 5:2-9 said: "you yourselves are fully aware that the day of the Lord will come like a thief in the night. While people are saying, 'There is peace and security,' then sudden destruction will come upon them as labor pains come upon a pregnant woman, and they

[246] Richard Bauckham, The Theology of Revelation, p. 35.
[247] Richard Bauckham, 1 – 2 Thessalonians, (IVPNTC), p. 217.

But you are not in darkness, brothers, for that day to ⸱ a thief. For you are all children of light, children of the ꜱᴀʏ⸱ of the night or of the darkness. So then let us not sleep, as others do, but let us keep awake and be sober. For those who sleep, sleep at night, and those who get drunk, are drunk at night. But since we belong to the day, let us be sober, having put on the breastplate of faith and love, and for a helmet the hope of salvation. For God has not destined us for wrath, but to obtain salvation through our Lord Jesus Christ." The consummation of [248]the 'day of the Lord' arrives unexpectedly for those unprepared, bringing judgment upon the unsuspecting.

What about a rebuilt temple and the great apostasy? Honestly, I'm not 100% sure and I've not seen anyone adequately answer those questions for me. [240]Some interpreters argue for a literal temple; the text itself does not decisively resolve the issue. I am convinced that as Paul said if we walk in the light then we will not be caught in the darkness and deception as the 'day of the Lord' comes to its conclusion. We don't have to speculate, Paul said we are not of the night or darkness. We need to pray, have a sober sound mind and realize we have been destined to obtain salvation through our Lord Jesus Christ. He will keep us just as he did the children of Israel during the Passover. He will give us the light we need to finish our race.

The bowls of wrath are going to come upon the world as a sudden surprise like a thief in the night. The delusion of the lawless one will blind with deceptive power those who take pleasure in unrighteousness because they have refused to love the truth and be saved. [240]The deception succeeds because of moral refusal, not intellectual ignorance. Paul said that the church will not be living in the darkness but will be filled with great light of the Holy Spirit because like the virgins in Jesus' parable we will be a praying people dedicated to the covenant of the cross.

Revelation views the prayers of the saints as instrumental in carrying out the purposes of God in the earth until the return of Christ. Jesus taught us to pray that the kingdom of God would come on earth as it is in heaven (Revelation 5:8). George Ladd says: "The prayers of the saints have a role in bringing upon the world the final expression of God's justice and wrath." The praying wheat of the kingdom and the

---

[248] Gene L. Green, The Letters to the Thessalonians, (PNTC), p. 226, 210, 324.

defiant rebellious tares will be separated as the fiery winds of God Spirit are blowing fiercely upon the very foundations of the earth (Revelation 8:1-5). Justice will prevail in the age to come we just need to stay humble, pray and love as Christ loves.

Divine Wrath Unleashed: Shaking the Foundations

We are now brought to the **fifth theme of foundations**. The wrath of God poured out upon the beast system is similar to the plagues poured out upon Egypt which destroyed the very foundations of their civilization. It was a beastly system that was opposed to God and held his covenant people in slavery. At the end of the age the heavenly principalities, powers and rulers of darkness are going to be shaken. The wrath of God is going to judge and destroy their ruling power so they can no longer deceive the nations.

Like the book of Hebrews, the book of Revelation employs the use of Temple imagery throughout it. The book of Hebrews was written to show the Jewish Christians that the earthly Temple was merely a type and shadow of the heavenly Temple that Christ entered. One of the main focuses of the book of Hebrews was to show them that there had been a complete transition from Mosaic law focused on an earthly priesthood, earthly Temple which was centered in Jerusalem and a temporary sacrificial system.

Hebrews Chapter 8:1 - 5 says: "we have such a high priest, one who is seated at the right hand of the throne of the Majesty in heaven, a minister in the holy places, in the true tent that the Lord set up, not man. For every high priest is appointed to offer gifts and sacrifices; thus it is necessary for this priest also to have something to offer. Now if he were on earth, he would not be a priest at all, since there are priests who offer gifts according to the law. They serve a copy and shadow of the heavenly things."

The earthly Temple just pointed to a greater reality. As the first martyr of the church quoted David the prophet saying in Acts 7:49 that: "Heaven is my throne, and the earth is my footstool. What kind of house will you build for me, says the Lord, or what is the place of my rest?" Right before he is stoned he is quoted as saying in verse 55 that Stephen: "full of the Holy Spirit, gazed into heaven and saw the glory of God, and Jesus standing at the right hand of God. And he said, "Behold, I see the heavens opened, and the Son of Man standing at the right hand of God."

The prayer of the church is to pray that God's kingdom would come on earth as it is in heaven.

The book of Hebrews wraps up in chapter 12 pointing us to the kingdom of God established through the risen king-priest Christ that cannot be shaken. It says in verses 22 - 24 that we have "come to Mt. Zion and to the city of the living God, the heavenly Jerusalem, and to innumerable angels in festal gathering, and to the assembly of the firstborn who are enrolled in heaven, and to God, the judge of all, and to the spirits of the righteous made perfect, and to Jesus, the mediator of a new covenant, and to the sprinkled blood that speaks a better word than the blood of Abel." In this age it's all about redemption, justification, propitiation and the blood of the cross that declares the grace of God. Yet, if you continue to read the author warns them of rejecting the cross and peers ahead to the return of Christ in judgment.

12:25 - 29 says: "See that you do not refuse him who is speaking. For if they did not escape when they refused him who warned them on earth, much less will we escape if we reject him who warns from heaven. At that time his voice shook the earth, but now he has promised, "Yet once more I will shake not only the earth but also the heavens." This phrase, "Yet once more," indicates the removal of things that are shaken—that is, things that have been made—in order that the things that cannot be shaken may remain. Therefore let us be grateful for receiving a kingdom that cannot be shaken, and thus let us offer to God acceptable worship, with reverence and awe, for our God is a consuming fire."

The powers of heaven will be shaking with the kingdom of the Son of Man being established upon this earth at Christ's return where every knee will bow both in the heavens and upon the earth. [249]Revelation unveils the spiritual dimension behind earthly events. The book of Revelation is the unveiling of the heavenly powers that have deceived and corrupted the nations. It shows us the shaking and removal of these powers ushering us into the transition of the kingdom of heaven fully coming upon the earth and it must be preceded by the fire of God's judgement.

---

[249] Richard Bauckham, The Theology of the Book of Revelation, p. 17.

Judgment: Restoring Justice and Righteousness

It now brings us to our **sixth theme of judgment**. A man corrupted the earth, Adam. One man's disobedience brought so much corruption, pain and heartache. The Last Adam paid for our sins, defeated the power of death and is ruling as the risen king from heaven. [250]Christ as the 'last Adam' inaugurates a new humanity. The book of Revelation shows us that the blood-soaked king is going to turn up the heat just prior to his return. The bowls of wrath are the preparatory. [251]The bowls represent the final climactic outpouring of God's judgements upon those who submit to the beast.

Judgment is about setting things straight, it's about justice and rewards. It's about the removal of those things that oppose the rule of Christ. At the return of Christ, he is going to set up his government ruling in righteousness and peace. The man Christ Jesus along with his body made up of both Jew and Gentile will judge the nations and the demonic powers that deceived them. [252]The saints participate in the administration of the kingdom.

History is moving towards this final climatic event. All of history is pointing to what Revelation unveils. It is the return of Christ to this earth in flaming fire with the armies of heaven to release creation from Adam's sin and judge the powers of darkness that have corrupted its inhabitants. Peter says that like in the days of Noah it will be universal, but instead of water it will be the cleansing fire of God's judgment (II Peter 3:5-13). [253]The imagery of flaming fire echoes Old Testament theophany and the final judgment traditions.

As a result of the cleansing fire of God's judgment there will arise a new temple in the midst of a creation released from the curse of sin and death. The redemptive story finds it's completeness in this age at the consummation of the 'day of the Lord'. At the last trumpet Christ descends setting his feet on the Mt. of Olives ushering us into the age to come where Christ will rule upon this earth through his body made up of both Jew and Gentile from the city of Jerusalem.

---

[250] Gordon D. Fee, The First Epistle to the Corinthians, (NICNT), p. 788.

[251] Grant Osborne, Revelation (BECNT), p. 569.

[252] George E. Ladd, The Blessed Hope, p. 567.

[253] Gene L. Green, The Letters to the Thessalonians, p. 302.

The millennial reign of Christ is only mentioned in Revelation chapter 20, and I take a premillennial view. I take this view because when looking at the Hebrew prophets I can't help but see the fulfillment of Christ reining over the nations. He reigns from the throne of David and not just from heaven, but upon this earth as the Messianic king of the Jews. If the millennial reign was to be done through the church in this present age, then the last 2,000 years have shown this to be an utter failure. Exactly what that is going to look like we will have to wait to see, but [254]creation awaits liberation tied to the resurrection and final redemption.

The Hebrew prophets are correct. The lion of the tribe of Judah will rule from the city of the king. His return is connected to the mystery of Israel, the resurrection of the dead and is a fulfillment of the lineage, land and prophetic purpose of the children of Abraham. [255]The promise of Davidic rule includes a future earthly dimension, and [256]the Old Testament anticipates a messianic reign over the nations.

I'm convinced that there are things about this period during the consummation of the 'day of the Lord' that we just will not understand until we see the words of the prophets coming to pass. It will happen during the end of this age as the overlapping of the age to come is happening. In much the same way it happened during Christ first coming as the age of Mosaic law was being overthrown by the age of grace established through the first coming of the Messiah.

Reconciliation: The Mystery of Christ's Uniting Plan

It brings us to the **seventh theme of reconciliation**. Paul opens the book of Ephesians explaining to us the mystery that God "set forth in Christ as a plan for the fullness of time, to unite all things in him, things in heaven and things on earth." [257]Christ is the one in who God purposes to unite the fragmented universe. It truly is all about Christ who is the Alpha and Omega. [258]The plan of God is cosmic in scope: heaven and earth are brought into unity under Christ's lordship (Phi. 2:9-11).

---

[254] Thomas Schreiner, Romans, p. 436.
[255] Darrell Bock, Luke 1:1-9:50, (BECNT), p. 181.
[256] George E. Ladd, The Presence of the Future, p. 285.
[257] Andrew T. Lincoln, Ephesians (WBC), p. 33.
[258] Frank Thielman, Ephesians (BECNT), p. 67

In this age we are getting to taste the age to come, but a fuller reconciliation is coming. It's the hope of our faith and fully realized through the resurrection of the dead. We don't know exactly what this time is going to look like because we are only given glimpses, but we know that it will be filled with the glory of God because it will be a further unveiling of the kingdom of God (Habakkuk 2:14). Romans 8 talks of the creation itself being released from corruption at the resurrection. [259]The whole creation awaits the resurrection of believers because its own liberation is tied to theirs.

Romans 8:22-23 says, "the creation itself will be set free from its bondage to corruption and obtain the freedom of the glory of the children of God. For we know that the whole creation has been groaning together in the pains of childbirth until now. And not only the creation, but we ourselves, who have the first fruits of the Spirit, groan inwardly as we wait eagerly for adoption as sons, the redemption of our bodies."

It will surpass anything that we know in this age because it will be the Messianic age of resurrection. It's the reconciliation when the perfect Christ returns in power and death is swallowed up with resurrection life. [260]The resurrection marks the final victory over death, fulfilling Isaiah's promise.

In our role as ambassadors in this current evil age, we are tasked with guiding others toward this mystery and encouraging them to repent. [261]The ministry of reconciliation is grounded in the accomplished work of Christ and oriented toward the coming consummation. We are commissioned to carry out this mission until the last trumpet. [262]Participation in Christ's rule is both present (spiritually) and future (consummately). In this age we are being prepared to rule and reign with Christ in the age to come because [263]believer's future reign with Christ is consistent New Testament expectation.

All of us have a responsibility to be faithful stewards over the gift of life that we have received through the wisdom and power of the cross. [264]The parable of the talents teaches accountability in light of the Lord's

---

[259] Thomas Schreiner, Romans (BECNT), p. 436.

[260] Gordon D. Fee, I Corinthians (NICNT), p. 805.

[261] David E. Garland, 2 Corinthians (NAC), p. 306.

[262] Anthony Hoekema, The Bible and the Future, p. 54.

[263] Grant Osborne, Revelation (BECNT), p. 198.

[264] R.T. France, The Gospel of Matthew, (NICNT), p. 953.

return. We each have a responsibility to discover, develop and put into practical use the gifts we have each received (To get more details on this subject I recommend reading my book: Empowered – Discover You Gifts, Develop Your Gifts and Do Your Part). As the author of Hebrews encourages us as we see the day approaching to "lay aside every weight, and sin which clings so closely, and let us run with endurance the race that is set before us."

I want to end with this exhortation out of the book of Ephesians which closely resembles Jesus parable about the praying virgins being filled with the oil of the Spirit (Matthew 25:1-13). [265]The parable emphasizes readiness for the delayed but certain return of Christ because the church lives between the authority already given to Jesus and the consummation yet to come.

Ephesians 5: 15-18 says, "Awake, O sleeper, and arise from the dead, and Christ will shine on you." Look carefully then how you walk, not as unwise but as wise, making the best use of the time, because the days are evil. Therefore do not be foolish, but understand what the will of the Lord is. And do not get drunk with wine, for that is debauchery, but be filled with the Spirit." Let's finish the original mission of the Great Commission in the power of the Holy Spirit.

---

[265] Ibid, p. 349.

www.ingramcontent.com/pod-product-compliance
Lightning Source LLC
LaVergne TN
LVHW051223080426
835513LV00016B/1381